"There's nothing academic about cohort marketing. It's global. It's practical. And it adds richness, texture, and definition to one's target market."

— Jeff Manning, Executive Director, California Milk Processor Board
(Godfather of the "Got Milk?" advertising campaign)

"To target an age bracket, you've got to figure out birth cohorts — and to do that, you've got to read this book by Meredith and Schewe, and read it carefully. It brims with color, wisdom, and the latest social science findings on a topic of growing importance to marketers worldwide."

— Neil Howe, Coauthor of *Millennials Rising: The Next Great Generation*

"I am impressed with this book's contribution to helping businesses better 'map' consumer attitudes, values, and behavior. It enormously broadens the marketers' ability to profile their target markets and more accurately match their market offerings to cohort groups and individuals. Cohort analysis and the Lifestage Analytic Matrix are substantial additions to the marketers' toolkit — and not only is it a solid contribution to market analysis, but it's also a joy to read!"

— Philip Kotler, PhD, Professor of Marketing,
Kellogg Graduate School of Management, Northwestern University

"Dr. Schewe's latest book should be on the must reading list for all direct marketers. In our catalogue and e commerce businesses we have discovered that many of the old rules of target marketing no longer apply. We have been using generational cohort marketing for our catalogue positioning with great success. This is not a book of theory. It offers actionable opportunities in every chapter."

— Bob Allen, President/CEO, The Vermont Country Store

"This book teaches what they don't teach you in business school marketing classes — what people are really like and how to relate to them. Schewe and Meredith provide a fascinating portrayal of generational cohorts that should stimulate ideas in anyone interested in developing consumer business."

— Wayne A. Marks, Senior Vice President, Customer Experience Practice,
The Forum Corporation

"Back when I was working for Nestle, I was introduced to Geoff Meredith's generational cohort theory and experienced its successful application to chocolate beverages, a category that was in dire need of excitement and innovation. I witnessed a narrowly defined 2-D consumer target transform into a 3-D consumer landscape that helped us identify several highly profitable new business opportunities. Like all great strides in Marketing theory, this new approach was an obvious epiphany . . . one that makes sense immediately despite the realization that no one has done this before."

— Lisa Steere, Executive Vice President of Marketing, Gloria Jean's Coffees

"Cohort analysis really works. We have used it as a primary tool to help us understand motivations and differences in consumption patterns in 14 countries around the world. This book describes the concept in a way that brings it to life and is fun reading."

— David Garrett, Director, Consumer Insight and Opportunity Planning,
Coca-Cola North America

Defining Markets, Defining Moments

America's 7 Generational Cohorts, Their Shared Experiences, and Why Businesses Should Care

By Geoffrey E. Meredith

AND

Charles D. Schewe, PhD

With Janice Karlovich

Hungry Minds™

Best-Selling Books · Digital Downloads · e-Books · Answer Networks
e-Newsletters · Branded Web Sites · e-Learning

New York, NY · Cleveland, OH · Indianapolis, IN

Defining Markets, Defining Moments: America's 7 Generational Cohorts, Their Shared Experiences, and Why Businesses Should Care

Published by
Hungry Minds, Inc.
909 Third Avenue
New York, NY 10022
www.hungryminds.com

Library of Congress Control Number: 2001090698

ISBN: 0-7645-5394-1

Printed in the United States of America

10 9 8 7 6 5 4 3 2 1

Distributed in the United States by Hungry Minds, Inc.

For general information on Hungry Minds' products and services please contact our Customer Care Department within the U.S. at 800-762-2974, outside the U.S. at 317-572-3993 or fax 317-572-4002.

For sales inquiries and reseller information, including discounts, premium and bulk quantity sales, and foreign-language translations, please contact our Customer Care Department at 800-434-3422, fax 317-572-4002, or write to Hungry Minds, Inc., Attn: Customer Care Department, 10475 Crosspoint Boulevard, Indianapolis, IN 46256.

DEDICATION

This book is dedicated to

Sara Christie Schewe

[1975–1996]

and

Christopher Geoffrey Meredith

[1974–1998]

Two fabulous souls who never lived to know the impact of their defining moments.

We miss them terribly.

ACKNOWLEDGMENTS

Writing a book is a journey with many side trips! It starts with the vision of a destination, but the meanderings along the way can lead to a destination different from the original. Our journey was helped by many "travel agents" and guides — and we wish to thank them for their help.

We could not have conceived the content for our book without the help of our early colleagues at Age Wave who contributed to shaping and breathing life into the Lifestage Analytic Matrix™. Michael Rybarski was present at its creation on a paper napkin in a suite at the Waldorf Astoria. Wayne Marks, Mary Anne FitzGerald, and Janet Dunn all helped expand, enrich, and polish it as a way of structuring our analytic approach to client problems. And it was our work there in the early 1990s that spawned the concept of cohort value differences.

As we began developing the manuscript, we happily found help in feedback given to early drafts. Those who graciously gave of their time include: Bob Allen, Bob Haiman, Rosie Hardenberger, Alex Hiam, Jeff Manning, Michael Montgelas, Eric Nelson, Larry Shaw, Bob Stoops, and George Waldman. We also must mention Bob Linsenman, our agent, for getting our manuscript to the top of the pile.

Providing us with great research assistance were Stephanie Noble, a University of Massachusetts doctoral student then and Assistant Professor at the University of Mississippi now, and Ute Jahns, an MBA student at the University of Massachusetts. Their painstaking attention to detail was most appreciated.

The last chapter on extending generational cohort analysis to global markets owes much to other Lifestage associates. Paulo Cesar Motta of Catholic University of Rio de Janeiro [PUC] and Dimitri Shalin of the University of Nevada Las Vegas had their hands and minds in the Brazilian and Russian cohort developments respectively. Ute Jahns is responsible for much of the work on the German cohorts. We thank them profusely for their intellectual contributions.

Professor Sidney Levy of the University of Arizona, who has provided marketing professionals decades' worth of understanding of sociology, gave his ideas to the book development. David Garrett of Coca-Cola poured over the manuscript and provided many insightful and highly detailed responses that lifted the manuscript's quality. Both of these technical reviewers deserve the tip of our hats.

And we clearly applaud and appreciate the excitement, the energy, and the execution of those at Hungry Minds. Without them, this book would not be a success. These wonderful people include Melisa Duffy, Kate Fischer, Holly McGuire, Marc Mikulich, Kathy Nebenhaus, Suzanne Snyder, and Kevin Thornton. And Celia Rocks has been the propellant for publicity — she is just simply great!

And, of course, we thank our families — especially our wives, Valerie and Anne, and husband, Ken — who gave us their inspiration and their patience. They stood by us as we spent the countless hours of time that could have been spent with them. But they, too, saw the vision of what this could be. And we must show gratitude to our children, Leigh and Charlie, who gave us insights into their cohorts and defining moments. And then there is Sean who, growing in Janice's body throughout the manuscript's development, is a defining moment for his mother.

Without all these wonderful people, this book just could not have happened, and we are grateful to them all.

TABLE OF CONTENTS

ABOUT THE AUTHORS

Geoffrey E. Meredith is President and founder of Lifestage Matrix Marketing®, the strategic planning and marketing consulting company that pioneered cohort and lifestage segmentation techniques, especially as they apply to the global aging phenomenon. Clients include the Coca-Cola Company, Nestle, Levi's, Kodak, SCI, and Kellogg's. Prior to starting Lifestage Matrix Marketing in 1992, he spent over 20 years in advertising and marketing, holding Senior Vice President and General Manager positions at Ogilvy & Mather, Ketchum Communications, Age Wave, Inc., and Hal Riney & Partners. He has extensive experience with clients in financial services (The Prudential, Bank of America), packaged goods (Procter & Gamble, Pillsbury, 7-Up, Clorox, Campbell Soup), healthcare (Aetna, Blue Cross and Blue Shield), consumer electronics (Pacific Bell, Fujitsu America, Convergent Technologies), cable television (Viacom, Goodlife Television Network) and retail (McDonald's, Marine World, Princess Tours). Geoff is currently acting as Executive Vice President and Chief Marketing Officer of connectME.tv, a broadband video telephony and Internet access company. A noted writer and keynote speaker, he has lectured in the Stanford, USF and St. Mary's MBA programs. He has a BA from Princeton University in Art and Archeology, and an MBA from Stanford.

You can reach Geoff at:
Geoffrey E. Meredith
Lifestage Matrix Marketing
3517 Eagle Point Road
Lafayette, California 94549-2329
925.283.4806 [Voice]
925.283.4276 [Fax]
Lifestage@aol.com [email]

Charles D. Schewe is Professor of Marketing at the Eugene M. Isenberg School of Management at the University of Massachusetts at Amherst and principal in Lifestage Matrix Marketing. Dr. Schewe has researched and written extensively about the marketing implications of the aging process. For three years, Dr. Schewe was executive consultant for Age Wave, the

Emeryville, California, strategic planning and consulting company that focused on the Aging of America. His client engagements included K Mart, Grand Metropolitan, Prudential Bache, Nabisco, Sara Lee, Procter & Gamble, and Lucky Stores. He has also advised IBM, Spalding Sports Worldwide, and Kraft General Foods. It was at Age Wave that he met Geoff, and shortly thereafter they joined in Lifestage Matrix Marketing. The author of over 50 articles in academic journals, and more than 10 books, including the bestselling *Portable MBA in Marketing,* Dr. Schewe has been the keynote speaker for a wide range of U.S. and global audiences. His talks are wildly received. He received his PhD from the Kellogg Graduate School of Management at Northwestern University, as well as an MBA and BA from the University of Michigan. He was a Fulbright Scholar and frequent visiting professor to Lund University in Sweden as well as other universities in Europe and South America.

You can reach Charles at:
Charles D. Schewe, PhD
Lifestage Matrix Marketing
23 Ash Lane
Amherst, Massachusetts 01002
413.256.0914 [Voice]
413.253.3338 [Fax]
Schewe@mktg.umass.edu [email]

Janice Karlovich is a freelance writer and a proud member of the Generation X Cohort. She has a BS in journalism from the University of Illinois at Urbana-Champaign, and has written for such publications as *The Chicago Tribune;* the *New York Times;* and *The Fort Wayne, Indiana, Journal-Gazette.* She also does marketing communications writing for several Fortune 500 companies and other clients from her home-based office. Janice lives in Michigan with her husband, son, and two border collies.

PROLOGUE

Mark Twain once remarked that "Age is a thing of mind over matter. If you don't mind, it don't matter." Twain was an unusually perceptive man, but he was primarily a writer, not a businessman. And for anyone in the world of business, age does indeed matter! And this book will show you why.

The age that matters is not old age, but rather the time when one is emerging from youth and becoming an adult — the age from about 17–23. At that particular time of late adolescence and early adulthood, we seem to shed our self- and family-focused mental mind-set, strap on a set of receptors, and become far more involved in what is going on around us. This is a particularly impressionable time, a time when core values are being formed. And, the events that happen to us at that age forge values that do not change over our life's journey.

Some of these events are unique to each of us. For instance, if you make the athletic team in your senior year in high school, you — as an individual — may be forever focused on sports. Or, if one of your parents is laid off as a result of downsizing, you — as an individual — may forever look for job security. These events are personal events, felt only by you and a few around you. However, there are events that we share with many others that have a broad impact. For example, there were those of us who served alongside millions of others and fought a common enemy in World War II. We who did tend to submerge our individuality and are quintessential "team players." Or, there were those of us who sat together in front of the TV and heard the words "One small step for man . . . ." Those of us who did share an appreciation of our century's technological advances. Many of us suffered through gas lines during the oil crisis of 1973, and we who did support a strong and independent nation. Today, we find our lives meeting and merging digitally with others, as our lifestyles integrate more and more with the Internet. We think this is causing a global synchronization of values segments, but only time will tell.

These kinds of shared major events can have an impact on one's life at any age. A man in his 30s who was drafted in 1943 had his career and life put on hold for at least two years; he was forever changed by World

War II. But his core values actually had been formed a decade before, and he was basically the same person when he was discharged in 1945 as he was the day he got his dog tags. However, a man who was drafted at age 18 in 1943 was a fundamentally different person on VJ-Day. His core values, and those of the people who came of age with him during that time, were formed and fixed by World War II. His group — his "generational cohort" — was forever bonded by the values created by that war. Major shared events such as these, which happen during the key coming-of-age years stated above, forge groups of people together with common value sets. That is what this book is about.

We have learned that the most significant of these shared external events create values that stay with us throughout our entire lives, largely unchanged. These values are shaped by events that have two characteristics: The events must have social consequences, and they must be known and experienced by relatively large groups of people. We call these events "defining moments," and they become the glue that bonds certain age clusters together and separates them from contiguous but different clusters. They form distinct segments with a common thread and provide the basis for effective target marketing. We have borrowed the term "cohorts" from sociologists to define these age groups. Our generational cohort groups are aged not by decades, but rather by certain defining moments when that group was coming of age.

We began researching different age groups in the early 1990s, refining our theories and helping our clients utilize them over the next five years. As 1995 began, we published our understandings in an article titled "The Power of Cohorts" in *American Demographics* magazine (December, 1994; 22–29). We were overwhelmed by the response it created in the business world. Some of the most sophisticated American marketing companies contacted us to learn more, and our work for them both in the United States and abroad has helped us refine and expand our understanding of the generational cohort phenomenon. We have addressed many other groups in a variety of venues and found their responses equally as enthusiastic — so we knew we had to write this book.

Our understanding of defining moments, generational cohorts, and resultant common bonds has enhanced the marketing of a wide range of clients — from multinational giants, such as Coca-Cola, Levi Strauss, Nestle and Kellogg's — to smaller companies in the cable television, catalog, restaurant, and even funeral industries. We believe that you will find our ideas as presented in this book groundbreaking yet enjoyable to read, as we provide fascinating case histories from our work and other sources. We find these examples compelling, and we hope you are as drawn in by them as we have been. Most importantly, we believe the ideas set forth in this book will spur your thinking and your resulting marketing executions into new and more profitable realms. At least, that is our hope.

And here's an added, unexpected bonus: While this book is not intended to be a self-help book, we believe that in reading it, you will discover a lot about yourself, your grandparents, parents, siblings, children, friends, co-workers and others. You will see why people of other ages think and act as they do. This, we hope, will keep you wanting to turn the page.

So read on, have fun, and — by understanding generational cohorts and the essence of Multi-Dimensional Marketing™ — we hope you find new ways to make successful marketing happen!

— *GEOFFREY E. MEREDITH, MBA*
LAFAYETTE, CALIFORNIA

— *CHARLES D. SCHEWE, PHD*
AMHERST, MASSACHUSETTS

September 11, 2001: A New Defining Moment

When airplanes hijacked by terrorist fanatics slammed into the World Trade Center and the Pentagon, a soft, sun-slanted September morning was transformed into a new and tragic defining moment in United States history.

Defining moments are key to this book, because what they define are *generational cohorts*, our new market segmentation concept. Generational cohorts are the people with whom we are born, who travel through our lives, and who experience similar events, especially those events in the critical late adolescent/early adulthood years. At the heart of the cohort concept is the idea that major events that take place while we are coming of age imprint core values on us, values that don't change for the rest of our lives. These "defining moments" often are dramatic and momentous events: wars, political dislocations, assassinations, or economic upheavals. Pearl Harbor was one such event; the assassination of President John F. Kennedy was another. September 11, 2001, was clearly such a defining moment, one that will forge values and bond what we call the N-Gen Cohort forever through sharing this common location in history.

Like Pearl Harbor Day, September 11 has engendered a pride, a gut appreciation of the freedom of movement and freedom from fear we as Americans have enjoyed that others, such as the Israelis, have not. The seed of the motivating value based on fear of physical harm was planted for many school-age N-Gens by the Columbine shootings, but September 11 has for some widened that fear and made it more intense. A trusting innocence was lost that Tuesday morning.

By highlighting those freedoms we as a nation share, the World Trade Center/Pentagon disaster will have a coalescing effect on the N-Gen Cohort, making them consciously aware of their membership as *Americans* sharing this moment in history. As we show in Chapter 9, the core values of the N-Gen Cohort are in many ways more similar to those of the World War II Cohort (their grandparents) than to the Gen X Cohort (their immediate predecessors). To those values — teamwork, acceptance of authority, hard work to get ahead, a repudiation of the "free agent" mentality — the events of September 11 have now added the core value of intense *patriotism,* yet another commonality with their 1940s value-mates.

Defining moments also tend to intensify those core values that may be lying dormant throughout society as a whole. Despite the coarsening of our popular culture, we believe that America in 2001 is built on a bedrock of family values, of decency and courage and concern for neighbors and countrymen. The events of September 11 have thrown a spotlight on these values; we have, at least for a time, put our differences and personal strivings aside to focus on those things that really matter: family, loved ones, and quality of life, not material possessions.

Pearl Harbor was the moment that defined the break between the Depression Cohort and the World War II Cohort (although the war itself became an extended defining event). The assassination of President Kennedy was the defining moment that separates the Leading-Edge Baby Boomer value set from that of the Postwar Cohort. It is too soon to know if the September 11 tragedy will be the moment that forms a break between the current N-Gen Cohort and a new one, or simply reshapes and intensifies the character of the current one. For the N-Gen Cohort, it is, however, a defining moment indeed.

— Geoff Meredith and Charles Schewe
September 14, 2001

CHAPTER 1

TOWARD A NEW ERA OF MARKETING

As a marketing consultant preparing for two client meetings in the early 1990s, Geoff Meredith, one of the authors of this book, faced a serious dilemma. It had nothing to do with the larger issues of how to market a 500-branch supermarket chain to customers over age 65, or whether Baby Boomers will eat prunes in their old age. No, his dilemma cut to the root of a much more fundamental problem, one that many of you have no doubt struggled with yourselves — what to wear.

Because our Lifestage Matrix Marketing headquarters are in San Francisco's East Bay, it made sense to schedule client meetings that are 40 minutes away in downtown San Francisco on the same day. This made even more sense when you consider that two of our clients — Levi Strauss and Bank of America — were located just a few blocks from each other. But because the two companies' corporate cultures are practically polar opposites, figuring out what to wear posed a challenging clothing problem for Geoff, who was handling both accounts.

At Levi's Plaza, as you would expect, the attire was decidedly casual — jeans, jean jackets, T-shirts even. To show up for a consulting engagement in a suit would reflect a complete lack of understanding of the core corporate culture. Bank of America, however, five blocks to the east, still functioned with old-fashioned banking values and dress codes. Showing up at the bank in jeans was unthinkable. So there Geoff stood, puzzling at his closet door — suit and tie, or jeans and loafers? It seemed a question for the ages.

It would be nearly impossible to find one ensemble that was appropriate for both sets of clients, Geoff told himself. And then suddenly it hit him. The solution was to carry an extra outfit for a quick change between appointments. Following the meeting at Levi Strauss, Geoff drove to the bank's parking garage and made a bee-line to the men's room, where he made a hasty change out of his jeans (Levi's, of course) and slipped into the requisite pin-striped flannel suit, white shirt, and muted tie. He arrived at the bank looking a mirror image of the conservatively dressed bankers that were our clients.

Why all this fuss about what to wear? This story shows the importance of "tailoring" your marketing approach to meet the very real needs and expectations of your clients and customers. Different companies have different cultures that affect everything from flex time to dress codes. And more often than not, these cultures reflect not just the age, but the *coming-of-age* experiences of the key executives in command. Levi Strauss's CEO, Bob Haas, was in his late 40s when Levi's went to great lengths to get the new relaxed dress code established throughout Corporate America. He was a Baby Boomer who came of age during the live-and-let-live '60s. Bank of America was still strongly under the influence of Tom Clausen, in his 60s and a quintessential member of the more traditional set of Americans who came of age in the post–World War II era. The two cultures couldn't have been more different.

We have found that these same kinds of differences also exist among customers of consumer products and services. The challenge is treating customers as individuals, taking into consideration their unique values and tastes, while at the same time maximizing resources and strategic marketing executions.

Before we delve into the many fascinating nuances of generational cohorts, let's first take a brief look at how the field of marketing is evolving to incorporate the individual tastes of specific market segments.

Death of the Dress Code

The death of the dress code reflects the relaxed attitudes of Baby Boomers and younger cohorts, who want to be comfortable and casual *all* the time. This is what we call a "generational cohort effect." Unlike older people, they have little interest in adhering to inherited social codes about professionalism and appropriate dress. Consider these facts:

✦ According to several recent surveys, 80% of North America's major corporations have now switched to business casual, and half of all employees go to work in casual clothes every day.

✦ Companies have been forced to spell out the do's and don'ts of acceptable business casual attire, including advice such as "Anything you would wear to a gym, beach, trendy bar, or to clean the garage, please leave at home." After a Tennessee credit union went casual a few years ago, one employee actually came to work wearing flip-flops. He was asked to go home and change.

✦ The Washington Opera and other prestigious opera houses and theaters have been trying to attract younger audiences by loosening up dress codes, or doing away with them altogether.

FROM "ONE SIZE FITS ALL" TO "ONE-ON-ONE"

During the last half of the twentieth century, strategic marketing moved from the premise of *mass* marketing to market segmentation. Henry

Ford's "Let 'em have any color they want as long as it's black!" Model T philosophy gave way to carving out groups of customers with some common thread and transforming them into targetable segments. The latter strategy — market segmentation — has been employed faithfully by marketers and advertisers for years, like a trusted family friend. The strategic market planning of the 1980s and the "value marketing" of the 1990s both rested on this premise of partitioning the mass market.

Throughout the 1990s, however, a technologically based reshaping of competition began to take hold. It looked like it might be the final nail in the coffin for mass marketing, and the death knell for its offspring — market segmentation. In a landmark 1993 book, *The One To One Future: Building Relationships One Customer at a Time,* Don Peppers and Martha Rogers ignited the idea that today's technologies allow marketers to collaborate with customers on a personal "one-on-one" basis to satisfy their needs.[1] The recent eruption of home fax machines and e-mail allows individualized promotions to be transmitted directly to interested customers.

At the same time, database marketing also gained acceptance. For example, Fingerhut, the huge Minnesota mail-order company, was a leader in this area, capturing as many as 1,400 pieces of information about a single household and using the information to design personalized pitches such as, "Here's wishing your daughter, Mary, a Happy Sweet Sixteenth Birthday on June 12." Database personalization is getting more and more sophisticated all the time. At the Ritz-Carlton Hotel, ordering a Cobb salad from room service without tomatoes or onions is recorded in the corporate information system. On a later visit to the Ritz — at any of their locations — the Cobb salad automatically is served *sans* tomatoes and onions. With seemingly no effort at all, the Ritz delights and "wows" regular customers with exceptional service.

Playing off this database marketing, we have seen the rise of concepts such as "learning organizations," where companies constantly mine databases to learn how to better serve and satisfy their customers, and "mass customization," where products are made to order to meet the individual tastes of each consumer. Dell, for example, lets customers go online to order computers configured exactly to their specifications. "Cookies" imbedded in a user's IP address let marketers track and record your every stop on the Internet. (However, a plan to merge this data with conventional demographic databases was discovered, and almost put the Internet marketing firm DoubleClick out of business due to privacy concerns.) And, TiVo (the first digital recorder, which encodes and records video content on a hard drive, not tape) is programmed to begin recording new TV shows it thinks the owner will like, based on the types of show recorded in the past!

Seth Godin's 1999 book, *Permission Marketing,* enhanced this idea of personalized marketing even further. The old way of marketing, whereby advertisers use increasingly intrusive tactics to get your attention (and which Godin calls "interruption marketing,") is giving way to a more personal approach — literally asking consumers permission to offer them goods and services.[2] An example of this is the "opt-in" approach some marketers are using on the Internet. Rather than sending out "spam" (the online equivalent of interruption marketing), the "opt-in" process requires consumers to pre-approve e-mails, streamed video content or other communications, asking for specific permission to send them. One step stronger than the one-to-one concept, permission marketing gives the power of communication to the customer. This is quite a change from the old mass marketing approach.

During the late 1980s and early 1990s, "Generational Marketing" began to get a lot of media attention, spurred in part by the fact that the oldest members of the Baby Boomer Generation were about to turn 50. The whole notion of generations is a familiar one, from the "Lost Generation" of F. Scott Fitzgerald in the '20s to the "Silent Generation" of the '50s to the "Pepsi Generation" of the '80s. These generations were then shoehorned into decades; some fit into a decade pretty well, others didn't. A 1997 book by J. Walker Smith and Ann Clurman on generational marketing, *Rocking the Ages,*[3] took a different tack, defining the generations as:

✦ **Matures** born from 1909–1945

✦ **Boomers** born from 1946–1964

✦ **Generation X** born from 1965 to the early 1980s

However, although the premise that people of a similar age behave similarly is sound, these groupings are so large that they are essentially useless as marketing tools. A more precise means of age segmentation is needed, and we have found it: generational cohort segmentation.

By adding the powerful concept of *generational cohorts,* we are offering marketers a new model that takes much of the guesswork out of strategy development and helps marketers focus in on the underlying factors that drive consumer purchasing behavior. This new approach to marketing is based on accepted sociological theory and academic research, but it has very practical applications, as you will see in detail in later chapters. Our clients have used this marketing approach with much success, and so can you. It offers a new strategic thrust for capturing the hearts and minds of your customers. It also provides you with a toolkit of proven marketplace executions that will lead to greater sales.

COMING OF AGE WITH YOUR COHORT

Our approach focuses on the idea that to develop a rapport with and understanding of your customers, you must tap into the latent feelings and values formed when they were coming of age, a time that for most of us falls roughly between the ages of 17 and 23. While in this age span, your customers likely fell in love for the first time, became economic beings, developed their own value systems, explored new ideas, and, essentially, became adults. "Coming of age" is a very powerful time, and the values that are instilled then last a lifetime. We use the term "generational cohort" to refer to groups of people who went through this important stage at roughly the same time. (*Webster's New World College Dictionary* defines *cohort* as any group or "band." It stems from Latin, where a cohort was one of 10 divisions in a Roman legion. It was adapted as a sociological term by Karl Mannheim in Germany in the 1930s, as explained in more detail later in this chapter.)

DEFINING GENERATIONAL COHORTS

Generational cohorts are the people we are born with, travel through our lives with, and experience similar events with, especially those events at the critical late adolescent and early adulthood years. At the heart of the cohort concept is the idea that events that are happening when we are coming of age imprint core values. These "defining moments" can include such things as wars, political dislocations, assassinations, or economic upheavals. They can also be major technological changes, such as the invention of the atom bomb or the automobile, and especially in the area of communications — for example, the advancement from silent movies to talkies; radio; the rise of television; or the Internet.

Events that take place when we first become "economic adults" affect our life-long attitudes toward jobs, money, spending and saving, food and eating patterns, apparel, and much more. Events going on when we become sexually mature and sexually active influence our long-term core values about permissiveness, tolerance, and sexual behavior.

UNDERSTANDING COHORT VALUES AND EFFECTS

The values engendered by key historical events are manifested in different ways. As a generalization, *each cohort tends to value most that which it lacked when coming of age.* For example, people who came of age during the Great Depression still value financial security. Those who came of age during the Eisenhower era following World War II, a time of conformity and social repression, were titillated by expressions of rebellion and forbidden sexuality, embodied by James Dean, Marilyn Monroe, Elvis, and *Playboy.*

In fact, sexual attitudes are the prototypical cohort effect. (Cohort *effects* are the ways in which cohort *values* are exhibited or expressed.) A survey published not long ago by the National Opinion Research Center at the University of Chicago illustrates this point — even if their conclusion was backward.[4] The press release on the survey was headlined "Older people becoming more sexually tolerant as they age!" The study showed that respondents in the 40+ age brackets exhibited much greater acceptance of homosexuality, premarital sex, oral sex, and other sexual activities than they had in previous studies. But people weren't becoming more tolerant as they aged — rather, the cohort (Boomers, in this case) that had been sexually tolerant ever since its formative years was simply moving into the survey's older age brackets. Despite its relative lack of newsworthiness, the headline should have read, "Sexually tolerant people are getting older."

A related phenomenon is that the kind of music that you listened to when you first fell in love is likely to be the music format you most prefer for the rest of your life. The Rolling Stones have enormous appeal today because the Baby Boomers liked the Stones when they were teens, and they continued to like them into their 20s, 30s, and 40s. In other words, now that Boomers have begun to turn 50, they haven't suddenly switched to Glenn Miller. Likewise, today's Gen-Xers will likely still be listening to Nirvana and Pearl Jam when they approach retirement. Cohort effects do not change with one's age or stage of life. That's why they can be such useful marketing tools.

EXPLORING THE ORIGINS OF GENERATIONAL COHORT THEORY

Until now, the concept of generational cohort analysis has been almost totally ignored as a marketing tool. But the foundations of the cohort concept as a recognized academic construct date back to the 1920s. In this section, we'll take a step back and look at a timeline of key events in the development of cohort theory.

The idea of cohorts was first articulated by the German philosopher and sociologist Karl Mannheim in an attempt to understand and explain the political attitudes and behavior of German youth after World War I. Mannheim raised the notion of groups of people bound together by historical events in his 1928 analysis titled "The Problem of Generations." Mannheim — and almost all later sociologists — used this cohort hypothesis to examine political attitudes and behavior, postulating that "late adolescence and early adulthood are the formative years during which a distinct personal outlook on politics emerges."[5]

Mannheim specifies that the beginning point of this attitudinal development begins at about age 17, and suggests that by age 25 the process is over. (We think that for most individuals it is over a couple of years earlier — Mannheim was more interested in the concept than in precise demarcations.) He clearly differentiates between the concept of *cohort,* which is societally determined, and *generation,* which is biologically determined, and suggests that cohorts are only formed when political and historical events occur and make an important impact or impression on that society.

During a time of great social stability, or in peasant societies with little mass communication, for example, cohort formation will not occur; values can't be influenced by events that didn't happen, or that people didn't know about. It explains why one cohort can be quite lengthy — as for example, the Postwar Cohort in the United States, composed of people coming of age from 1946–1963, a 17-year period. The time frame is that long because things were pretty stable during that period; although there were some value-influencing events, such as the Korean War, there just weren't any huge historical disruptions that would cause an entirely new cohort to form.

In 1959, American demographer Norman B. Ryder adopted Mannheim's thesis and published "The Cohort as a Concept in the Study of Social Change."[6] Since that time, cohort analysis has been widely recognized and accepted in sociology. Ryder was a demographer, not a sociologist, and he introduced the notion of *demographic metabolism,* in which babies are continually added to society and elderly people die, making it ever changing.

Ryder goes on to say, "Each cohort has a distinctive composition and character," reflecting those events when they were becoming adults, the formative years when they completed their schooling, when they married, or when they entered the work force.

Numerous papers followed Ryder's, but almost all continued to be in the area of sociopolitical analysis, as in Neal Cutler's "Political Socialization Research as Generational Analysis: The Cohort Approach vs. the Lineage Approach,"[7] which again drew the distinction between cohorts and generations. In his 1979 book, *The People Puzzle,* human resource consultant Morris Massey also used a rudimentary form of cohort analysis to suggest how people of different age groups could learn to understand each other and get along better.[8]

Early on, Ryder called for empirical research to validate the coming-of-age hypothesis, but it wasn't until 1985 that the challenge was accepted by the Institute of Social Research at the University of Michigan at Ann Arbor. Under the direction of Drs. Howard Schuman and Jacqueline Scott, the institute did a nationally projectable study titled "Generations and Collective Memories,"[9] in which people were asked to report the historical events that seemed most important to them, and why. Surprise: The most important events came from their adolescence and early adulthood!

This study was repeated several years later in the United Kingdom by Dr. Scott and her colleague Lillian Zak and resulted in the same conclusions, even that the cohorts were much alike.[10] This is perhaps not unexpected, given the extremely close cultural and historical ties between the United Kingdom and the United States. On the other hand, countries with very different cultures and histories might be expected to have very different cohort structures, because the defining moments will be very different — and indeed we have found this to be the case, as discussed in Chapter 10, "Taking Generational Cohort Analysis Global."

Turning to more marketing-related research, a number of longitudinal studies using historical data for various product categories have been published. Dr. Joseph O. Rentz conducted two such studies while he was a marketing professor at the University of Georgia. The first study dealt with the consumption of colas, relied on historical category data from the Coca-Cola Company, and clearly showed that cola consumption is a cohort effect: the younger the individual, the greater the propensity to consume cola, and the higher the per capita consumption.[11] His second study was of coffee consumption data provided by the Maxwell House Division of General Foods (before it was acquired by Kraft), and showed equally strong cohort effects for coffee as for colas, *although in the reverse age-direction.* In the case of coffee, the *older* the cohort, the greater the propensity to consume coffee, and the higher the per capita consumption.[12] The studies make an extremely strong case (at least for the coffee and cola categories) that cohort effects are a major — indeed, *the* major — influence on consumption.

Turning these kinds of academic insights and understandings into actionable marketing programs that influence the consumption of one brand over another is the basis of our consulting practice. We have replicated Professor Rentz's analysis in numerous other categories, including breakfast cereals, prunes, chocolate beverages, restaurants, financial services, and apparel. And it is perhaps not coincidental that Coca-Cola and General Foods have been two of our clients.

Several other marketing-related studies have been undertaken by Professor Morris B. Holbrook of Columbia University and Professor Robert M. Schindler of Rutgers University-Camden. They have looked at cohort effects and musical preferences and found that people like the kind of music that was popular when they were coming of age[13] — a finding that we (by design) and others (largely by intuition) have used to great effect in a wide range of marketing campaigns.

Schindler and Holbrook have also done studies in the apparel and movie categories with similar results. In one report, they show that men prefer clothing styles that were popular when they were in their 20s,[14] and that the preference for motion pictures peaks for those movies popular when they were in early adulthood.[15] This last study has important implications for the use of nostalgia in building advertising and marketing appeals.

UNDERSTANDING COHORT ANALYSIS AS A MARKETING TOOL

As noted above, the idea that different age groups are unique is the essence of generational marketing, which maintains that a new generation begins when a person has children, roughly in 25-year periods.

But using Mannheim's theory as a guide, we have concluded that popular generational breakdowns — Matures (55 and up), Boomers (36–54), and Xers (35 and under), and so forth — are really too broad to be useful as marketing targets. For example, if you are 55 today, how much do you really have in common with people in their 80s? Not much, we suspect. And if you're 35, how similar are your buying habits to those of a 16-year-old? In our country and culture, the answer is usually "not very," because people of these ages have different core values. Why? They were influenced by different "defining moments" — those key events that bound them into different cohorts.

DEFINING MOMENTS CREATE TIES THAT BIND

We all experience a wide range of events during our coming-of-age years. Not all are defining moments, however. Only those that are strong enough to have a lasting social consequence become defining moments. The death of President John F. Kennedy in 1963 was just such an event. It stole the enthusiasm and excitement for a new tomorrow that characterized the Camelot days. The death of John Lennon in 1980, however, another event that shocked the world, was not a defining moment because it had no lasting significant social consequences. Table 1.1 shows a comprehensive list of important historical events of the twentieth century. These were compiled in a recent study done by Stephanie Noble, a professor at the University of Mississippi.[16] Her methodology and results are similar to that of the earlier University of Michigan research into the lasting impact made by such defining moments. It should be noted however, that for some of the most recent events we can't be sure just yet that they are truly defining moments.

Table 1.1: Important Historical Events of the Twentieth and Twenty-First Centuries

Time period events occurred	Events
1930–1939	✦ Depression
	✦ Franklin Roosevelt's New Deal
	✦ Implementation of Social Security
	✦ Social reform
	✦ Labor reform
1940–1949	✦ World War II
	✦ Pearl Harbor
	✦ D-Day invasion
	✦ A-Bomb/Hiroshima
	✦ GI Bill of Rights
1950–1959	✦ Korean War
	✦ Advent of television
	✦ Sputnik
	✦ Equal Education Act
	✦ Polio/Salk's vaccine
	✦ Civil Rights movement
1960–1964	✦ Social change of '60s
	✦ Cuban missile crisis
	✦ John F. Kennedy assassination
	✦ Equal Rights/Civil Rights Act
1965–1969	✦ Robert Kennedy assassination
	✦ Woodstock
	✦ Man walks on moon
	✦ Martin Luther King, Jr. assassination
1965–1973	✦ Vietnam

Time period events occurred	Events
1970–1979	✦ Kent State riots
	✦ Watergate/Nixon
	✦ Oil crisis; '70s inflation
	✦ Stock market decline
	✦ Women's rights movement
Throughout 1980s	✦ The Reagan Years
	✦ Height of HIV/AIDS scare
	✦ Stock market rise
1985–1989	✦ *Challenger* explosion
	✦ Fall of Berlin Wall
1990–1994	✦ Gulf War
	✦ Advent of the personal computer
	✦ Breakup of USSR
	✦ World Trade Center bombing
	✦ Waco
1995–1999	✦ President Clinton's affair
	✦ Advent of the Internet
	✦ O.J. Simpson trial
	✦ Oklahoma City bombing
	✦ Columbine shooting
2001	✦ Terrorist attack on World Trade Center and Pentagon

Source: Stephanie Noble, University of Mississippi

These defining moments influence a cohort group's preferences, desires, attitudes, and buying behaviors in ways that remain with them virtually unchanged for the rest of their lives. This includes attitudes about everything from appropriate dress to family responsibilities to job satisfaction. Defining moments create generational cohort homogeneity that is missed in generational marketing. As a result, evoking strategic cohort words, symbols, and memories can bring substantial rewards for marketers. Using sociological research and the significant historical and social events of the last century as our guide, we have identified seven distinct American cohorts.

IDENTIFYING THE SEVEN DISTINCT AMERICAN COHORTS

At the beginning of the twenty-first century, we can use these defining moments to group living American adults into seven distinct cohorts (see Table 1.2):

✦ **Depression Cohort:** Aged 80–89 in 2001. This group's coming-of-age experience consisted of economic strife, elevated unemployment rates, and the need to take menial jobs to survive. Financial security — what they most lacked when coming of age — rules their thinking.

✦ **World War II Cohort:** Aged 74–79 in 2001. Sacrifice for the common good was widely accepted among members of the World War II Cohort, as evidenced by women working in factories for the war effort and men going off to fight. Overall, this cohort was focused on defeating a common enemy, and their members are more team-oriented and patriotic than those of other generational cohorts.

✦ **Postwar Cohort:** Aged 56–73 in 2001. These individuals experienced a time of remarkable economic growth and social tranquillity, a time of family togetherness, school dress codes, and moving to the suburbs. While there were some elements of unrest (the Korean conflict, McCarthyism), overall this was a pretty tranquil time, which is why this is such a long cohort.

✦ **Leading-Edge Baby Boomer Cohort:** Aged 47–55 in 2001. This group remembers the assassinations of John and Robert Kennedy and Martin Luther King, Jr. It was the loss of JFK that first shaped this cohort's values. They became adults during the Vietnam War and watched as the first man walked on the moon. Leading-Edge Boomers are very aware of their cohort grouping, and are very self-assured and self-centered: They championed causes with fervor because they were sure of being right (Greenpeace, civil rights, women's lib), and felt equally justified in being hedonistic and self-indulgent (pot, "free love," sensuality). Because of their position following the "birth dearth" of the Depression years, they had (and continue to have) an influence on society disproportionate to their numbers, being smaller as a group than the later Boomer cohort which followed.

✦ **Trailing-Edge Baby Boomer Cohort:** Aged 36–46 in 2001. This group witnessed the fall of Vietnam, Watergate, and Nixon's resignation. The oil embargo, raging inflation rate, and the more than 30% decline in the S&P Index led these individuals to be far less optimistic about their financial future than the Leading-Edge Boomers, whom they feel got the biggest opportunities in jobs, houses and investments.

✦ **Generation X Cohort:** Aged 24–35 in 2001. These are the latchkey children of the '80s, who have received the most negative publicity. Perhaps because many have seen first-hand the trauma of divorce, this cohort has delayed marriage and children, and they don't take those commitments lightly. More than other groups, this cohort accepts cultural diversity and puts quality of personal life ahead of work life. They're "free agents," not "team players." Despite a rocky start into adulthood, this group shows a spirit of entrepreneurship unmatched by any other cohort. Take a look at many Internet start-ups and you'll find successful Gen-Xers who did it their way.

✦ **N Generation Cohort:** Aged 17–23 in 2001. We call the youngest cohort the "N Generation," or "N-Gens," because the advent of the Internet is a defining event for them, and because they will be the "engine" of growth over the next two decades. They are also known as "Gen Y" or "Millenials," and while still a work in progress, their core value structure seems to be quite different from that of Gen X. They are more idealistic and team-oriented, without the cynical, "What's in it for me?" free-agent mind-set of many Xers.

TABLE 1.2: COHORT MARKETING GROUPS

Cohort	Born	Coming of age	Age in 2001	Percentage of adult pop.	Defining moments
Depression	1912–1921	1930–1939	80–89	13 million, 5%	◆ Great Depression
World War II	1922–1927	1940–1945	74–79	17 million, 7%	◆ World War II
Postwar	1928–1945	1946–1962	56–73	47 million, 21%	◆ End of World War II ◆ Moving to the suburbs ◆ Korean War ◆ Emergence of rock 'n' roll ◆ Good economic times ◆ Cold War ◆ McCarthyism ◆ Civil Rights movements
Leading-Edge Boomers (I)	1946–1954	1963–1972	47–55	31 million, 14%	◆ Assassination of JFK, RFK, and Martin Luther King, Jr. ◆ Vietnam War ◆ First man on the moon
Trailing-Edge Boomers (II)	1955–1965	1973–1983	36–46	49 million, 22%	◆ Fall of Vietnam ◆ Nixon resigns ◆ Watergate ◆ Energy crisis
Generation X	1966–1976	1984–1994	25–35	42 million, 19%	◆ Reaganomics ◆ *Challenger* explosion ◆ Gulf War ◆ Stock Market crash of 1987 ◆ Fall of Berlin Wall ◆ AIDS crisis
N Generation	1977–?	1995–?	24 and under	26 million (aged 17–23), 12%	◆ The Internet ◆ Columbine school shootings ◆ Clinton's impeachment ◆ Good economic times ◆ Terrorist attack on World Trade Center and Pentagon

In all, we have identified seven adult generational cohort groups that are alive in the United States today. By the time you reach the end of this book, you will be intimately acquainted with each of them. But, for now, we simply want to introduce you to the concept and give you a feel as to how each cohort differs from the one before and after it.

Multi-Dimensional Marketing™: Five Factors

Over the years in our research and consulting work, we have refined the concept of generational cohort analysis, combined it with other variables that affect purchasing behavior, and used it to develop the concept of Multi-Dimensional Marketing™. In a nutshell, this model provides a way to look at customers not just as flat statistics on a page, but as multidimensional beings, motivated and driven by a complex matrix of demographics, physiology, and emotion. Generational cohort analysis is the key new element in Multi-Dimensional Marketing. It provides us with information about the defining moments and values formed during a cohort's coming-of-age experience. These core values typically don't change over time, so they provide us with a reliable way to connect with people again and again on a very personal level. But cohort analysis is only one piece of the puzzle. In all, there are five factors that influence buying behavior and make up Multi-Dimensional Marketing:

+ **Cohort Values:** The members of our cohort group are people who are about our age and with whom we shared important historical events when we were coming of age together. These shared experiences help shape our cohort group's long-term values, which we carry through life virtually unchanged.

+ **Lifestages:** These are the roles we take on or act out over our lifetime: spouse, parent, divorcee, retiree, and so on. Lifestages define our attitudes, outlooks and daily activities, but different cohorts often react to the same lifestage in completely different ways.

+ **Physiographics:** These are changes in bodily appearance and function as we age. For example, older people are more likely to suffer from reduced grip strength, while middle-aged people are just beginning to notice gray hair.

✦ **Emotions and affinities:** Our age affects our attitudes about a wide range of issues. For example, teens tend to worry about their appearance, while new parents tend to put their child's needs ahead of their own.

✦ **Socioeconomics:** This includes our financial, educational, career, marital, and other social and economic states. While important to keep in mind, a person's socioeconomic status tells us little about the underlying motives for consumption behavior.

Arrayed as a matrix — the Lifestage Analytic Matrix™ — these five factors become the primary tool for applying the conceptual framework of Multi-Dimensional Marketing in real-world situations. The Lifestage Analytic Matrix is described more fully in Chapter 2, "What Makes Us Tick: Using the Lifestage Analytic Matrix™," and the five factors are detailed on a cohort-by-cohort basis in chapters 3–9. All these factors can be of greater or lesser importance depending on the particular product category of interest. Over time, these factors continue to combine in new ways to impact the purchasing behavior of the ever-savvy American consumer.

Four of the five factors — lifestages, physiographics, affinities, and socioeconomics — are typically determined by age. For example:

✦ Individuals generally marry for the first time in their 20s and become empty-nesters at about age 50.

✦ Eyes generally begin to falter in the mid-40s, and hearing tends to waiver as one reaches 60.

✦ Income peaks at age 49.

These are all "aging effects." However, what is so new and different about our Multi-Dimensional Marketing approach is the discovery that the cohort-values factor overlays the other four factors and shapes how they impact marketplace behavior. Baby Boomers, for example, who overwhelmingly favor staying and looking young, demand appearance-enhancing eyewear to compensate for flagging eyes. Older generational cohort groups, meanwhile, were not so concerned with such features when they first began to experience visual impairment.

To cite another example: We believe that the Leading-Edge Baby Boomer Cohort, who gave their children lots of independence when they were growing up, will bring this same approach to grandparenting, creating new markets for companies that provide support for "distance grandparenting" — offering online customized gift giving for busy Leading-Edge Boomer grandparents. Older cohort groups, however, showed a much greater involvement in being "companions" with their grandchildren. Such understanding of the cohort values factor allows strong strategic and tactical guidelines for future success. Our approach puts cohort values as the central determinant of how these other forces drive behavior.

Five New Rules of Multi-Dimensional Marketing

A large number of marketers may already think they're doing something similar to cohort marketing because they're doing segmentation based on age. But cohorts don't divide on commonly used age breaks (18–34, 45–54, and so on), and each common age grouping has a continually changing cohort composition as one cohort exits and another one enters. It takes a lot of insight and analysis to figure out when one cohort ends and another one begins, and even those companies who try base their approach largely on intuition with no underlying theoretical structure to make it work. As a result, sometimes they guess right and things work out very well. Other times, they get it horribly wrong. The approach outlined in this book will help you to devise a reliable marketing strategy that consistently taps into the underlying factors that drive consumer purchasing behavior. To help you do this, we have developed five new rules for marketing in the twenty-first century. These rules are discussed in the sections that follow.

Rule #1: Demographics don't do the job anymore

In the past, sophisticated marketers, such as Procter & Gamble or Kraft General Foods, relied heavily on defining their marketing targets in

---

Which Cohort Are You?

Take a moment to think back to your own coming-of-age
years. The clothes you wore and the music you listened
to when you were 17–23 tell a lot about which cohort
group you likely belong to. To discover your true cohort
identity, take this short quiz.

When you were 17–23:

1. What kind of music did you listen to?
    A. Ricky Martin / 98°
    B. Pearl Jam / REM
    C. Bob Seger / Santana
    D. Rolling Stones / The Beatles
    E. Elvis Presley / Frankie Avalon
    F. Glenn Miller / Tommy Dorsey

2. What was your favorite activity?
    A. Chatting with friends on the Internet
    B. Watching MTV
    C. Disco dancing
    D. Smoking pot and protesting against "The
        Establishment"
    E. Hanging out at the drive-in
    F. Listening to big band music on the radio

---

terms of demographics, such as gender, age, income and education.
These categories used to define people pretty well — if you knew these
things, you pretty much knew who you were talking to. But they don't
today. Here's why:

As marketing consultants, one of our mantras is to "touch the
consumer." So we do a lot of consumer research, especially focus groups.
When we pick respondents, our clients usually begin by specifying a
demographic profile. A typical example might be men, aged 55–64,
household incomes of $50,000 or more, and at least some college
education. This is a pretty usual marketing target, one that you can

3. How did you dress?
   A. Capri pants, tie-dye, and platform shoes
   B. Oversized pants and flannel shirts
   C. Polo shirts, loafers and feathered bangs
   D. Tie-dye, bell bottoms and sandals
   E. Poodle skirts, saddle shoes, or like James Dean
   F. Military uniform, plain suits, unadorned blouses

4. Which TV shows or movies did you like?
   A. Dawson's Creek / The Blair Witch Project
   B. The Simpsons / The Breakfast Club
   C. Rocky / Star Wars
   D. The Mod Squad / Easy Rider
   E. I Love Lucy / Rear Window
   F. Casablanca / Yankee Doodle Dandy

If most of your answers came up:	Then you most likely fit into this cohort group:
A	N Generation
B	Generation X
C	Trailing-Edge Baby Boomer
D	Leading-Edge Baby Boomer
E	Postwar
F	World War II

specify when buying media, among other things — it's a traditional way of defining a marketing segment.

And so, sitting in the focus group in front of the one-way mirror, we often find two men, both fitting the same demographic profile: both 61 years old, making $55,000 and $63,000 respectively, both college graduates. We want them to talk about their motivations for buying or not buying a particular product.

While they appear the same demographically, in reality they couldn't be more different. One took early retirement at 59½, is living off his pension and IRAs, and is mostly puttering around the house, driving his wife crazy, and setting off on forays across the country in his Winnebago to see his grandkids. The other is a newlywed of two years (for the third time), has a toddler around the house, and is working harder than ever before to make alimony payments, save for the toddler's college education, and put away a little for his own retirement — which looks like it will be a long way off.

Identical demographics. Radically different lives. Why? Because these men are in very different *lifestages.* In the past, lifestages used to happen predictably. You went to school, you got a job, you got married and had a family, you worked for a long time, you retired for a little while, then you died. And you did all these things at more or less the same age as everybody else.

Today, it's much different. People are going back to school after working for years, getting married several times, retiring early, retiring late, or not retiring at all, and due to an increased life expectancy, doing it all a lot longer than they used to.

RULE #2: GENERATIONAL COHORTS
REINTERPRET LIFESTAGES

When Mazda first introduced the Miata in 1986, the company envisioned it as an entry-level vehicle for young, mostly single people: sporty, but small and inexpensive. And so the introductory advertising and brochures for the '86 Miata featured a group of young 20-somethings frolicking on the beach with their new Miata.

So, imagine Mazda's surprise when the first trend analysis of sales were compiled, and the median age of the Miata buyer was 42! Forty-two-year-olds weren't supposed to buy sporty cars — if anything, the auto industry had envisioned them as ready to trade in their family station wagons for a more luxurious, more comfortable vehicle that better suited their move from the child-rearing lifestage into the empty-nesting one. Middle-age was upon them — they should be buying Buicks or Oldsmobiles, not Miatas, or so Mazda thought.

But the people turning 42 in 1988 were born in 1946 — the leading edge of the Baby Boomer Cohort. Continually striving for youth, hedonistic and self-indulgent, the Boomers weren't about to become middle-aged (and aren't quite yet — although it's squarely upon them). Many had always wanted a sports car, but could never afford or justify one in their early marriage, early family, and early career lifestages. But now that they were empty-nesters, they were finally going to fulfill their dream. The empty-nesting lifestage that meant middle-aged comfort (and middle-aged vehicles) for older cohorts meant a chance to recapture youth for the Boomers. Same lifestage — different cohort — radically different results.

So you can see that simply assuming that tomorrow's young, middle-aged, and older adults will respond to marketing in similar ways as they do today could lead to disastrous results. Thanks to Boomers, who broke the mold and loosened up attitudes at both ends of the age spectrum, each age group responds differently to each new lifestage they enter. Suddenly everybody's unique. Boomers are redefining middle age, and Gen-Xers will likely do the same when their time comes.

RULE #3: NEW COHORTS MEAN NEW BEHAVIORS

If demographics no longer segment customers adequately, what does? There is a complex but predictable relationship between generational cohort values and other age-related motivators, such as lifestages (Are you a student or a grandmother?), physiology (Do you suffer from arthritis, or are you at your physical peak?), and other factors. In fact, by combining all of the various factors into a multi-dimensional matrix (see Chapter 2, "What Makes Us Tick: Using the Lifestage Analytic Matrix™"), the future can often be predicted with a fair amount of certainty. How? In part by looking at all of the buying factors and laying the driver of cohort values over the top. Doing so gives you a good idea as to how Generation X will react to parenting, or how the Baby Boomers will handle retirement. That's the power of Multi-Dimensional Marketing, what's different about it, and what this book is all about.

Since cohorts offer the only real constant in the equation, they are the key to Multi-Dimensional Marketing. How people react to the aging process is largely determined during their coming-of-age years. For example, the Baby Boomers have fought middle age every step of the way, using plastic surgery, day spas, hair dyes, and sports cars to help them hold on to their youth any way they can.

By focusing on the intersection point of cohort values and other age-related motivators, you can flesh out details about consumers and learn to develop a kind of portrait of your target audience. This will provide you with a stronger understanding of whom you're selling to, and what products and messages this group will find most appealing. You can also tailor marketing campaigns (even for the same product) to emphasize different attributes or benefits for maximum appeal to different cohorts.

RULE #4: VALUES DEFINE GENERATIONAL COHORTS, AND CORE VALUES DON'T CHANGE

As one of our clients said to us recently, "In an ever faster world of change, the one constant is values!" And because values define cohorts, knowing the cohort value structure is an invaluable marketing tool.

Values come in many shapes and sizes. Some values are permanent in scope, such as self-fulfillment or security. We call these *core values*. Other values can be characterized as superficial and changeable, such as convenience, or acquiring material possessions. These, we call *changeable values*.

"Hassle-Free" Holidays Reflect Changing Cohort Values

Decorating for Christmas used to be an important holiday tradition for most families. But that is changing as busy Baby Boomers reach their peak income years, and look to pay others to do these and other time-consuming tasks.

In some upscale suburbs, for example, business is booming for many landscaping companies, who charge anywhere from $450 to $3,000 or more to install residential outdoor Christmas lighting displays. The service includes set up, removal, the purchase of lights, and in some cases, round-the-clock service to fix the lights should something go wrong. All customers need to do is write a check and flip the switch.

This kind of "hassle-free" decorating is becoming all the rage, and is just one more example of how changing cohort values are affecting nearly every aspect of life—even holiday traditions.

Core values are molded by external events at the time they are being formed, and they do not change to any significant degree during the course of one's life. In most cases, these core values define a specific cohort and provide cues for behavior. One does not journey through life alternately looking for security, then showing no concern for it, then wanting security again. If we value security, we always seek it out.

Although changeable values are not as long-served as core values, they often provide the means to *achieving* our core values in different lifestages. For example, acquiring material possessions may enhance self-fulfillment in one's younger years, while having more things might not rank as important as one grows older. Older people may well choose other means for attaining self-fulfillment, such as building a strong relationship with their grandchildren. The means change over time, but the core value of self-fulfillment remains constant.

In some cases, deficits most influence people's value structure — they value most that which was most lacking during their value-forming years. For example, those who felt less nurtured as they were coming of age deem the value of belonging as most important. The value of security is most important for those who felt threatened as they matured. In other cases, the value structure is most influenced by emulation. In these cases, people tend to value most that which was demonstrated by strong role models, such as their parents or teachers.

Our research clearly shows that generational cohort values are more closely related to core values and provide ongoing cues for human — and consumer — behavior. And because these values do not change over one's life, they provide a solid platform on which to build brand equity. They are emotional motivators that offer opportunities for age-directed, cohort-directed marketing campaigns that work.

RULE #5: YOUNGER GENERATIONAL COHORTS ARE CONVERGING GLOBALLY

If you have traveled to any developed countries in recent years, you probably have noticed how similar the teenagers and 20-somethings are to those in the United States. You see it in their clothing, music, movies, television programming, even in their overall lifestyles. The basic youth uniform of sneakers, jeans, T-shirts with logos, and billed hats (often worn backwards) has found its way into virtually every nook and cranny of the economically developed world. Our work with clients has demonstrated that the underlying value systems of the youngest generational cohorts are likewise becoming increasingly similar worldwide.

We speculate that this "synchronization" of the youngest cohorts globally is due to the Internet's linking people together, or to the advent of truly global communication in general. It didn't used to be like this. For example, our research into numerous countries finds that World War II is most often mentioned as an event that defined cohorts. However, the *values* that same event generated in different countries differ. Consider the United States, France, and Japan. Our work has clearly shown that those Americans who came of age during World War II are the most patriotic of all cohorts. Those who came of age in France at the same time, while ultimately triumphant, actually had the war fought on their soil. With the entire society actually living the war (unlike those who stayed at home in the United States), the French World War II cohort group values peace and tranquility, stability in home life, and material possessions. The corresponding Japanese cohort group displays a longing for things such as control and mastery of their world and self-confidence, because both were lacking as a result of their defeat. One defining moment, three different value sets. And in many countries of South America, World War II did not directly or significantly impact populations at all. For them, there *is* no "World War II Cohort."

But that was 50 years ago, when one country or region could go about its business relatively isolated from the rest of the world. Today, we have the Internet, which enables instant access to communication and information anywhere in the world. We have advanced communication media that broadcast messages instantly and pervasively all over the planet: MTV, the Superstation, and CNN are virtually everywhere. STAR (the satellite broadcasting system owned by News Corp.) beams its way into much of Asia, even into otherwise sequestered China. And you can see new American movies all around the globe, and not much later than we do here in the States.

The media that transmit and often interpret defining moments have allowed impressionable late adolescents and early adults the opportunity to share in events. And the ease of transportation has made the world more and more accessible to young adults. In 1998, for example, 125,000 American students studied abroad, up from 76,000 in 1996. And increasingly, they have ventured to developing countries, spreading similar values. The result of this mass-globalization of information and entertainment, combined with ease of travel, has been that values for global generational cohorts are increasingly becoming similar. So what are some of the expressions of global values shared by youth around the world? Young adults in developed countries are pushing off responsibility by marrying later in life. Japanese males, for example, on average marry at age 30. Young adults in more and more countries are accepting early divorce in first marriages, and at a younger age. Cohabitation and a more casual philosophy about sex are increasingly accepted by today's global youth. These are Gen-X value manifestations, as valid in most developed countries as they are in the United States. And the N-Gen seems even more aligned worldwide.

HITTING THE MOVING TARGET

In 1996, the first of the demographically-defined Leading-Edge Boomer cohort turned 50. The Census Bureau predicts that the number of Americans 50 and older should grow from 79.6 million in 2000 to about 96.4 million by 2020 — an increase of about 21%. This represents the greatest gain of any age group. The two Boomer cohorts — Leading-Edge and Trailing-Edge — will be the largest population of 50+ consumers the United States has ever seen. And because the Boomers have driven everything in our popular culture since the days when they were babies, we believe they will continue to do so in the future. Our motto is "50 ain't what it used to be!" — and we predict that the demographic shift from a predominantly youthful population to a largely middle-aged and older-base population will have profound effects upon the composition of the marketplace and the way in which goods and services are consumed for years to come.

Changing demographics are having a powerful impact on all aspects of society. For example, as we saw with Levi Strauss and Bank of America, the move from business suits to Casual Friday, to Business Casual, to jeans and T-shirts in the American workplace is a direct result of Baby Boomers hitting middle age and taking over positions of authority in U.S. companies. Boomers, who thumbed their noses at authority and wore tie-dyed shirts, bell-bottoms, and long hair in their youth, have now risen to power in many organizations. They have thrown established suit-and-tie dress codes out the window. Business casual dress codes reflect Boomers' casual attitudes toward just about everything. These attitudes have trickled down to nearly every corner of society, including marketing. And because of their sheer numbers, the influence of the combined Boomer cohorts is expected to grow as more and more flood into their peak income years. This will have major implications on business and marketing for years to come.

In this day and age, it's critical to realize that age demographics are a moving target. For example, a common marketing target today is the demographic break of people aged 50–64. However, this common age break in 1990 was composed completely of the Postwar Cohort. Today, it's one-third Boomers, two-thirds Postwar, and 10 years from now, as Figure 1.1 clearly shows, it will be completely Boomers. The same age bracket — three entirely different groups of people. In some cases, the lifestage transitions will be the same. For example, due to the biological imperatives of childrearing, people in their mid-50s and early 60s will mostly be experiencing the empty-nest lifestage. So, if your market target is based on empty-nesters, targeting the 50–64 age bracket may make some sense. However, if you're marketing based on values, you must understand that the values held by those in that age cluster change every few years as a different cohort, with its own unique values, moves in and then out of that age bracket.

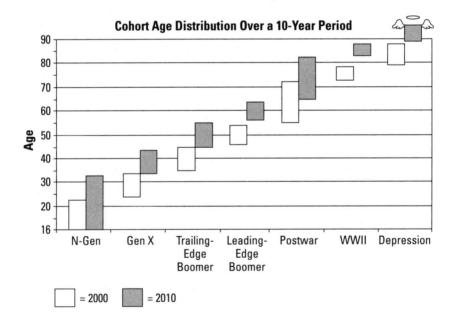

Figure 1.1: U.S. Cohort Composition, 2000 and 2010. Age segmentation is a moving target.

Finally, as the age distribution in the United States changes, so will consumers' wants and needs. These cohorts will impose their values and preferences on the way they carry out their lives. Grandparenting, for instance, is likely to take on very different rights and responsibilities as the individualistic, indulgent "Me Generation" Trailing-Edge Baby Boomers move into this lifestage. And what will happen as today's teens become parents? Understanding generational cohort values and plotting them alongside lifestages and other factors will allow for better forecasting of changes and quicker response in meeting marketplace wants and desires.

USING GENERATIONAL COHORTS IN YOUR OWN MARKETING

Because demographics don't define people the way they once did, and because of differences in the way various cohorts approach new lifestages, old marketing strategies no longer apply. That's why we have developed Multi-Dimensional Marketing — to eliminate the guesswork and provide marketers with a firm foundation on which to build effective marketing strategies.

Understanding what motivates the customer is the crux of successful marketing. Generational cohort values drive many behaviors, including consumption. These values tell us much about what people in various age groups desire and prefer, and why they do what they do. They also provide the platform for developing reliable marketing strategies and executions. Evoking cohort coming-of-age experiences is a powerful but subtle way of tapping into cohort values, a way to communicate very strongly that "This is for you — we understand you!" Here are a few examples of successful marketing strategies:

✦ Cohort values helped shape the tenor of the programming offered by one of our clients, the GoodLife TV Network, a cable television network that focuses on viewers over the age of 49. Understanding cohorts and their values helped GoodLife better strategically meet the unique interests of its audience. For example, *Bonanza, Make Room for Daddy,* and *Ozzie and Harriet* all reflect the stability of the family that is so central to the Postwar Cohort. The depiction of the American family in each of those programs is a far cry from the depiction of the American family in the 2000 Oscar winner *American Beauty.*

✦ A catalog company with whom we have worked offers a large array of products that are not only hard to find today, but also are highly reminiscent of customers' coming-of-age experiences. Most of the catalog's buyers are over the age of 50 and love such products as old-fashioned and modest boy-leg women's swimsuits, cotton muumuu dresses, Bissell carpet sweepers, and Polar Ice aftershave, which to older male cohorts quickly conjures up memories of their first barbershop shave. These products are put into black-and-white catalogs that show drawings of the products, not photographs. The catalogs themselves are nostalgic, conjuring up strong memories of old Sears & Roebuck catalogs from the early twentieth century. The company has even developed special cohort-specific catalogs that speak to customers with the language, icons, symbols and values of their youth.

✦ For another of our clients, we used "cohort icons" — pictures of heroes of a particular cohort and language of the times — on direct mail envelopes. This campaign resulted in new subscription response rates for cable television companies (Multiple System Operators — "MSOs") that were six times greater than previously achieved!

✦ Specific products can be developed that directly reflect the values of different cohort groups. Boomers prefer informality, and once they rose into the ranks of management, they were the ones who gave us Casual Fridays. Catering to this preference, Levi Strauss developed a line of casual slacks targeting Baby Boomers. Dockers are now part of the unofficial office uniform for many men.

✦ Promotional messages targeting cohorts can reflect cohort values. Print ads for Polo clothing targeting Generation X depict lifestyles focused on quality of life, a value prized by today's 20- and 30-somethings. Ethnic and racial diversity, embraced by Generation X and the N Generation is reflected in the context of advertisements such as Benetton, Calvin Klein and the Gap.

As you delve deeper into this book, you will see execution after execution that incorporates generational cohort values as the fundamental foundation upon which our marketing program is based.

The use of age to demarcate cohort segments is the way to get started, but don't rely on outdated, over-broad age segments, such as 55+. Age is a highly usable segmentation variable because most media can be purchased on the basis of age. That is, a marketer can buy space or time in newspapers, magazines, television, and radio with the cost based on the delivery of a particular age demographic, as can lists suitable for direct mail or telemarketing campaigns. But efficiently delivering the message to people of a particular age is meaningless if that message doesn't resonate with the viewer.

Generational cohort segmentation isn't just a theoretical tool — it can be easily implemented. And knowing the motivators that emanate from shared coming-of-age experiences provides the basis for the message. Sophisticated marketers' growing love affair with database management suggests that targeting by age segment can provide an easy key to unlocking success. So whether you employ congregate marketing by targeting segments, or use the contemporary one-to-one marketing approach, generational cohorts and Multi-Dimensional Marketing can improve your strategic and tactical executions.

RETHINKING YOUR MARKETING STRATEGY

Consumers are more savvy than ever before, demanding personal attention and products that suit their lifestyles. They do not want to be encumbered with mistargeted or misguided products and promotions. A Multi-Dimensional Marketing approach can provide a sense of familiarity and personal appeal to these savvy consumers, bringing them one step closer to making a purchase and providing the groundwork for building long-term relationships.

We hope to redirect marketing efforts away from so-called "tried and true" twentieth-century approaches that so often focused only on demographics and over-broad characterizations. These approaches may have worked for you in the past. But chances are they won't work for you in the future. Now is the time to start rethinking your marketing strategy. Multi-Dimensional Marketing will give you a more accurate view of the motivators affecting buying decisions for a wide range of consumers.

Multi-Dimensional Marketing can also help in designing more effective communication campaigns. Utilizing music, movie stars, or other icons that cohorts identified with in their past is an effective selling technique. These tactics work because they rely on nostalgia — reminding individuals of the good old days. Many companies have already begun to use this tactic, as evidenced by the growing number of commercials with songs, logos, and actual commercial footage from the past. Volkswagen used this strategy to reintroduce the Beetle. The strategy was to provide Leading-Edge Baby Boomers with a warm familiarity that reminded them of their youth, while tapping into the "retro" affinities of younger cohorts.

Furthermore, if you are using permission marketing or one-to-one marketing, or even some form of mass marketing as part of your strategy, your communications will only be more powerful if cohort-related signals are embedded in the message. Whatever approach you choose, Multi-Dimensional Marketing offers a wealth of opportunity to grab the minds, hearts and pocketbooks of today's marketplace.

In chapters 3–9, we will introduce you to the seven distinct American cohorts we have discovered and show you how to use Multi-Dimensional Marketing to target your marketing efforts to individual cohort groups for the greatest possible returns. We have included practical how-to tips with each cohort chapter that we hope you will find useful. We recommend that you first read Chapter 2, "What Makes Us Tick: Using the Life-stage Analytic Matrix™," which describes the basic theory behind Multi-Dimensional Marketing, then feel free to hop around to the chapters that best describe your target customer base. Or better yet, read them all to catch the full flavor of generational cohorts and their roles in Multi-Dimensional Marketing — and because new cohorts are entering the old age-defined targets all the time. We guarantee an enjoyable ride through this book, but, more importantly, a more productive approach to successful marketing.

ENDNOTES

1. Don Peppers and Martha Rodgers, *The One to One Future: Building Relationships One Customer at a Time.* New York: Doubleday, 1993.

2. Seth Godin, *Permission Marketing: Turning Strangers into Friends and Friends into Customers.* New York: Simon & Schuster, 1999.

3. J. Walker Smith and Ann Clurman, *Rocking the Ages: The Yankelovich Report on Generational Marketing.* New York: HarperCollins, 1997.

4. University of Chicago. General Social Surveys conducted for the National Data Program for the Social Sciences at the National Opinion Research Center, 1972–98.

5. Karl Mannheim, "Das Problem der Generationen." 1928. Reprinted in *Essays on the Sociology of Knowledge.* London: Routledge, 1928.

6. Norman B. Ryder, "The Cohort as a Concept in the Study of Social Change." Presented at the Annual Meeting of The American Sociological Association. August 1959. Reprinted in the *American Sociological Review* 30 (1965): 843–861.

7. Neal Cutler, "Political Socialization Research as Generational Analysis: The Cohort Approach vs. the Lineage Approach." In *Handbook of Political Socialization: Theory and Research,* edited by Stanley Allen Renton. New York: Free Press, 1977.

8. Morris Massey, *The People Puzzle: Understanding Yourself and Others.* Reston, VA: Prentice Hall, 1979.

9. Howard Schuman and Jacqueline Scott, "Generations and Collective Memories." *American Sociological Review* 54 (1989): 359–381.

10. Jacqueline Scott and Lillian Zak, "Collective Memories in Britain and the United States." *Public Opinion Quarterly* 57 (1993): 315–331.

11. Joseph O. Rentz, Fred D. Reynolds, and Roy G. Stout, "Analyzing Changing Consumption Patterns with Cohort Analysis." *Journal of Marketing Research* XX (February 1983): 12–20.

12. Joseph O. Rentz and Fred D. Reynolds, "Forecasting the Effects of an Aging Population on Product Consumption: An Age-Period-Cohort Framework." *Journal of Marketing Research* XXVIII (August 1991): 355–360.

13. Morris B. Holbrook and Robert M. Schindler, "Some Exploratory Findings in the Development of Musical Tastes." *Journal of Consumer Research* 16 (June 1989): 119–124.

14. Robert M. Schindler and Morris B. Holbrook, "Critical Periods in the Development of Men's and Women's Tastes in Personal Appearance." *Psychology and Marketing* 10 (Nov/Dec 1993): 549–564.

15. Morris B. Holbrook and Robert M. Schindler, "Market Segmentation Based on Age and Attitude Towards the Past: Concepts, Methods, and Findings Concerning Nostalgic Influences on Customer Tastes." *Journal of Business Research* 37 (September 1996): 27–39.

16. Stephanie M. Noble and Charles D. Schewe, "Cohort Segmentation: An Exploration of Its Validity," *Journal of Business Research* (forthcoming).

CHAPTER 2

WHAT MAKES US TICK: USING THE LIFESTAGE ANALYTIC MATRIX™

Imagine that you are a marketing executive for a company called General Beverages. The company has two divisions: coffee and cola. Being the astute marketer that you are, you know that during the last 40 years, per capita coffee consumption has risen and per capita cola consumption has fallen as a function of age.

You also know that the population is aging. The number of persons 18–34 years old will increase by only six million in the first decade of the new millennium, while the number of adults aged 50 or older (spurred on by the Baby Boomers) will grow by almost 17 million.

Given these facts, which division has the brighter prospect for future growth: coffee or cola?

You might use traditional cross-sectional age analysis and quickly conclude that coffee will remain king at General Beverages. Your conclusion would likely be based on the premise that historic consumption rates will continue into the future. An aging population should boost the demand for coffee and cut the demand for cola, right?

On the surface, this conclusion seems perfectly obvious, but unfortunately, it isn't that simple.

A generational cohort analysis of cola and coffee consumption yields the exact opposite outcome from an age analysis of the same problem. Studies show that younger, cola-intensive cohorts will continue to consume soft drinks even as they age. Meanwhile, older, coffee-intensive groups will age and move out of the marketplace. And indeed, per capita coffee consumption continues to fall. The widely heralded success of Starbucks and other "designer coffee" brands is a drop in the bucket compared to the falloff in regular coffee drinking in millions of homes and offices. The numbers effect is compounded by the fact that much of Starbucks' product is in fact *milk* — think lattes — not coffee at all. Baby Boomers and younger consumers who drink much less coffee than older cohorts will replace habitual coffee drinkers. In other words, people who grew up drinking cola will most likely continue to do so later in life. Thus, cola consumption should increase as the younger population ages. In fact, one of the fastest growing beverage segments today, next to bottled water, is people who drink cola for breakfast. And surprise: They aren't seniors! This would indicate that despite an aging population, General Beverages should focus on its cola division for growing profits.

This example clearly shows how generational cohort analysis can provide powerful insights that often run completely counter to conventional marketing wisdom. And yet the cohort approach has been almost completely ignored as a consciously applied marketing discipline — until now. Some astute marketers have intuitively used cohort effects very successfully in isolated cases without really understanding what they were doing, but their efforts were more guesswork than anything else. Chapter 1, "Toward a New Era of Marketing," gives you an overview of cohort theory and helps to answer the question, "What advantages does generational cohort analysis offer over current marketing methodologies?" But cohort analysis alone is not enough — it is the interplay of cohort values with the four other elements of Multi-Dimensional Marketing™ that drives attitudes and behavior. This chapter will show that interaction, and how it can be understood and utilized through the Lifestage Analytic Matrix™.

THE LIFESTAGE ANALYTIC MATRIX

Although which generational cohort group a person belongs to is important, it is not the only determinant of attitudes and behavior, particularly purchasing behavior. By defining core values for the seven cohort groups, and anchoring those values to coming-of-age events and birth years, we have devised an extremely powerful and predictive marketing tool that is easy to use and highly practical. We call it the Lifestage Analytic Matrix, and it is the key to Multi-Dimensional Marketing. Core cohort values don't change. But other factors determining behavior do change, and arraying the changeable factors against the non-changeable ones is the basis for the Lifestage Analytic Matrix.

The matrix can help marketers get their arms around the factors that influence consumer behavior — those that change, those that don't, and how they intersect. It helps to illustrate what is and isn't a segment-discriminator (i.e., what makes one segment behave differently from another), what is likely to change as an individual ages, and what will likely stay the same. Marketers can then selectively invoke coming-of-age values to generate powerful emotions and motivations, which can result in increased sales.

A generalized schematic diagram of this Matrix is shown below in Figure 2.1. The various items and events are not, in most cases, intended to be rigidly aligned with the ages depicted on the horizontal axis. Rather, they are there for illustrative purposes only, to provide a sense of how the events might generally flow. This Matrix allows you to dissect a market based on age and to see the key forces that influence wants, needs, desires and preferences. By going vertically up the matrix, you can gain a balanced picture of the individuals that comprise a particular age segment.

Trying to keep track of all of the various factors that influence consumer purchasing behavior can be a frustrating and time-consuming experience. Why? Because although their cohort values don't change, consumers are not static — they are constantly adapting to new forces in the marketplace, their home and work lives, and their own personal tastes. As we have discussed, marketers often segment consumers on demographic factors such as age, gender, income, education, and geography. Although these approaches can be successful, emerging cohorts upset the status quo, making the old approaches obsolete. New models are needed to keep pace.

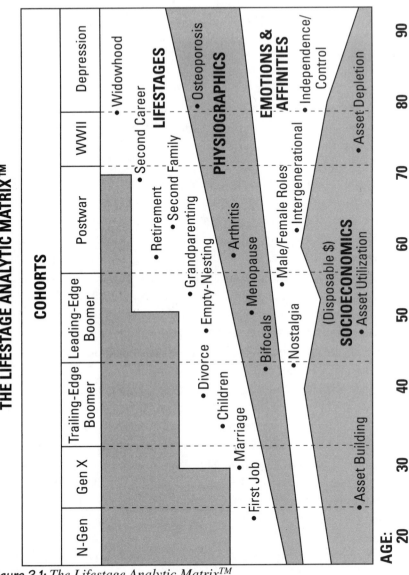

Figure 2.1: The Lifestage Analytic Matrix^{TM}

Figuring out the key drivers of attitudes and behavior is the essence of marketing — but these drivers are different in every product category. The trick is to determine which of the five factors in the Lifestage Analytic Matrix are critical in any given category. If they are primarily cohort-motivated, then the drivers are relatively fixed for any given segment, and the way to predict future behavior is a straight-line extrapolation of a particular cohort's past. If they are lifestage-motivated, then the intersection of cohort and lifestage becomes critical: How will cohort A manifest lifestage B? Physiographics and affinities are closely correlated with age, and are the sole driver in some categories, such as pharmaceuticals and other health-related items, but are relatively inconsequential in others. Socioeconomics are important for high-ticket or status items, such as cars or cruises, but not in low-cost categories, such as coffee or colas. Which cells in the Matrix are key? That is the core question.

The Lifestage Analytic Matrix usually by itself doesn't answer the question, "Which factors are driving attitudes and behavior in this particular category?" Instead, it provides a structure for answering the question and points out the right places to look for the answers, usually through some kind of market research. Often we have found that the necessary market research to provide the answers already exists within a company — the data just needs to be reanalyzed from a Multi-Dimensional Marketing perspective, and structured via the Matrix. Other times, new research, especially crafted from a cohort or lifestage perspective, is needed. Qualitative research (focus groups or one-on-ones) can usually provide invaluable insights. From time to time, when a very precise segment definition is essential, a quantitative study may be required.

The five factors in the Matrix divide the market into distinct segments, and help predict upcoming changes. As you will see in subsequent chapters, different cohorts can and do experience and react to the same lifestage at different ages, and in very different ways. The Matrix is not the answer — but it is the question that leads to the answer.

As you can see from the Matrix, the five crucial factors influencing people's attitudes, behavior, and buying patterns as they age are:

+ Cohorts.

+ Lifestages.

+ Physiographics.

+ Emotions and Affinities.

+ Socioeconomics.

We've covered cohorts in some depth (see chapter 1); in the remainder of this chapter, we'll take a closer look at the other four factors to help determine which are likely to be key in any given product or service category. Then, beginning with Chapter 3, "The Depression Cohort," we use the Lifestage Analytic Matrix to create a Multi-Dimensional Marketing snapshot of each generational cohort. These snapshots are more detailed and focused on marketing implications than the examples given for the Lifestage Analytic Matrix, but they are derived from the same theoretical background.

ALL THE WORLD'S A STAGE

Lifestages are the roles we take on, or act out, over our lifetime. They can include student, spouse, parent, divorcee, retiree, and so on. Lifestages bring with them new rights and responsibilities. You only need think of the role of a new parent to understand the radical change in lifestyle that this lifestage presents. Lifestages define your attitudes, outlooks, and daily activities. In our work, we have identified over 25 different lifestages that dot one's lifetime, some as obvious as those just noted, others less obvious, such as:

- ✦ Buying a first car or home.

- ✦ Switching careers.

- ✦ Going through menopause.

- ✦ Remarrying a third or fourth time.

- ✦ Paying off a mortgage.

- ✦ Taking care of a parent.

- ✦ Dating in older age.

And recent years have given us increasingly prevalent new lifestages to consider, including:

- ✦ Cohabitation: 50% of marriages today are preceded by this lifestage.

- ✦ Deliberately having children out of wedlock: We call it "The Madonna Effect."

✦ Financially independent career women seeking divorce and custody of their children.

✦ "Boomeranging Children": When the adult child, perhaps with children of his or her own, returns to the nest.

In the past, the progression from one lifestage to another used to be fairly predictable and linear. You went to school, got a job, got married *once,* worked for a long time, had children (who eventually left home), retired for a short time, and died. Today, the progression is more cyclic. Second (or third or fourth) marriages, second families, and second careers can and do happen in various sequences and with less regard to age. Often in our focus groups we find men, for instance, who share quite different lifestages even though they are the same age. As we noted in chapter 1, one 55-year-old may be preparing for retirement and focusing on his IRA investments, while another is a brand-spanking new father on his third marriage who's focusing on buying a car seat and baby diapers. And while some of the lifestages are traditional, such as parenting and grandparenting, others are quite new. Eldercare, for example, only became common when aging parents began to live long enough to exhaust their financial resources — a relatively recent phenomenon.

Lifestage analysis is important to marketers for two reasons:

1. It enables you to recognize the diversity of lifestage alternatives today, and not to pigeonhole a particular group on the basis of simple demographics.

2. It allows you to recognize additional marketing opportunities that were previously missed. Every time an individual moves from one lifestage to another, it represents a change in mind-set and behavior. This provides a very real opportunity for marketing intervention. Needs change, attitudes change, behavior changes — and brands or categories of products or services can change at that time, too.

YOU CAN RUN (OR JOG) BUT YOU CAN'T HIDE

Whereas demographics paint a portrait of markets by descriptors such as age, gender, income, geography, and the like, physiographics mark the changes in bodily appearance and function as one journeys through life.

In some product or service categories — and thus in some cells of the Lifestage Analytic Matrix — physiographics don't play a very important role. In designing a new financial services product for example, cohort values (such as risk aversion) are much more important than physiographics. Having said this, when *retailing* a financial service, such things as wheelchair accessibility or well-lit office space to accommodate aging eyesight can be critical. Conversely, if one is designing a new food brand for an older cohort, such factors as stomach irritation, chewability, or intensity of flavor — all dependent on physiographic elements — can play a major role.

In youth, we find acne and gawkiness as prevalent physical concerns. About age 30, our metabolism slows and we begin to fight weight gain. Balding and premature graying start to show through if they are in our DNA. Our 40s give us other markers of aging — presbyopia (the inability to focus near or far), and slower recovery from the aches and pains of exercise, for instance. The 50s and beyond are even less kind, as the real signs of aging begin to appear. While not all individuals face these adjustments at the same chronological time in life, for the most part we find these bodily alterations occurring at rather defined periods. Arthritis generally hits as early as one's 40s, wrinkling of the skin is more pronounced in one's 50s, while hearing loss typically does not happen until one's 60s. And so it goes. While many aging effects are well known, many more are less obvious. For example, as we age:

+ Fingernails and toenails become thick, tough, and more brittle.

+ Feet become larger as muscles weaken.

+ The nose broadens and ears get longer.

+ The skin of light-skinned people loses pigment and becomes less dark when exposed to the sun.

+ The eyes generally become dull and lusterless as new lens fiber growth outstrips the concomitant shedding of old lens fibers.

+ Body height shrinks; men lose one inch in height and women two inches on average over their lifetime as they age.

But have faith. Physical changes can be accommodated. For example, Rogaine and Grecian Formula 16 attend to hair issues, while collagen injections, at least temporarily, counter the reduction in skin elasticity. Eyeglasses and contact lenses can also be tinted to literally erase the aging effect of the yellowing of the cornea. And less obvious, many older adult living communities decorate their walls with peach, light blue, mauve, and other tones that compliment the normal lightening of the skin.

Aging is not a disease but rather a "normal" and unavoidable phenomenon that begins when we are born. It provides you, as a marketer, with an opportunity to expand your market by accommodating for the natural changes that take place. But that can only happen if you better understand the physiology of the aging process yourself and incorporate appropriate compensations into your products and marketing activities. This is particularly true today, with a population that is aging in larger numbers than ever before. The Matrix cells relating to physiographics should always be considered, to help anticipate and accommodate aging-related marketing issues.

Understanding aging effects creates a competitive advantage for expanding market share for your company, by improving the quality of life and the general satisfaction of your customers. Up to now, we'll bet few of your competitors have dealt with them. Many of the accommodations you can make are easy, once you use the Matrix to better understand where they are applicable.

For example, we helped a large supermarket chain position itself for the retiree lifestage market segment by looking at the Matrix cells where that lifestage and the appropriate physiographic factors intersected. To gain further insight, we did "walk-arounds" with older customers. It was incredibly enlightening. One woman in her early 70s indicated that her favorite Swiss cheese was located just out of her reach (arm span and range of motion decrease with age as well as height). We found that having a small, short (but very stable!) stool nearby allowed her to get to her cherished brand. She loved that idea. Later at the seafood counter, she complained that she could not see the quality of the options in the display. Overhead fluorescent lighting was reflecting off an angled Plexiglas cover on the counter display. Aging brings with it a difficulty in adapting to glare, and this deficit increases rapidly in one's 40s. The natural inclination is to avoid any problems, not ask for help, and move on to the next aisle. This results in lost sales for the supermarket.

Our shopper also found some of her favorite paper towel products located on the top shelf, and household cleaner Ajax on the bottom shelf. But her osteoporosis didn't allow her to easily raise her head to scan the top shelf, and her bifocals blurred her vision of the Ajax down below.

Just think of the possibilities for literally thrilling older customers in the supermarket by accommodating these kinds of changes in bodily ability. And keep in mind that aging effects are not just limited to senior citizens. Adjustments can be made for people of almost any age.

Some accommodations to aging are very subtle, even downright sneaky. A study of 7,000 women over the age of 54 found that even those who gain no weight might see a dramatic change in their shape over time because of shifts in bone structure and the relentless tug of gravity. Shoulders, for instance, generally rotate forward so blouses stretch across the shoulder blades and fit loosely in the chest. Wolf Form Co., however, a maker of dress forms used by dressmakers since 1931, helps the aging woman applaud her ability to still wear the same dress size she wore in college. Sixty years ago a size 10 dress form had a 34.5-inch bust, a 24.5-inch waist, and a 34.5-inch hipline. Today, there is no standard size 10 form, but the smallest one Wolf makes has a 35.5-inch bust, a 26-inch waist, and a 37-inch hipline. So if you're a dress marketer, not only do you have to consider cohort preferences in *fashion,* you have to consider physiographic ones as well — and how these factors interact.

Understanding the nuances of aging can open strategic windows unnoticed by others. Younger cohorts are not as wrapped up in physical problems. But as they age and experience "the Big 3-0," they start to focus more on bodily issues. And as Baby Boomers continue to move into middle and older ages, accommodations will increasingly become an important value-added feature to everything they buy. After all, they have always pursued holding on to their youth. It's a strong cohort value, and there is no reason to think they will relinquish that pursuit in the future. It's another example of how cohort and physiographic factors intersect.

AFFINITY EFFECTS: WHAT TURNS YOU ON

At various times in our lives, we are drawn more strongly toward things that touch us emotionally. These are the desires and wants that arise because we are of a certain age. For example, in our late teens, we dote on our appearance and prize being socially accepted by peers. In our 20s, we seek socialization, meeting possible mates, and just simply having fun. Once married, we focus on gaining an identity as a couple and on gathering material possessions. The childrearing years focus inward on children's education, personal career development, and home maintenance. As the children leave the nest, a whole new set of interests come into play: enjoying experiences rather than possessions, having fun, living a healthful lifestyle, and feeling financially secure. Certain emotions and affinities become much stronger as we age. These emotional touchstones, marketers understand and acknowledge them, can tap deep motivational pools.

The affinities that we find important change throughout life. These are also related to aging effects. For example, bodily appearance is very important when we are young and single. It remains important throughout marriage for most people, but in our later years, the focus starts to switch to retarding the effects of the aging process — wrinkle creams, work outs, and healthier eating reflect this evolution. Oil of Olay, Gold's Gym, and Stouffer's Lean Cuisine help to accommodate these changing needs. And we have found that concern for dieting for physical appearance reasons falls off after age 59. Dieting then becomes focused on health effects.

In our research, we have found over 50 affinities that play a strong role as we journey through life. Some of these affinities include:

- ✦ **Home:** The environment affording security and happiness, a belief in the ability of one's home to provide stability for family life.

- ✦ **Learning:** An interest in following intellectual pursuits, to attain knowledge.

- ✦ **Novelty:** The need for change and diversity, to experience the unusual, and to be amazed or mystified.

- ✦ **Nostalgia:** The desire for persons, things, or situations of the past, and enjoyment in reminiscing.

Many affinities are the outward manifestations of cohort values, and as such they have deep roots. But the affinities tend to change more over a lifetime, and some become much stronger the older we get. These affinities are not all in play at the same time. Younger adults tend to be more drawn to acceptance and learning. Those in the full nest would embrace home, work ethic, and recognition, while nostalgia often kicks in as the empty nest and the "Big 5-0" approach. And in older age, recognition and novelty become more important.

TABLE 2.1: TYPICAL AFFINITIES

Cohort	Affinity
Depression Cohort	**A yearning for intergenerational experiences:** The older people get, the less they want to interact only with people their own age. This has strong implications for advertising. Executions that depict only one age group rather than a mix of ages will generally not be well received, even if those seeing the ad can't quite articulate why it's unappealing.
World War II Cohort	**Convergence of male and female roles:** It has long been observed that as people age, male and female roles switch over or converge. That is, men become less aggressive and more compassionate, while women become more independent and assertive. A number of factors cause this, including hormonal changes (men's testosterone levels decrease) and lifestage (men may no longer be the "hunters" and women the sole "nest-tenders").
Postwar Cohort	**Emphasis on experience, not things:** Most mature adults have passed through the acquisitive stage of life, and are for the most part no longer seeking additional possessions. Rather, they tend to more highly value their time, and what they do with it — enjoying enriching experiences (especially with others) that they can savor.

Increased spirituality is an affinity that seems to get stronger with older age. Although the older cohorts tend to be more religious to begin with, we don't think this is just a cohort function — for example, the Postwar Cohort seems to be getting more spiritual the older they become. Kenner's line of Special Blessings dolls, which have hands that bend into a praying position, takes this affinity into account. A print advertising campaign targeted grandparents with copy that focused on the joy of religious faith. The ad showed a little girl kneeling and praying with her doll while her grandmother peeked through her bedroom door. Table 2.1 shows some other examples of common affinities shared by people in the seven cohort groups.

Cohort	Affinity
Leading-Edge Boomer Cohort	**Challenge authority:** The civil rights, anti-war, women's rights, nuclear power and environmental protests of the '60s and '70s solidified a blatant disrespect for authority that this group still carries with them today. This has carried over into many sectors, including politics, schools, and the workplace.
Trailing-Edge Boomer Cohort	**Sexual freedom:** Birth control pills, the women's movement and the sexual revolution contributed to a growing trend toward sexual freedom among this cohort in the '70s and '80s. While times have changed, these days, this affinity translates into more liberal attitudes toward living together, premarital sex, nudity, adult themes on TV, and more.
Generation X Cohort	**Social and ethnic diversity:** Growing up, this group was exposed to many different ethnic groups and many have learned to value diversity much more than their parents did. In general, young people typically are more tolerant, and this group seems much more open to social, ethnic, and religious diversity than older groups.
N Generation Cohort	**Brand consciousness:** This cohort tends to be very brand conscious due to the economic prosperity that has accompanied them into adulthood. But some brands that appealed to older cohorts, such as Levi's and Reebok, have little appeal with this group in part because they are so associated with this cohort's parents.

Understanding these changing preferences as different cohorts cycle through the various lifestages can open new marketing opportunities to you. Take a closer look at the desire for experiences that becomes more important as we age. Between about ages 40–60, enjoyment shifts away from possessions to "catered experiences," such as going to restaurants, sporting events, attending art shows, and traveling. And after age 60, the focus shifts to "being experiences," such as interpersonal relationships, philosophical introspection, and a higher connectedness with life. People in this age category have a keener appreciation for the simpler things in life. Getting in touch with oneself, enjoying a walk or a sunset, or having a friendly conversation all gain in importance — and certainly present cues to advertisers for appropriate backdrops to messages. Products, and especially services, that generate these feelings also play to this affinity.

SOCIOECONOMICS: GOT MONEY?

Socioeconomics include our financial, educational, career, marital and other social and economic states. They are constantly used to segment markets, but it must be remembered that they really describe only part of the market. They tell us little about the underlying motives for making a purchase — only for example, whether a purchase is affordable or not. In some cases, as for high-ticket items like luxury cars or designer suits, this becomes the first, and perhaps most important, factor to consider. For most products, however, it's only one element with cost-benefit trade-offs. In low-cost categories, such as most packaged goods and foods, it's not a key factor at all.

That said, socioeconomics do provide some very key insights that help fill out the market picture and show where market potential is heading. In our case, they underlie the importance of various age groupings. As we start this new millennium, we are experiencing the first wave of a huge demographic shift that will impact the marketing landscape for the next three decades: the aging of the population.

At present, 11% of the population is 65 years of age or older. By 2010, one in seven Americans will be age 65 or above. And right now half of those over 65 are 75 years of age and older. The median age of the population in 2000 is 36.3, up from 32.3 in 1988 and 30.2 in 1950. These are enormous changes in such a short span of time — usually, median age changes happen with the rapidity of glaciers!

Spurred on by advances in public health, sanitation, nutrition, and medical science, our average life span has soared from 47 years in 1900 to 76 today, the greatest increase in life span ever. Women have a seven-year advantage over men, with an average life expectancy of 78 years today. A male reaching age 55 in 2000 can expect to live an additional 22 years to age 77 while a female at 55 can expect to live to 82. And if lucky enough to hit 65, a man can expect to reach 81 and a woman 85 years. What's more, one of the fastest growing age segments today is people over age 85. But let's not forget about the tidal wave of the two Baby Boomer Cohorts — the demographically-defined bulge of those 76 million born between 1946 and 1964. Their parents began minting children at a clip of 3.8 per family right after the end of the war, and that mass production of children lasted for 18 years. The Baby Boomers have shaped marketing ever since they came on the scene. They *were* the Pepsi Generation. In the '80s and '90s, they ran up the stock market with their 401(k)s. Now, they are making their mark with day spas and SUVs. You can be sure that they will continue to pursue their interests and spearhead consumption for decades to come, especially now that they are entering their peak income years.

We are also beginning to see Boomer offspring creating yet another demographic wave. Sometimes called "the piglet in the python," in direct reference to their parents' impact as the "pig in the python," the annual number of births in America began rising again in the early 1980s. This ended the "birth dearth" that followed the Baby Boom. Between 1989–1993, U.S. births were greater than 4 million for the first time since the early 1960s. There are about 60 million in this new wave. They are as young as 7 and as old as 24 in 2001. This is the first population segment since the Boomers that will make such a large impact, perhaps a huge footprint, on the marketplace as they move into adulthood and through various lifestages and evolving affinities. This bulge has its own unique characteristics. Blended families, dual-income parents, racial diversity, and especially technology are creating quite a different marketing landscape than that experienced by their Boomer parents.

This next wave is guaranteed to be different, yet because our Lifestage Analytic Matrix rests on the defining moments of our coming-of-age experience, it is really too early to define all of the values, attitudes, and preferences of this young cohort group. But we certainly believe that the impact of the Internet will be one defining moment for this age segment. The booming economy of the '90s is another. As we started the new century, the U.S. economy entered its ninth year of sustained growth, unemployment was at a 30-year low, and consumer confidence was at a 50-year high. Since the boom began in March 1991, 20 million new jobs have been created. Half of America's households own stock. We may be experiencing a momentary downturn as we write this in mid-2001, but we believe that economic growth will continue for at least another 5 years. (For our projections of what we think will happen after that, see the epilogue, titled "Predicting the Future.") And a robust economy will be a defining moment that will shape the way the N-Gen Cohort thinks about saving and spending. Although we haven't seen the end of the current boom and its inevitable move to the downside, if that decline happens abruptly (as discussed in the epilogue), it could be the moment that defines the successor to the N-Gen Cohort.

Figure 2.2 tracks the changes in population over the first decade of the twenty-first century. Overall, the U.S. population will advance 8.4%

over that period. You can see the impact Boomers will have on the middle-age market. That's clearly where the action is and will continue to be for some time. Those Boomers at the front end of the surge will increase the 55–64 age category a full 47.25% over the next decade, while those following up the rear will boost the 45–54 age group by almost 20%. In the 85+ group, population is expected to increase 33%, or 1.4 million persons during the same time frame. At the same time, Generation-Xers will replace Boomers in the 35–44 age category, causing that age group to *decline* by 12.5%. As the N-Gen moves into its early 20s, this group will lift the 18–24 segment by nearly as much as the youngest Boomers — although as a percentage of the total population, the N-Gen Cohort will have far less impact than either of the Boomer Cohorts in their youth.

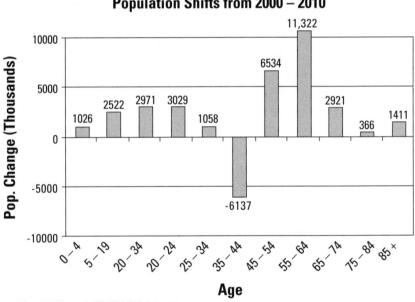

Figure 2.2: *Population Shifts from 2000–2010.*

Source: U.S. Bureau of the Census. 1997

When you look at the financial side of things, you can really see where the opportunities await in the next decade. The scenario shown in the Lifestage Analytic Matrix indicates that in early adulthood, asset accumulation begins. At about age 49, income peaks, and in later life, assets are depleted. Once again, the two Boomer Cohorts will be king, with Leading-Edge Boomers leading the way. In their peak years now, their disposable income is creating large increases for their late middle-age years. Figure 2.3, which documents disposable income, clearly shows their financial dominance. The Leading-Edge Boomers will power up disposable income by almost 50% in the 55–64 age group, and the Trailing-Edge Boomers will propel income forward in the 45–54 bracket by almost 18%. They have the numbers and the economic power. Each group shows increases except those in the 35–44 age category (which, by the way, are the "darlings" that so many marketers court and woo). The older age groups also show increases, almost as large as those in the 18–34 age group. And while income peaks near age 50, discretionary income does not. It continues upward into one's 60s as financial obligations such as mortgages, college tuition payments, and retirement savings dwindle.

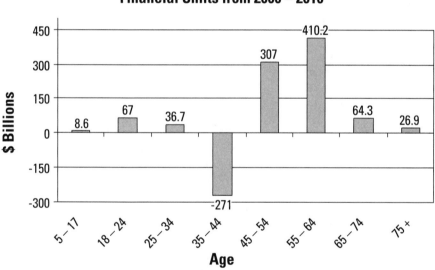

Financial Shifts from 2000 – 2010

Figure 2.3: *Financial Shifts from 2000–2010.*

Source: U.S. Bureau of the Census. 1997

So it is clear that marketers should continue to paint bull's-eyes on the two Boomer Cohorts as the most promising market segments in the coming years. Over the next decade, the Boomers will increase the 45–65 age group by almost 18 million persons and ramp up spending power by over $700 billion. Now that's serious buying power! The older-than-Boomer age segments will add almost 5 million to their numbers and increase spending power by almost a $100 billion. And they are not the serious savers their parents were — they are much more willing to spend. While the N-Gen is large, they will just be starting to test their earning power and so will not as yet offer the immediate sales potential of older groups.

Putting the Matrix to Work

Multi-Dimensional Marketing and the Lifestage Analytic Matrix provide a way to crosscut a wide range of motivating factors on the basis of age. If you know the age range of your target market, you can gain insights into the "drivers" of their consumption behavior. For far stronger results, target by cohort and use the intersection of lifestage, physiographic, affinity, and socioeconomic forces that come into play to predict and direct their buying behavior.

Consider the plight of Kellogg's. It has been the breakfast companion of millions of families for decades. For many children, the morning used to mean meeting Tony the Tiger at the breakfast table for a "Gr-r-reat" tasting bowl of Frosted Flakes, or listening to the "Snap, Krackle, and Pop" of the Rice Krispies elves. But the child-rearing lifestage today is quite a change from the 1950s. First of all, and most importantly, parents today are of a decidedly different cohort. Over the decade of the 1990s, parents have been predominantly Boomers, not Depression and World War II Cohorts. Their values are dramatically different. And the ways in which they carry out various lifestages are different, too, to say the least. That's why the old 1950s model for marketing isn't working for Kellogg's.

In 1999, it lost its market leadership to General Mills as its share dropped from 40% in 1988 to 31% in 1999. It even closed the Battle Creek, Michigan, plant of its flagship brand, Corn Flakes, and laid off 525 workers. Kellogg's stuck with what it believed were "tried and true" marketing schemes — emphasizing trade promotions, not consumer branding — and they had turned sour. Cereal category sales overall plunged $1 billion to $7.7 billion in 1999. Meanwhile its more nimble rivals, such as Post, were churning out new ideas that caught the eye of consumers.

Why are cereal category sales declining? The morning routine for today's Baby Boomers and their children has become hectic as the dual-career family gets ready for its day. With long commutes to work, who has time to sit and relax with a leisurely first meal? With 77% of Boomer mothers heading for jobs, they have little or no time to fix even the most meager of breakfasts. The convenience affinity has become critical to young families today: Anything that will help propel them faster out the door to school or their jobs is highly valued. But health is a key value for Boomers, too. After all, they want to maintain their youthfulness. So foods should be natural, healthy and fat free. These Boomers, as has been their history, offer a target market to be reckoned with.

Kellogg's is getting the picture: It is redefining itself as a snack-foods company. After a 27-year break in bringing a blockbuster product to market (Pop-Tarts in 1964), Kellogg's finally found its next hot product. In 1991, it brought out Nutri-Grain Cereal Bars, which could be eaten on the run and in place of the breakfast bowl of cereal. These bars meet the Boomer value for health and convenience, and have been a big success. Kellogg's has even tried to impact the decline in cereal category sales with an ad campaign that is almost generic, touting the benefits of cereal in general (with a somewhat contrived and not terribly successful attempt to ascribe these generic benefits to Kellogg's entries). An even bigger success might be for Kellogg's to lead the cereal industry in a joint effort to promote cereal — like milk ("Got Milk?"), beef ("It's what's for dinner"), pork ("the other white meat"), or raisins ("I heard it through the grapevine"). The Justice Department might have a problem, but that's another issue.

Today's marketplace offers many new challenges that were non-issues just a few decades ago. With the population shift away from a youth population to a largely middle-aged and older society, and life expectancies now reaching close to 80 years, the long-ignored "mature market" has gained greater significance than it ever has before. Insightful marketers recognize the differences that come with aging and are launching a new wave of products, packages, services, and promotions targeting older adult consumers.

But that doesn't mean you should discount younger consumers altogether. The N Generation represents the largest population surge since the Boomers. As teenagers, they have disposable incomes that far exceed that of older cohorts when they were the same age, and they are very willing to spend big bucks on CDs, computer games, designer clothes, movies, and other entertainment. But like Generation X, they grew up inundated with advertising and are more skeptical of marketing claims than older cohorts.

Finding out what makes each cohort group tick, then using that information to develop targeted marketing plans and tactics will help you achieve a competitive advantage in the marketplace. The next seven chapters will introduce you to each of the different generational cohort groups, giving you valuable insight into their defining moments, likes, dislikes and dreams — and specific examples of how to use these insights. It is our hope that this information will help you take your marketing to a whole new level of success.

CHAPTER 3

THE DEPRESSION COHORT

Funerals are not a topic most people like to discuss. But for the Depression Cohort, funeral preplanning is just one more way to reduce the uncertainties in life, both for them and their adult children. Like other life changes, death also represents a very real marketing opportunity. After all, try as we might, it's not a lifestage any of us can avoid!

One of our clients at Lifestage Matrix Marketing was SCI Corporation of Houston, Texas — the largest "deathcare" company in the world, with revenues in excess of $4 billion. SCI had acquired funeral homes and cemeteries all over the United States, nearly 2,000 in all. They own another 2,500 globally, and have about a 40% share of all funerals in France, and (as the industry phrases it!) nearly a quarter of deaths in the United Kingdom, Italy, and Australia.

The funeral business has traditionally been a local one, where people tend to patronize funeral homes their families have used in the past. But SCI wanted to create a *brand* of funeral homes. To do that, and to use the efficiencies of mass marketing, the funeral had to be standardized, and moved out of the realm of the local, neighborhood funeral parlor. Local funeral homes (and SCI) had tried selling preplanned funerals before, however, using one-on-one cold calls and individualized selling, but had met with limited success.

We helped SCI advertise their standardized, preplanned "Dignity Memorial Plan" package by targeting specific generational cohort appeals. For the Depression Cohort, the most powerful appeals targeted their frugality, and their sense of wanting to be self-sufficient. The advertising and sales messages that were most effective included (key phrases from research in italics):

◆ "Funeral costs have been going up faster than inflation — buy a preplanned funeral now and *lock in today's prices* forever."

◆ "Unscrupulous funeral directors can manipulate your children into spending far more for your funeral than you would wish. Buy a funeral package now and *make sure it's not more extravagant* than you want."

◆ "A la carte funeral pricing adds up amazingly quickly. Buy one of the packages now and everything is included in one low price. Complete funeral packages start at $2,495, *less than half the cost of an average funeral* in the United States today."

◆ "You remember how you had to struggle when you had a young family. Don't put the *financial burden* of your funeral on your children — prepay it today."

These messages appealed to the World War II Cohort, too, albeit not as strongly. For them the key thought was their ability to handle anything that came up, and the military (and Boy Scout) virtue of always being prepared. The most appealing message to them proved to be:

"You've planned for everything — from saving the world for democracy to saving for your retirement. Shouldn't you plan for your funeral, too?"

Interestingly enough, we learned that it was very difficult to sell preplanned funerals to people under about age 67 (the Postwar Cohort and younger). It seems there's just too much denial operating below that age. However, particularly for Leading-Edge Baby Boomers, the one appeal that did resonate was the exact opposite of what hit home for the Depression Cohort. Far from being concerned about costs, what most appealed to Boomers about preplanning their funerals was that they could do it their own way. The fact that they got to pick the flowers, the music, the sermon, and the clothes they would wear really appealed to them.

You're not going to see much preplanned funeral advertising targeting Leading-Edge Baby Boomers for a while yet. But when you do, the successful campaigns will play to Boomer's sense of individualism and narcissism: "Make your funeral as special as you were!"

This example illustrates what a great divide exists between the thinking of different generational cohort groups. And it shows some of the values held most dear by the Depression Cohort, aged 80–89 in 2001, who came of age from 1930–1939.

STEP BACK IN TIME

It's hard for most of us to fathom what life was like in the 1930s, so let's take a moment to step back into time to a typical Saturday night during the Great Depression:

> It's "bank night" at the movies, so you put on your fedora hat, help your new wife into your broken-down Ford Model T, and head out to the local theater. It's a big event for both of you. Most evenings you stay home and listen to "The Jack Benny Program," "Amos and Andy," and other radio shows. Times have been tough for everyone since the stock market crash four years ago. But Mr. Roosevelt said in his radio program that things were going to get better from now on — and you believe him. Although you were an A student in high school, you now load boxes down at the paper factory four days a week. And you feel lucky to do it. Many of your friends still can't find work. Money is tight, but you can afford to treat your wife to a night out now and then. You're going to see the newly released movie that everyone is talking about — "King Kong." At the box office, you pay 50 cents — 25 cents for each of you. As a special treat, you buy a roll of Necco wafers, which you and your wife share. Although you don't want to admit it, you secretly hope your number is

drawn in tonight's give-away sponsored by the local bank. Sure, it's a gimmick to try to bring in more customers, but you could really use the money. Your father just got laid off and your family needs help.

Welcome to 1933.

As you can imagine, the Great Depression wasn't a lot of fun for anyone, particularly if you were coming of age and just starting out on your own. Times were tough. At the height of the Depression in 1932–33, 16 million Americans were unemployed — roughly one-third of the work force. This was in sharp contrast to the booming prosperity of the "Roaring '20s," when credit and installment buying boomed, stock speculation took off, and productivity reached new heights.

Unfortunately, most farmers and unskilled workers were left out of this prosperity, and the country's ability to consume was much less than its ability to produce. Tariff and war-debt policies reduced the foreign market for U.S. goods, contributing to oversupply and low margins. In addition, easy credit and risky stock speculation created a house of cards that toppled on October 24, 1929 — Black Thursday — the day security values lost $6 billion. Suddenly, happy days were gone. Hard times were here to stay:

✦ In 1930 alone, more than 1,000 U.S. banks failed and closed.

✦ Within six months of the crash, four million Americans were unemployed.

✦ Those who managed to keep their jobs saw their incomes drop by 50% or more.

"BROTHER, CAN YOU SPARE A DIME?"

In 1932, the song "Brother, Can You Spare a Dime?" topped the music charts, reflecting the widespread suffering felt by millions of Americans. The '30s was a decade of hard times, scraping to get by, barely making ends meet, failed dreams, and lost hope. There were sacrifices at every turn. Hard-earned savings evaporated overnight. Opportunities for good jobs also disappeared as people took any job they could find, and suffered untold humiliation, just to feed their families. The economic, agricultural, and welfare policies of President Franklin D. Roosevelt's

New Deal helped to lessen the effects of the Depression and restore America's optimism and hope. But the hard times didn't really disappear until the war machine geared up for World War II in the early 1940s.

For most cohort groups, coming of age is typically a time filled with anticipation, optimism, and experimentation. But not for those unlucky enough to have been born between 1912–1921, and who came of age during the '30s. They couldn't have picked a worse time. The Great Depression inflicted deep wounds on this cohort group that never really healed, scarring them for life.

"IT'S A WONDERFUL LIFE"

Not surprisingly, this cohort felt bitter about what they missed. The 1947 Christmas classic *It's a Wonderful Life,* set during the Depression, features Jimmy Stewart's portrayal of the archetypal George Bailey and epitomizes the kinds of sacrifices this cohort was forced to make. Bailey had dreams of traveling to exotic places, but he delayed and eventually abandoned his dreams, choosing instead to help the family-run building and loan remain solvent during the Depression.

And yet, despite the disappointments of the Depression years, there were good times, too, as people pulled together to survive, replacing the joys once brought by material possessions with poignant moments shared with friends and family. Perhaps more than any other group, the Depression Cohort — 13 million of whom are still alive today — learned to appreciate simple pleasures and the true value of family, friends, and neighbors.

Major Events of the 1930s

+ Radio becomes a rapidly growing medium

+ Gangs control illegal liquor trade (Al Capone)

+ World population reaches 2 billion (1930)

+ Adolf Hitler becomes chancellor of Germany (1933)

+ Bank panic (1931)

+ FDR elected president (1932)

+ 21st amendment repeals prohibition (1933)

+ Amelia Earhart crosses Atlantic (1932)

+ Lindbergh's son is kidnapped (1932)

+ FDR's New Deal begins (1933)

+ Gone With the Wind is published (1936)

+ First coast-to-coast radio broadcast is of the Hindenburg disaster (1937)

+ Orson Welles's broadcast of War of the Worlds panics the country (1938)

+ Germany invades the Rhineland (1936) and Poland (1939).

RADIO AND THE MOVIES: "THE GREAT ESCAPE"

Rather than wallow in the misery that surrounded them, the Depression Cohort looked for escape anywhere they could find it. They were the first to be truly influenced by contemporary media: radio and especially motion pictures.

Radio provided free entertainment during hard times. Shows, such as "Your Hit Parade," "The Ed Sullivan Show," and soap operas whisked listeners away to another world, allowing them to forget their cares for 15 minutes or half an hour. And for advertisers, these shows helped shape a new generation of consumers.

Movies were another popular diversion. Horror movies, such as *Dracula* and *King Kong,* kept audiences on the edge of their seats, and Walt Disney's first feature-length cartoon, *Snow White and the Seven Dwarfs,* was applauded by children and adults alike. Other popular movies of the time included *Tarzan, Gone With the Wind,* and *The Wizard of Oz.* Movies of the '30s were all about escape. Despite hard times, by 1933, the number of weekly paid movie admissions exceeded that of the entire population, as millions found movies an inexpensive escape from their troubles. People often went to the movies several times a week.

Popular Radio Shows and Their Sponsors

✦ "Little Orphan Annie" (Ovaltine)

✦ "Jack Armstrong" (Wheaties)

✦ "Tom Mix" (Ralston Wheat Cereal)

✦ "Dick Tracy" (Quaker Oats)

To encourage audiences to spend the 25 cents for adults and 10 cents for children that it typically cost to see a movie, theaters would host "bank nights" where local banks would give away dishes, other prizes, or money to moviegoers. This helped boost the *value* movies provided viewers while increasing sales for theaters and helping banks to rebuild their tarnished image in the community.

At the theater, moviegoers bought Necco wafers, Tootsie Rolls, Hershey bars, or Boston Baked Beans from the candy counter—nostalgia products that are still around today.

SHARED VALUES FORGED FROM HARD TIMES

When hard times finally eased with the beginning of World War II, the Depression Cohort had forged a set of shared values that continues to affect their behavior to this day:

✦ **Practicality:** Everyone needs a sense of purpose.

✦ **Save for a rainy day:** Be conservative where money is concerned; doing without has its rewards.

✦ **Safety and security:** Safety and security must be guaranteed.

✦ **Friends and family:** Social connectedness is vital.

✦ **The good life:** Comfort and convenience are nice luxuries, not requirements for living.

Because of their conservative attitudes about money and their fear of uncertainty, the Depression Cohort has never been an easy market for marketers. But don't give up hope. This group still represents a market opportunity. It may require a little homework and patience on your part, but, with this initial investment up front, you can reap major rewards.

THE DEPRESSION COHORT TODAY

Now that the Depression Cohort is in its 80s, physiographics (the bodily changes that accompany the passage of time) primarily drive their behavior. Although many members of this cohort are still very active, chronic illnesses such as arthritis, high blood pressure, diabetes, and heart disease are now making a larger impact on buying decisions than they ever have before.

But other factors, such as cohort values and social attitudes, also play an important role in influencing the buying behavior of the Depression Cohort. The Snapshot feature shows a Multi-Dimensional Marketing™ overview of the Depression Cohort, which we developed using the Lifestage Analytic Matrix™.

The Depression Cohort is now dealing with a host of heavy issues, from loss of a spouse to their lessening role in society to their own mortality. Aging often presents contradictions, and it challenges the elderly to confront values about the importance of youth, work, progress, and independence that they held in earlier years. As people age, it's these same values that now make them question their own value to society.

Devaluation of the old by advertisers and society in general often results in the elderly having a negative self-image and other less-than-desirable consequences. According to gerontologist Edwin T. Boling, "It is difficult to grow old in a society that values youth and devalues old age. Older people are made to feel they are useless, out-of-date, and incapable of adapting to new and changing conditions. In this environment, no wonder people clutch frantically to youth and try to deny and postpone old age as long as possible."[1]

85+ AS ONE OF THE FASTEST GROWING SEGMENTS

In marketing — and society for that matter — there is a tendency to want to write off the Depression Cohort as no longer viable. They're old and frail, dwindling in numbers, living in nursing homes, and no longer able to make decisions for themselves, or so the stereotype goes. While this may be true for some members of this generational cohort, it by no means describes the cohort as a whole.

Icons of the '30s

Clark Gable

Shirley Temple

Will Rogers

Judy Garland

Bette Davis

Al Capone

Louis Armstrong

Ella Fitzgerald

Jean Harlow

Babe Ruth

Jesse Owens

Snow White

In fact, Americans 85 and up represent one of the fastest growing segments of the population. Members of this group are remaining active longer and are healthier than their predecessors. This is largely due to tremendous strides in medicine, sanitation, healthier diets and lifestyles over the last century, and through their own sheer determination. Although today's 85+ are healthier, more active and more independent than ever before, they continue to be ignored by marketers as a serious consumer segment.

SNAPSHOT OF THE DEPRESSION COHORT

Name of cohort:	Depression
Born between:	1912–21
Coming of age:	1930–39
Age in 2001:	80–89
Population:	13 million ✦ 6%

Key cohort values and concerns:
- ✦ Sense of purpose
- ✦ Safety and security
- ✦ Waste not, want not
- ✦ Social connectedness and companionship
- ✦ Risk averse

Current and next lifestage:
- ✦ Great-grandparenting
- ✦ Nursing homes
- ✦ Widowhood
- ✦ Love and romance

Emotions and affinities:
- ✦ Sexual Intolerance
- ✦ Independence
- ✦ Active and positive
- ✦ Nostalgia
- ✦ "Grittiness" ("I can survive anything")
- ✦ Intergenerational experiences

Physiographic profile:
- ✦ Vision
- ✦ Hearing
- ✦ Taste and smell
- ✦ Touch
- ✦ Strength
- ✦ Information processing

Social activities and lifestyles:
- ✦ Family
- ✦ Church
- ✦ Local community

Purchasing behavior:
- ✦ Adult children help
- ✦ Value-conscious
- ✦ Comfort and convenience with decisions

TAPPING THE DEPRESSION COHORT MARKET

Members of the Depression Cohort obviously aren't the biggest risk takers out there, so if you're selling Internet stocks or skateboards you will want to look somewhere else. And many do not use credit cards — debt is a no-no. But, for example, if you're in the toy business, don't overlook the growing legions of great-grandparents who are looking to buy just the right gift for their great-grandchildren. And what about the need for services to make their lives more convenient and comfortable? Those still residing in their own homes (most of them, by the way) would welcome new forms of home maintenance services to lighten their load, or lawn maintenance, or pickup and delivery of their car for routine repairs.

Currently, the Depression Cohort comprises about 6% of all Americans, nearly 13 million persons. This may not seem like a huge number, but this generational cohort is an underserved market segment. Especially when you consider that Americans over age 75 have a median net worth of $92,300, and the lowest debt level of any age group (see Figure 3.1). In fact, 75% of this group have no debt of any kind — no mortgage, no car payments, no credit card debt. What does this mean for you as a marketer?

Percentage of 55+ Household Debt in 1998

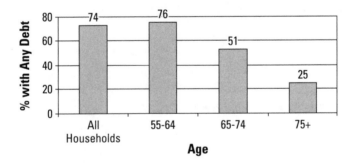

Figure 3.1: Older cohorts are highly debt-averse.

Accommodating the changes that accompany advanced age offers tremendous opportunities for new sales. In addition, since the 80+ crowd has really never been catered to, except by hospitals, nursing homes and retirement communities, the Depression Cohort represents an untapped market for many new and existing mainstream products.

STEP 1: LOOK AT KEY COHORT VALUES AND CONCERNS

As you saw in Chapter 2, "What Makes Us Tick: Using the Lifestage Analytic Matrix™," generational cohort values are largely determined by the defining moments we experience when coming of age. The Depression Cohort's coming-of-age years were fraught with hardship, sacrifice, and uncertainty. So it's not surprising that this group values hard work, security, and certainty more than anything else. This is just what they lacked during the hard times of the '30s.

GOD ISN'T FINISHED WITH ME YET

Members of the Depression Cohort are not "finished products," and there is a tremendous need for them to feel useful, to learn, and to grow personally. They are looking for a sense of purpose. This is particularly true following retirement, where job challenges and daily structure are suddenly removed. But it's true in later years as well.

Marketers provide a number of gateways to personal achievement. Educational travel, higher education programs for older people, and volunteer programs aimed at older adults are all common. In recent years, there has been a boom in programs and activities aimed at the senior market. Here are just a few examples:

✦ Senior exercise classes, including Tai Chi and Yoga, which emphasize balance and flexibility, are becoming mainstream activities for members of the Depression Cohort.

✦ Art programs and museums that offer the 80+ group a creative outlet provide much more than just an afternoon of activity. They can, in fact, offer opportunities for self-expression and greater life satisfaction.

BETTER SAFE THAN SORRY

Because of the hardships they experienced in the '30s, the Depression Cohort has sought safety and security ever since. They look to alleviate fears of the unknown. Positioning your product or service as offering security reflects the psychological need to feel safe. The 80+ crowd overwhelmingly prefer large, luxury automobiles to smaller models in part because they offer sturdiness, greater weight, and are perceived as safer. Financial security is also a major concern. This cohort is one of compulsive savers. In fact, many are still saving well into their 80s, when according to conventional economic theory, they should be depleting accumulated resources. Unlike their children or grandchildren, they often submit to reduced lifestyles rather than spend some of their core savings. Debt levels are very low (see Figure 3.2), and more than 60% of this group has outstanding debt of less than $2,000, including mortgages. Almost all of those who utilize credit cards at all pay off the balance in full every month — no revolving charges in this group! Quite a change from today's credit card society. So what are they saving for? At this late date, many are now saving to pay for future medical costs, nursing home care, and to pass on inheritances to their children and grandchildren. They don't want their families to have to deal with uncertainty should another Depression strike.

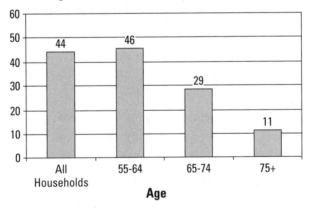

Figure 3.2: *55+ Credit Card Holders with Debt (%).*

Safety and security also apply to personal protection. There is an obvious need for protection that increases with age. The around-the-clock security that has become a must for senior living communities, the home alarm systems, and the deadbolt locks on apartments and hotels that older people prefer over the contemporary plastic card entry systems reflect this need. Residential community marketers need to be

Inheritance — A Tale of Two Cohorts

The generational cohort effect that influences attitudes toward inheritance is particularly pervasive, according to research done by the insurance industry.

Although the original and primary function of life insurance is to provide for widows and orphans in the event of the untimely death of the family breadwinner, another clear purpose is to provide an inheritance, a legacy for one's heirs, after a death in old age.

But two contiguous cohorts have highly dissimilar attitudes toward leaving an inheritance — one is a prime target for an inheritance-need insurance sale, the other couldn't be less interested.

The Depression Cohort, those between ages 80–89 in 2001, feel an acute need to leave a legacy for their survivors, especially their children. A typical expression of this attitude might go something like this: "It is very important to me to leave something for the kids after I'm gone. You never know what's going to happen to the country and the economy, and I want to be sure they never have to go through what I did during the Depression."

On the other side of the watershed is the World War II Cohort — those 10–15 years younger. This cohort uniformly has almost no interest in leaving a legacy for their children. With them, a characteristic comment is: "My kids are so much better off than I was at their age. And they don't know the value of money. They get a few dollars, and it's a new car or a fancy dinner or a trip to Florida. Their idea of saving is to pay down some of their credit cards. Leaving them anything would be silly."

aware that their communities should have their security personnel in uniform — it adds greater credibility. The same is true for cable repair, lawn care, and delivery persons. This cohort came of age when uniforms meant something, and the sight of a uniform reduces anxiety.

While many products by their nature are geared toward security, effective security positioning can employ some clever subtleties. Kimberly-Clark, for example, successfully positioned Depend undergarments, a line of absorbent products for people with bladder-control problems. Avoiding the sensitive issue of incontinence — an affliction that affects 10 million Americans, mostly older women — the campaign focused on the product's solution instead of the problem. With beloved actress and dancer June Allyson, from Hollywood's Golden era, as spokesperson, the ad campaign focused on the secure lifestyle obtainable using Depend undergarments. June Allyson could speak with sincerity and conviction because her own mother had suffered from the problem. This provided the key positioning ingredient.

TOGETHER IS BETTER

Many members of the Depression Cohort live alone, and most of them are women. In all, 53% of people between the ages of 75–85 live alone, as do 71% of those aged 85 and older. And because women typically outlive men by seven years, you can see why most older widowers remarry (see Figure 3.3).

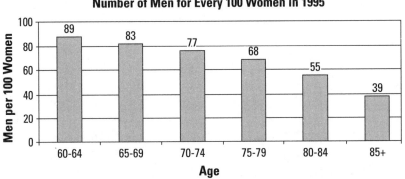

Number of Men for Every 100 Women in 1995

Figure 3.3: The ratio of women to men greatly increases with age.

Source: U.S. Bureau of the Census

It's easy to become isolated, so opportunities for social connectedness and companionship are highly valued. Especially as friends pass away, older adults need to maintain relationships — even create new ones.

Many products and services can enhance social networks for the Depression Cohort. Senior centers with their dances, games, teas, and craft programs clearly encourage social interaction. Older adults have a definite tendency to use community services, such as senior centers, and joint venturing with them can help your company gain legitimacy and create a competitive advantage when targeting this segment.

Most members of this cohort are looking not to save time, as younger cohorts are, but to fill time. Banks and other businesses have begun to tap into the available free time of older seniors. They offer their facilities for use by senior groups, or organize travel clubs or discussion groups that appeal to older people. Grocery stores are another good example. Our work for a large supermarket chain found that the early morning hours were prime shopping time for older shoppers. And it was often their main social event of the day. They loved it when stockers would help them find groceries they couldn't locate, rather than merely pointing them to the right aisle. They beamed as they chatted away with these helpers.

Studies have shown that people (especially men) who have a spouse, family member, or companion to live with are more likely to live longer than someone who doesn't. So you can see that social connectedness is important not just to mental well-being, but for physical health as well. And luckily for men, women tend to be better informed about nutrition and help keep their partners eating healthy.

Much of the Depression Cohort members' social interaction is with relatives, and interactions with grandchildren are more common than with friends. So keep this in mind — appropriate association of a company's goods or services with social interactions, especially with family, can be a very effective positioning strategy. Even connecting with animals is a popular form of social interaction. Although the majority of the Depression Cohort still live in their homes, some nursing homes even set aside time for dogs and other pets to come to the facility for the amusement and appreciation of the residents.

MONEY UNDER THE MATTRESS

When it comes to finances, the Depression Cohort is naturally conservative and risk averse. They have lived in fear of risk their whole lives, and that is not going to change. Because they are so risk-averse, the financial industry has courted this cohort with a whole host of conservative financial products. Some of these include reverse mortgages, CDs, and life insurance. Credit card companies have pretty much written off the Depression Cohort because of their aversion to buying anything on credit. This stems back to the Depression days, when buying on credit often meant you were poor and could not pay your bills. It was a sign of disgrace. In a time of deflation (something no other cohort has ever experienced), debt also meant paying off purchases with more expensive money. So emphasize safety and security when targeting this group, and avoid all mention of buy now, pay later credit schemes.

WASTE NOT, WANT NOT

Having lived through the Depression, this cohort prefers to pay more for a smaller serving, rather than throw something away. As a result, single-serving products are now becoming popular. Maxwell House Filter Pack Singles, Pillsbury single-serve cakes, and Orville Redenbacher single-serve microwave popcorn (for those without dentures!) are all examples of products consumed by this cohort. These smaller portions are also popular because they accommodate for smaller appetites among many older consumers.

But that's not all. Remember, this is the cohort that told their children to clean their plates because it would be sinful to throw away food when there were poor children starving overseas. Any effort to avoid being wasteful — less unnecessary packaging, smaller portions in restaurants, and so on — will be rewarded by this cohort.

STEP 2: ANALYZE CURRENT AND NEXT LIFESTAGE

The Depression Cohort has been retired for years, and that lifestage no longer presents the adjustments it once did. Grandparenting is also old hat. For this group, their biggest challenge now is in maintaining their independence and fighting the stigmas and stereotypes that accompany old age.

GREAT-GRANDPARENTING: THE GULF WIDENS

Now that the Depression Cohort is in its 80s, grandparenting has taken on a more formal role than in years past. Grandchildren are most likely adults now, and because of age differences, there is a widening gulf between the Depression Cohort and their great-grandchildren.

Depression Cohort grandparents are more likely to give a gift of money. They may be unable to physically get to the store, or they may not know what the kids like, or they may find the maze of products at toy superstores confusing and intimidating. And besides, money is what this group values most, having spent their lives toiling and saving to build the sizable nest eggs they will eventually pass on.

NURSING HOMES: A NEW IMAGE

Most people consider nursing homes as something to avoid. But nursing home owners are trying to change their image. Some are adopting new philosophies to enliven the often-depressing places where many people spend their final years. These facilities are filled with plants, pets, children, and activities. The homier feel helps to raise residents' spirits, and can even help to prolong their lives and reduce the need for medication. At some facilities, dogs go from room to room, looking for treats, and birds perch on residents' fingers.

Assisted-living centers, which offer more of a home-like setting, and different levels of assistance, are also popular with the Depression Cohort because they help them maintain their independence and dignity as long as possible. These types of communities are offering more options to older people who are living longer, more active lives than ever before.

WIDOWHOOD: HOME ALONE

Loneliness and depression are major problems for this age group. Widowhood (or widowerhood) contributes to the loneliness many older people feel. Cruise lines can help alleviate loneliness and increase sales by subtly appealing to widows, in part by providing older (or widowed) companions on board. Researchers have found heart patients without a spouse or confidante were twice as likely to die within six months of their first heart attack or cardiac arrest compared to those who were still married or who had friends to talk to. In this case, having a support group or someone to talk to may be as effective as medical treatment. Even having a pet can help ease loneliness. Ralston-Purina has a pet companion program for the older cohorts that provides animal companionship, helps find homes for pets — and also helps sell pet food!

IN THE MOOD FOR LOVE

Contrary to popular belief, falling in love, with all of its attendant emotions, is not just for the young. Older people experience the same emotional excitement, nervousness, and rapid heartbeats as the young. They find just as many thrills in candlelight dinners, hand-holding, and affection as do younger couples. Indeed, most older people are just as capable of fulfilled sexual behavior as younger people, if they are in circumstances where their somewhat repressed sexual tendencies (see "Old-Fashioned Passion," below) can be relaxed. In those instances, they often find themselves feeling less pressed to "perform," and more experienced and hence adequate, and thus often more satisfied than earlier in their lives.

Meeting significant others, dating, and romance are particularly important to enhancing an older person's feelings of acceptance and self-worth. This is especially true for single women over age 65, who outnumber single men in the same age group eight to one.

Many marketing opportunities exist for positioning on this too-often neglected desire. Products can be particularly cued to this dimension of aging. For example, AT&T has positioned long distance service as a way to flirt again, depicting an elderly couple conversing on the telephone. Church gatherings and adult education classes are good places to meet companions. Music festivals, art shows, and bus excursions sponsored by banks and insurance companies all bring together older people with common interests. Dances put on and promoted by Medicare HMOs are still another way for mature daters to enjoy a relationship of passion and romance.

STEP 3: EXAMINE EMOTIONS AND AFFINITIES

The emotional and affinity effects of coming to age in the Depression era are closely tied to that cohort's values. Because the Depression Cohort "got burned" early on, they tend to be much more conservative than younger cohorts. They usually respect authority and are more likely to accept conventional views.

OLD-FASHIONED PASSION

In general, this cohort exhibited "cohort-skipping" behavior toward sex. That is, they rejected the relatively open sexual attitudes that prevailed from the end of World War I through the Roaring '20s, and reverted to the more Victorian pre–World War I mind-set. The cohort skipping effect shows up in a number of areas; in music and the arts, it's known as "the grandfather law," where styles harken back not to the period immediately before, but to the one before that. For many women of the Depression Cohort, sex was not something they looked forward to, or derived much pleasure from. It was something a wife submitted to for her husband's satisfaction. And obviously, it was also the way to have children. Most women did not come to expect fulfillment from sex as younger cohorts have. One reason for lower levels of fulfillment was the lack of reliable birth control, which, because children were often not desired in this period of economic hardship, tended to generate anxiety and decrease sensuality.

Because the Depression Cohort did not have the sexual freedom that Baby Boomers had, for example, they never developed much tolerance for discussions about sexual fulfillment or alternative lifestyles. As a result, marketers would be well-advised to avoid sexual innuendoes or themes in targeting this group. Romance, however, can effectively be used to tap this cohort, provided that sex is not directly mentioned.

INDEPENDENCE TO THE DEATH

Maintaining independence is a top priority for the Depression Cohort. They fear losing their independence more than they fear dying. As a result, home-based services for the elderly, such as home healthcare, housekeeping, and lawn services, are booming. These services make older people's lives easier and more enjoyable, allowing them to remain in their homes and in control. Much of the success of home-based services stems not necessarily from a direct demand from people using the services, but from insurance companies' desire to reduce healthcare costs, and adult children's lack of time to help their parents. Regardless, older cohorts are major beneficiaries of this new emphasis on home-based services.

Adult day-care centers also help those in the Depression Cohort maintain their independence. They provide a social outlet and stimulating activities, which help to ease loneliness and depression for seniors living alone. Adult day care can be a lifeline that helps ease the isolation of old age. According to the *Wall Street Journal,* adult day-care centers have multiplied tenfold since the mid-1980s, and this growth will likely increase in coming years.[2]

Multistage retirement communities are another way the Depression Cohort can maintain some of its independence, while getting the medical care or other help they need. These communities allow residents to gradually increase the level of care they require, while providing a familiar and secure setting.

"LEAPIN' LIZARDS!" AND OTHER MEMORIES

Older generational cohorts enjoy reminiscing about "the good old days," and your product promotion can help remind them of their youth. Although aging does cause some decrease in short-term memory, long-term memory stays intact. Older people often prefer that which is familiar to that which is new. Fond memories of childhood, youth, and young adulthood make nostalgia a most effective positioning approach.

These days, there are entire nostalgia industries geared toward older Americans. Take the Vermont Country Store catalog, for example. This black-and-white catalog has an old-fashioned feel to it, and it offers many products that are old favorites of the Depression Cohort, but virtually unheard of by younger groups. The catalog features hard-to-find products the Depression Cohort remembers from its youth, including Maypo maple-flavored hot cereal, Skybar candy bars, Necco wafers, and Fels-Naptha bar soap. The catalog is, in fact, one big nostalgia trip sure to delight older customers.

Fads of the 1930s

+ Jitterbug dancing
+ Swing music
+ Gangster movies
+ Little Orphan Annie
+ The Marx brothers
+ Horror movies
+ Zoot suits
+ Saddle shoes
+ Nonsense songs, such as "Three Little Fishies" or "Mairsy Doats"

Another example is *Reminisce* magazine. Billed as "The magazine that brings back the good times," it showcases stories that come from its readers in many cases. Among its features are "Fond Flashbacks," "Our Most Memorable Meal" (submitted by subscribers), "I've Kept it All These Years," and "Ads from the Old Days." This endearing publication trades on nostalgia.

Each issue tugs at the heartstrings of the Depression Cohort, and gives readers a warm memory of pleasurable times.

AGE IS A STATE OF MIND

If you want to be successful marketing to the Depression Cohort, use positive role models that emphasize this group's dignity, vitality, healthy lifestyle, determination, and considerable life experience. Since most older people tend to see themselves as 15 years younger than they really are, use younger models to portray their "cognitive age," rather than their chronological age.

People who are models of successful aging can also gain quick attention and positive attribution in marketing. Marketing consultant and champion of positive aging Ken Dychtwald has coined the term "elder-hero" to describe older people, such as Jimmy Carter, Paul Newman, or Lena Horne, who are revered and respected for their personal or professional accomplishments. These icons of successful aging make wonderful product endorsers.

Former Apollo astronaut and Ohio senator John Glenn is a member of the Depression Cohort and is an excellent example of an elderhero. In 1998, at age 77, Glenn defied skeptics and returned to space on the space shuttle *Discovery,* making him the world's oldest astronaut. The trip turned him into a major role model for senior citizens, both today and well into the future.

Just look around and you will find many examples of active, healthy older Americans that dispel popular negative stereotypes:

- ✦ Noel Johnson, who died at age 95, spent the last 25 years of his life setting age records in everything from the half mile to the New York City Marathon. He had turned his life around while in his late 60s after a doctor gave him only six months to live. He began walking, then running, and proved that an active life helps promote longevity. He wrote two books about his experiences: *A Dud at 70, a Stud at 80;* and *The Living Proof.* He ran his last New York City Marathon, a grueling route of 26.2 miles, at age 90. He later commented, "I'd rather be 92 years young than 70 years old."

- ✦ Male bodybuilders are competing in senior contests well into their 70s.

- ✦ The Sun City, Arizona, Poms perform rousing pompon routines, complete with back flips, cartwheels and splits. The average age — 73, and some members of the squad are even older. Instead of calling themselves senior citizens or "the elderly," they like to think of themselves as having reached "the age of elegance."

- ✦ Local and state spelling bees geared specifically for senior citizens are attracting large followings, dispelling stereotypes that this cohort is feeble and content to watch TV all day long.

Wouldn't people like these make fabulous spokespersons or endorsers for your product?

ELDERHEROES TO THE RESCUE

Although we are in an age of so-called political correctness, in the advertising world, senior citizens are still targets of ridicule. Stereotypes of older Americans as feeble and foolish abound, sending the subtle message that growing older is something to avoid at all costs. There are a few exceptions; Home Savings of America featured George Fenneman (former announcer on Groucho Marx's "You Bet Your Life" program) as spokesperson, embodying the virtues of conservativism and thrift. It was extremely well received by members of the Depression Cohort audience.

Modern Maturity, the monthly magazine published by AARP, rejects about 30% of the ads submitted for consideration because of negative portrayals of older Americans. The magazine seeks to inspire its readers with vitality, not depress them about physical ailments they may or may not have.

The impact of negative stereotypes isn't just psychological. Negative stereotypes about aging can also hurt how people function, researchers have shown. A recent study found that healthy older people could suddenly walk faster and shuffled less when they were subconsciously shown positive images of aging. And how well a person walks often predicts their future health and independence, because falls can become major health problems.

INTERGENERATIONAL EXPERIENCES

The older people get, the less they want to interact only with people their own age. This has strong implications for advertising. Commercial and print ad settings that depict only one age group rather than a mix of ages will generally not be well received, even if those seeing the ad can't quite articulate why it's unappealing.

Modern Maturity magazine provided a series of "How to" advertisements suggesting promotional and communication approaches that other advertisers could use to win the hearts of mature Americans. One ad advised showing older adults with people of other ages, backgrounds and races, depicting them as involved in the world, not separate from it. Other ads advocated depictions of active, vital seniors, engaged in physical activities such as fitness walking, bowling, or canoeing. The more astute advertisers have paid heed, and have taken these suggestions to heart.

STEP 4: BUILD A PHYSIOGRAPHIC PROFILE

We realize that a lot of you would rather lose your left kidney than engage in a frank discussion about the physical realities of the aging process. But be brave. Understanding and reflecting life's physical changes in your marketing and communication strategies will help you connect with older audiences, such as the Depression Cohort, and it could even help to enhance their quality of life. Look at it this way — it's one more great opportunity to build a competitive advantage! For members of this cohort, physiographics now plays a much greater role than it ever has before. They are very aware of their aches and pains, and have learned to adapt to reduced physical capabilities. So for this group, it's not just what you sell, but how you sell it that is important.

Let's take a look at the following six main areas of physiographic change: vision, hearing, taste and smell, touch, strength, and information processing.

VISION: "WHAT YOU SEE IS WHAT YOU GET!"

Older generational cohorts are involved in a higher percentage of accidents per miles driven than any other age group except the youngest drivers, according to *USA Today*.[3] This has a lot to do with slower reflexes and poor vision. In Englewood, Colorado, and other communities, cities are replacing existing street signs with larger, brighter ones to accommodate the growing number of older drivers. Other improvements include wider, brighter pavement markings, more reflective bumps along center lines, and redesigned intersections with left-turn lanes and signals. Florida has also launched an elderly road-user program, which encourages communities to widen, brighten and enlarge pavement markings, signs, and signals.

With age comes a diminished capability to distinguish between colors, especially pastels and the green-blue-violet portion of the color spectrum. This is due to the yellowing of the eye's lens, and is particularly pronounced after age 70. By using significant color contrast — yellow on black is best — marketers can enhance the older consumer's ability to see packaging, brochures, displays, and other marketing materials, as will using at least a 13-point, serif typeface.

While a Depression Cohort individual needs up to three times as much light as a 20-year old, aging also brings reduced acuity because of an inability to accommodate for glare. Glare can be found in glossy, shiny finishes used on packaging, posters, floors in retail stores, even fluorescent lights reflecting off supermarket meat and fish displays. As a result, older cohort consumers may want to buy your product, but they can't see it, so they pass it right up. By reducing the use of glossy finishes on packaging and paying close attention to lighting, you will make older cohort consumers more likely to purchase your product.

HEARING: "NOW, LISTEN UP!"

Hearing loss is found more often in men than women, and is more pronounced for higher tone frequencies. Of persons aged 65 or older, 25% experience hearing problems, and more than 30% of people over 75 have hearing difficulties. The ability to discriminate between different tones is most problematic for low- and high-pitched sounds. In targeting older adults, choose spokespersons with deeper voices.

Aging also brings greater difficulty in separating out background noise from key messages. As a result, radio and television commercials should focus on the main message and avoid background clutter, such as music, voices, or other sounds.

TASTE AND SMELL: "THAT'S HOW THEY USED TO TASTE!"

A decline in taste sensitivity begins at about age 50. By age 80, two-thirds of one's taste buds have atrophied. Loss is greatest for sweet tastes, whereas sour tastes seem to be least affected. We once did some focus groups with Depression Cohort respondents, and had a cookie tasting. The "regular" chocolate flavor was not much liked, and there was general agreement that the company must have sharply reduced the chocolate content. (In fact, it hadn't.) Then we had them try the new "double fudge" version. Aha! "That's the way they used to taste!" Because 80% of taste is attributed to smell, odor amplification seems to offer the best means of enhancing the palatability of foods and beverages.

Interestingly, appearance can also play a part. Another of our clients had a problem with their packaged sausages. As with the sweetness of the cookies, the Depression Cohort unanimously felt the spiciness level of the sausages had diminished. Again, it hadn't. But simply adding more spices would have potentially caused stomach irritation. The solution: Increase the intensity of the red *color* in the spice flakes used in the sausages. Suddenly, the perceived spiciness was just right — "just the way it used to be!"

TOUCH: "THAT OLD FEELING!"

Touch and temperature sensitivity begins to decline after middle age. At age 65, a five-degree change in temperature is needed to equal the sensitivity a 30-year-old would have for a one-degree change. This decrease is greater in areas such as the palms of hands, soles of feet, and hairless parts of the face. Pain thresholds also increase with age. Many products can be fabricated of materials with greater texture or contrast, which enhance sensitivity.

Generally, 80+ individuals prefer more warmth in winter, are less able to endure extreme heat in summer, and are particularly uncomfortable in a draft. Heating, ventilating, and air-conditioning systems clearly should accommodate these changes.

STRENGTH: "THOSE DARN PILL BOTTLES!"

For the Depression Cohort, muscle strength, coordination, and grip strength are also diminished, making it difficult to do simple tasks once completed with little or no trouble at all, things like walking up and down stairs, opening jars, or opening prescription medicines. Arthritis and rheumatism only make matters worse.

In fact, the inability to open products is a major complaint of the Depression Cohort. According to the Consumer Product Safety Commission, up to 60% of older people are unable to open some types of child-resistant packaging, including medication. A few minor modifications, such as switching to easier-to-open child-resistant caps and widening tear strips, can make a world of difference for older consumers. Other substitutions can also be made, such as use of Velcro strips instead of buttons, door handles instead of doorknobs. In residences, older generational cohorts appreciate handrails that allow their fingers to fully encompass the circumference of the railing.

To prevent atrophy, muscles need to be used, and weight training is the best way for even the Depression Cohort to compensate for muscular deterioration. Exercise and activity need only be moderate, such as that found in mall-walking programs, the exercise classes in many senior centers, and other fitness programs.

A New "Twist" on Packaging

Here's the challenge: Develop a childproof cap that older consumers with declining grip strength can easily open, but that can foil the prying hands of toddlers.

Since new packaging regulations requiring that caps be more accommodating for physiographic changes took effect in 1998, pharmaceutical and packaging companies have begun to experiment. Here is what they've come up with:

The key Involves inserting a key into grooves on top of the cap, eliminating the press-and-turn motion (Sanner of America, Inc.)

The lock Uses a combination lock device (Searle)

The trapdoor Includes a small door and tiny plastic shock absorbers for removing it (Searle)

The quarter turn Uses a tapered bottle design and four locking grooves, and does not require palming of the cap to open (Searle/Kerr Group Inc.)

INFORMATION PROCESSING: "USE IT OR LOSE IT!"

The mental processes that shape the reception, comprehension, and storage and retrieval of information also slow as we age. These deficits potentially have the greatest effect on the communication process. To make sure your message gets through, follow these basic guidelines:

✦ For print communications, advertisements and promotional materials should be relatively uncluttered and simple in structure. Printed materials are preferable to radio and television, because they allow readers to process information at their own pace.

✦ For radio and television communications, use 60-second ads, rather than 30-second or 15-second spots. This contributes to better comprehension by older audiences.

✦ Keep messages simple, and present information in a straightforward, linear manner that is easy to process.

✦ Use pictures wherever possible. Visual cues help enhance the comprehension of written and spoken messages.

Use it or lose it. Sounds kind of harsh when referring to mental capacity and physical strength. But, according to researchers, staying active, both physically and mentally is the key to long life. This is a theme that the Depression Cohort is receptive to, so use it when designing your own marketing messages that target this group.

At age 85, New York financier and political adviser Bernard Baruch quipped, "To me, old age is always fifteen years older than I am." And this attitude is true of most older adults. Most members of the 50+ market see themselves as active, involved people who are 10–15 years younger than they really are. They expect to be represented and spoken to in this way by marketers.

You can also add value by offering products and services that encourage greater activity, both physically and mentally. In designing retirement communities, for example, put elevators some distance away from the dining room so that residents get some exercise after meals. Or, join with local colleges to provide on-site seminars, adding intellectual stimulation to their lives. Nostalgic games, such as Scrabble, Monopoly, Hearts, and Gin Rummy, help to keep the mind active. And retailers of all kinds can also devise ways to engage the Depression Cohort and keep them feeling young as part of the value they add to the shopping experience. It has worked for our clients. It can work for you, too.

STEP 5: UNDERSTAND SOCIAL ACTIVITIES AND LIFESTYLES

For the most part, social activities for this cohort are very limited, revolving mostly around their family, church, and local community. But these activities still offer opportunities for marketers.

FAMILY: TIES THAT BIND

For the Depression Cohort, social activities often revolve around family. As this group has aged, many of their friends have passed away. This has brought them closer to their families, who they now rely more heavily on for social companionship and assistance with household chores and financial decisions. In your ad campaigns, show older people interacting with family members of all ages. It can evoke powerful emotions.

CHURCH: "THE LITTLE BROWN CHURCH IN THE VALE"

Religion also often plays a large role in the lives of Depression Cohort members. With age, many people have an increased urgency for enhanced spirituality. For some this surfaces with more thoughts turned directly toward God, religion, and attending church and synagogue functions. Religion then becomes a social, as well as a spiritual, outlet. But even more subtly, doing what is right, obeying the laws of God and society, and avoiding all guilt-producing actions embody this need for psychologically knowing there will be a good life in the hereafter. You can show respect for spirituality in your marketing messages, while avoiding the specifics of any particular religion.

LOCAL COMMUNITY: FAMILIAR IS BEST

In most cases, the Depression Cohort prefers face-to-face interactions in their local community to catalog shopping, or electronic transactions that can be done from home. While a variety of communication tactics can be used to reach this market, personal, face-to-face contact often works best.

Realizing this, one California bank started supplying coffee and donuts at some of its branches and encouraged people to think of the bank as a meeting place. A Canadian bank offered tellerless ATM branches, but staffed the site with greeters who helped train older customers and others how to use the machines. This allowed the bank to reduce costs by not having tellers, but still allowed for personal service.

Wal-Mart's strategy to hire older adults as greeters not only provides flexible jobs for older workers, but it also makes older shoppers feel welcome in the store. To these shoppers, the greeters are not just obstacles to avoid while running in to pick up baby diapers or detergent, but friends and neighbors. This familiarity helps to boost older shoppers' comfort level and increases the odds that they will return to the store.

STEP 6: INVESTIGATE PURCHASING BEHAVIOR

Depression Cohort members have never been big spenders, and they are even less so now that they are in their 80s. Their lifestage and age constrain the range of products that they do buy, and their shared cohort value of frugality makes them particularly reticent spenders.

"DAUGHTER KNOWS BEST"

For some members of the Depression Cohort, adult children are now often heavily involved in the decision-making process. Consider health-care decisions. The Depression Cohort may be the consumer of the healthcare service, but the initiation ("Dad, have you seen your doctor lately?"), influence ("I heard about a new drug for that very problem, Mom."), decision, and even payment may be in the hands of the children. And certainly they are in on the evaluation of the care.

But what must be understood is that the children come from a different generational cohort, and are likely to have a very different set of preferences and demands. Healthcare is just one example of a service that often affects both older cohorts and their adult children. Eldercare, assisted living, nursing homes, and financial services are other categories in which multiple cohorts may be involved in the decision-making process.

The Consumer as Six Different People

Sometimes the buy-sell process involves just two parties — the buyer and the seller. Other times this exchange can include as many as six different parties. This is important to keep in mind when targeting various audiences, especially older cohorts. The six roles are:

Initiator The person who first recognizes an unsatisfied want or need.

Influencer The individual who provides information about how the want or need may be satisfied.

Decider The person who finally chooses an alternative that will satisfy the want or need.

Buyer The purchaser of the product.

Consumer The user of the product.

Evaluator The individual who provides feedback on the chosen product's ability to satisfy.

Source: Charles D. Schewe and Alexander Hiam, "The Portable MBA in Marketing." John Wiley & Sons, Inc., 1998.

VALUE-CONSCIOUS COUPON CLIPPERS

The Depression Cohort also tends to be very value-conscious. They don't spend frivolously, and they expect a lot for their money. Value, not image, drives this group's purchasing behavior. For larger purchases, such as televisions or appliances, they like to gather as much information as possible about the item before making a decision. So providing clear, easy-to-understand marketing materials are important to this group. Coupons, discounts, and promotions that emphasize value are also strong selling points.

LITTLE THINGS MEAN A LOT

Because of physical changes that have taken place over the years, this cohort is more apt to look for comfort and convenience than they once were. Eliminating hassles and avoiding products seen as difficult to use takes on increasing priority. Aging focuses less concern on *looking* good, and more on *feeling* good. Concern for comfort and convenience becomes a key need and offers yet another strategic positioning opportunity.

A whole host of products are designed to meet this need: Automatic card shufflers, rakes and shovel handles designed to avoid stooping, short garden wagons that allow sitting down while working outdoors, Velcro tabs instead of buttons, fuller-cut clothing, remote controls for lighting in the bedroom, and large-handled cutlery are just a few of the many products positioned on the need for comfort.

Retailers can often offer comfort to Depression Cohort customers very simply. Sometimes, it's as easy as putting chairs or benches in waiting areas where husbands or wives can sit and chat while their spouses do the shopping. This technique often proves to be popular with younger customers as well. These areas can also serve as excellent communication points for what amounts to a captive audience, the cost is minimal, and as Paco Underhill describes in *American Demographics* magazine, the consequences of *not* providing seating for uninvolved shoppers can sometimes lead to disastrous results:[4]

... If a store doesn't provide seating, people will stand or sit where they can, leading to potentially undesirable results. Envirosell witnessed a telling example in a study we did for a national lingerie manufacturer. While older women may be less concerned with generating cleavage as opposed to controlling it, their interest in the Wonderbra is nevertheless quite high. In one of the sites we examined, the Wonderbra display stood across from a windowsill on which uninvolved male shoppers tended to congregate. The peanut gallery of observers reached its apogee when two hard-of-hearing gentlemen parked themselves on the sill and loudly discussed whether each shopper who approached needed the product. No Wonderbras were sold during their 20-minute tenure.

The Depression Cohort group's need for comfort and convenience has also opened up a broad market for home-based services, such as lawn care, housekeeping, and meal services, which help older adults to remain in their homes and maintain their independence. A few hospitals now cater to this new take-out food market by selling frozen dinners to older people with special dietary restrictions. Holyoke Hospital in western Massachusetts, for instance, offers "Just What the Doctor Ordered" — entrees cooked in the hospital kitchen that are low in sodium, cholesterol, fat, and sugar, and are delivered to the homes of elderly adults. These types of services also offer important outlets for socialization.

Comfort and convenience are valued, but keep in mind that to the Depression Cohort, convenience isn't always about saving time. In fact, many in this cohort group are looking for ways to *fill* time. This is one reason they prefer tellers to ATMs (although lack of standardization between different ATMs and the need to remember a PIN also contribute to the preference for a live person). But passing time and the desire for social interaction also make going out to do something much more appealing than doing it from home.

CONCLUSION: "OLD AGE IS NOT A SIN"

The Depression Cohort's coming-of-age experience consisted of economic strife, elevated unemployment rates, and having to take menial jobs to survive. Financial security — what they most lacked when coming of age — rules their thinking.

Their physiological state tends to be the main driver of their needs and wants today. The Depression Cohort represents a widening market for convenience products and home-based services that will help them to maintain their dignity and independence. Table 3.1 shows a summary of key principles to keep in mind when targeting the Depression Cohort.

Former Prime Minister of Israel Golda Meir, who was a formidable older woman, once remarked, "Old age is not a sin." And that is certainly true. To marketers, old age can actually be a blessing in disguise. First, the older the market segment, the more precisely (and more efficiently) it can be targeted. For example, reaching Boomers via mass media takes big bucks, but reaching the Depression Cohort via big-band format radio is pretty cheap.

Marketers have notoriously ignored the older age segments. They do not want to have their products associated with the negative aspects of advanced age. Yet this very fact opens up an underserved market that is eager to be served. Clearly, when the Baby Boomers reach advanced age, their numbers will change marketers' focus. Then it will be "cool" to address older consumers.

Right now, older adults are ripe for being catered to in a much more ingenious manner. It doesn't take much — any small improvement can have an enormous impact on their lives . . . and on your sales! Generational cohort values are at the root of how to do this. Because this segment has been so often forgotten, much of the underlying understanding of what motivates their behavior is not well known. Hopefully, this chapter has shed some light on today's older adult marketplace and how you can tap into it.

TABLE 3.1: HOW TO TAP THE DEPRESSION COHORT MARKET

Cohort values	✦ Focus on financial security.
	✦ Offer guarantees that provide psychological security.
	✦ Stress risk aversion.
	✦ Use cohort-specific icons and nostalgia to powerfully, but-subliminally convey, "This is for you!"
	✦ Emphasize social companionship.
	✦ Display Victorian sexual values.
	✦ Reflect work as a reward (Protestant work ethic).
	✦ Show them sacrificing for the future.
	✦ Incorporate appreciation for group joining.
	✦ Depict the importance of the family.
	✦ Don't imply free-spending lifestyle — remember, "Waste not, want not."
Lifestages	✦ Great-grandparenting.
	✦ Widowhood.
	✦ Dating and romance in older age.
	✦ Use Elderheroes as inspirational spokespersons.
	✦ Help them to "fill time" rather than "save time."
Emotions and affinities	✦ Emphasize experiences, not "things."
	✦ Depict intergenerational experiences.
	✦ Focus on gaining independence and control over one's life.
	✦ Use nostalgia to remind them of their youth.
	✦ Emphasize a pride in one's skills.
	✦ Reflect the safe journey, a belief that one will achieve a heavenly end to life.
Physiographics	✦ Provide three times the light (in retail stores) as for a 20-year-old.
	✦ Avoid direct references to age and age-related problems.
	✦ Cast to cognitive age, not chronological age.
	✦ Use pictures and other visuals in communications for enhanced comprehension.
	✦ Reflect onset of nearsightedness.
	✦ Enhance taste in food products due to loss of taste buds and impact of medications.
	✦ Use fitness and health as "illness-preventing" rather than "youth enhancing."
	✦ Build less exertion into related tasks such as shopping, product acquisition, and product usage and consumption.

TABLE 3.1 (CONT.)

	✦ Use 13-point type or larger.
	✦ Avoid fluorescent colors, pastels, and colors in the blue-green portion of the spectrum.
	✦ Use contrasting colors to emphasize a package's opening features.
	✦ Increase the number of perforations in tear strips.
	✦ Widen tear strips.
	✦ Reduce the amount of carton sealant used.
	✦ Avoid any opening feature that requires consumers to grasp a small, thin string or component.
Social activities and lifestyles	✦ Emphasize intergenerational experiences with family, church, and local community.
	✦ Reflect organized religion.
Purchasing behavior	✦ Reflect adult children's role, and recognize they may make final decisions about some purchases.
	✦ Show them as value conscious and risk averse.

ENDNOTES

1. Edwin T. Boling, "Growing Old: Adjustment to Change." *Nursing Homes,* Vol. 36, No. 2 (March/April 1987): 20–23.

2. Sue Shellenbarger, "More Day-Care Centers Help the Aging Attend to the Aged." *The Wall Street Journal* (7 March 1994): sec. B, p. 1.

3. Linda Kanamine, "Spreading the word — with bigger street signs." *USA Today* (29 December 1994): sec. A, p. 6.

4. Paco Underhill, "Seniors in Stores." *American Demographics,* Vol. 18, Issue 4 (April 1996): 44 (5).

CHAPTER 4

THE WORLD WAR II COHORT

A t the Ramada Express Hotel and Casino in Laughlin, Nevada, guests begin their day with a rousing 7 a.m. flag raising ceremony. Later, at the hotel's American Heroes Museum, interactive displays put visitors into a 1940s virtual reality. Visitors can step back into a 1940s living room, or try on weighted components representing a World War II helmet, field pack, rifle, ammunition, and field radio equipment. Even the most robust youngsters find the equipment too heavy to wear comfortably. Then, they are reminded that this is the type of gear World War II GIs carried while landing on beachheads, slogging through swamps, and defending mountainside positions.

Daily, on the hour, an emotionally stirring multimedia program pays tribute to life in America from 1940 to the end of World War II. The program includes more than a thousand World War II images and popular songs of the times, all showcased with dazzling sound and lighting effects. From giant screens, young faces peer out through the years. Tears well up and conversations stop, as the acknowledgement of so much sacrifice makes a deep and lasting impression on many of the older folks in the audience who lived through the war. To top off the day, the hotel provides free live music in the lounge every afternoon, featuring swing and big band hits from the '40s and '50s.

Is this some kind of World War II time warp, or what? Although it may look and feel like you woke up in 1941, AZTAR Corporation's Laughlin resort transports senior guests on a brief, but vivid, sentimental journey back to their youth. The atmosphere, surroundings, and customer service at the hotel and casino are all geared to the World War II Cohort. This model for mature marketing, known as "Back to the 1940s," began in November 1996 and continues to attract more than 100,000 visitors each year. The program leaves guests with a truly unforgettable experience that goes beyond a typical night's stay at a casino resort hotel. This trip back in time targets those who lived through World War II and helps to build brand loyalty for Ramada Express.

World War II as a Defining Moment

The World War II Cohort was unified by common enemies, shared experiences, and — especially for the 16 million who served in the military — a sense of postponement and delay. In World War I, the average duration of service was less than 12 months, but in World War II, the average was 33 months — nearly three times longer. Marriages, careers, and children were all put on hold until the war was over. This sense of postponement made the World War II Cohort an intensely romantic one. The yearning for loved ones left behind and for those who left to fight is reflected in the music, books, and movies of the time.

While for many the war was an unpleasant experience, for many others it was the apex of their lives. They had the opportunity to do noble and heroic things, such as liberating Paris and rescuing concentration camp inmates, fighting for their country, and making romantic sacrifices and grand gestures (think *Casablanca*). And they had a defined role — Captain, Sergeant, Major — which was frequently more important in status than any other they would ever have again. They had a measure of freedom from social norms and an opportunity to travel, some to exotic foreign shores, others just away from the towns and farm fields of their youth. It was something they would never forget.

Sacrifice for a common good was widely accepted among members of the World War II Cohort, as evidenced by women watching their husbands and boyfriends leave — some forever — and men heading into an unknown world that often mixed boredom and terror in equal measure.

KILROY WAS HERE

Popular culture reflected the romance and uncertainty of the times. The big band sounds of Glenn Miller, Tommy Dorsey, and Benny Goodman were popular during this time, while Frank Sinatra was a heartthrob to millions of teenage girls.

Hollywood's portrayal of the war included everything from romantic dramas, such as *Casablanca* with Ingrid Bergman and Humphrey Bogart, to cartoon spoofs, including *Der Fuehrer's Face* with Donald Duck.

The line of graffiti "Kilroy was here," along with a drawing of the big-nosed mascot, became a popular joke among soldiers. It appeared everywhere, from bathroom walls to bombed-out buildings to dirty jeep windshields. It seemed that the more remote or unbelievable the location, the more the soldiers liked it. Kilroy was an inane metaphor for the unfathomable situations soldiers — many of whom had never left home before — suddenly found themselves in during the war.

THE "GOOD WAR"

What Was Popular in the '40s

Popular movies of the early '40s

> *Blondie for Victory* (Penny Singleton and Arthur Lake)
>
> *Casablanca* (Humphrey Bogart and Ingrid Bergman)
>
> *For Me and My Gal* (Gene Kelly and Judy Garland)
>
> *Yankee Doodle Dandy* (James Cagney)

Hit songs of the early '40s

> "Chattanooga Choo Choo"
>
> "White Christmas"
>
> "Somebody Else is Taking My Place"
>
> "As Time Goes By"
>
> "I'll Be Seeing You"
>
> "It's Been a Long, Long Time"
>
> "Sentimental Journey"

Popular books of the early '40s

> Sales of the Bible increased 25% throughout the war
>
> *The White Cliffs of Dover*, Alice Miller
>
> *Berlin Diary*, William Shirer
>
> *See Here, Private Hargrove*, Marion Hargrove
>
> *Here Is Your War*, Ernie Pyle
>
> *Guadalcanal Diary*, Richard Tregaskis

World War II officially began on Sept. 1, 1939, with Germany's invasion of Poland. This prompted Britain and France to declare war on Germany a few days later. Though determined to maintain its neutrality, the United States was gradually drawn closer to the war, providing aid to Britain and instituting the first peacetime draft in the nation's history in 1940. Efforts to reach a peaceful settlement ended Dec. 7, 1941, when Japan attacked Pearl Harbor without warning, killing 2,400 servicemen.

The war itself was cast in very simple terms — evil dictators in Germany, Italy, and Japan bent on world domination versus the Allied forces of goodness and freedom. Propaganda playing off these stereotypes only made it easier for the United States to mobilize public opinion behind the war and to support the war machine.

By 1944, the United States was producing bombers, jeeps, and armaments at amazing rates that far surpassed those of the Axis powers. For workers, the payoff was sometimes deeply personal. One story that inspired many on the home front involved a seaman whose life belt had saved him from drowning when his ship went down off of Guadalcanal. He later discovered a stamp on the belt indicating it had come from his hometown of Akron, Ohio — and that it had been inspected and packed by his own mother! It was these kinds of stories that inspired the can-do spirit of many Americans and helped win the war for the Allies.[1]

ROSIE THE RIVETER — "WE CAN DO IT!"

With so many men fighting overseas, America's wartime industry relied heavily on women to keep up the pace. Between 1940–1944, the number of employed women rose from 12 million to 18.2 million, many lured into factories by rousing propaganda of how their contributions were needed to win the war. The image of "Rosie the Riveter" became a popular one throughout the war, as women took on the new role of wage earner. Previously, women had aspired to more traditional roles of wife and mother, but the war provided new opportunities. After the war, some of the female factory workers doubtless welcomed returning to their time-honored, if more limited functions. Others chafed at returning to domestic status, and set the stage for the mass entry of women into the workforce a decade later. Even today, Rosie is a symbol of feminine independence and power, and is used as such in advertisements to invoke that concept.

With the population of eligible males depleted by overseas service, deaths, and war injuries, women competed more overtly for mates than ever before. This was the first cohort to wear makeup as part of the daily routine — partly to enhance their appeal for the smaller number of males around, and partly to signal general sexual interest and dating availability.

The Real Rosie

The real-life "Rosie the Riveter" was Rose Monroe. She was a young mother of two who went to work at Ford's Willow Run Aircraft Factory in Ypsilanti, Michigan, during the war. She and her co-workers riveted together B-24 and B-29 bombers that were flown in combat missions by American pilots overseas.

By 1942, there was already a popular war song called "Rosie the Riveter," and the famous poster of a fictional Rosie with the title "We Can Do It!" was recognized around the world.

Then one day a film company came to Willow Run to produce a documentary on War Bonds. One actor noticed that there was a real-life Rosie on the riveting line — Rose Monroe. She was young, attractive, and full of life. So she was chosen to portray Rosie the Riveter in the film they were making.

Rose Monroe became the real-life embodiment of Rosies all over America, a symbol of strength and pride for all women who made an invaluable contribution to winning the war.

"YOU'VE DONE YOUR BIT — NOW DO YOUR BEST!"

Even before the United States officially entered what was to become the bloodiest and most costly war in history, it had already undertaken the largest and most ambitious advertising campaign ever. Its goal? To sell wartime government programs and war bonds to the American public. The War Advertising Council and the War Finance Committee promoted voluntary compliance with war bond buying quotas and rationing programs, while at the same time boosting home-front morale. According to the John W. Hartman Center for Sales, Advertising, and Marketing History at Duke University, where a collection of these ads are archived, these organizations produced the greatest volume of advertising and publicity ever given to any product or agency in the history of America. Some of these ads are now in the public domain, and are thus usable today for evoking nostalgic responses.

"FOOD IS A WEAPON!"

During the war, Americans were called upon to make sacrifices that are difficult for younger generational cohorts to even imagine today. Food was strictly rationed, and staples, such as meat, coffee, butter, cheese, and sugar, were controlled by a complicated point system that required retailers and consumers to keep track of ration stamps, stickers, and coupons. To supplement their diets, many people became part-time farmers, tending "victory gardens." Even in cities, where space was tight, people tilled small plots of vegetables in whatever space they could find. As a result, even today, gardening is a popular hobby for the World War II Cohort.

"Food is a weapon!" was a frequently heard watchword. Advertisements directed at patriotic women called for "Meatless Days," and provided recipes that used bread scraps or leftovers. The government asked that women prepare only what their families would eat in one sitting.

Harkening back to the concept that each cohort covets what it most lacked during its coming-of-age years, the World War II Cohort's food preferences lean strongly to the fresh: fresh meat, fresh eggs, and fresh vegetables. Most abhor what they often ate out of necessity during that time: Spam.

"USE IT UP, WEAR IT OUT, MAKE IT DO, OR DO WITHOUT!"

Gasoline was also strictly rationed, with most drivers limited to only three gallons of gas per week. Mileage-ration stickers had to be displayed on windshields, and rubber was in such short supply that old tires first had to be turned in before ration cards could be issued to buy new ones. Advertisements pleaded for citizens to "Cooperate With Your Government — Use Less Gas." Imagine the reaction of today's cynical 20-somethings to such a message! But those were different times. For the World War II Cohort, who came of age during a time of crisis, the message hit home.

To boost the supply of raw materials needed for defense, Americans joined in nationwide scrap drives, targeting everything from iron and steel to paper, nylon stockings, and cooking grease. Advertisements appealed directly to women, suggesting, for example, that the storage of waste fats could directly aid a wounded soldier. The glycerin in recycled fats was used in gunpowder, sulfa anti-infection drugs, smallpox vaccines, and ammunition. Advertisements encouraging paper recycling showed a number of uses for scrap paper, including use in shell containers, blasting kegs, bomb rings, and parachute flares. Interestingly, while the recycling concept was accepted and followed as a necessary part of the winning war effort, once the war was over it became too much trouble to bother with. This was doubtless exacerbated by the sudden abundance of "stuff" after the war ended. During the conflict itself, however, recycling or doing without, however inconvenient, was their most tangible contribution to the war effort.

"I'll buy bonds!"

The war bond campaign was a unique blending of patriotism and consumerism. Seeking to stir the conscience of Americans at home, it invoked both Americans' financial and moral stake in the war. By the end of the war, more than 85 million Americans (Depression or older cohorts as well as World War II Cohorts) had invested $185.7 billion in war bonds, a number unmatched by any other country. The sale of war bonds provided a way for those on the home front to express their patriotism and contribute to the national defense.

In WWII, the Average Shoe Size Was 6

At the Ramada Express American Hero's Museum, visitors are reminded of how much times have changed since World War II.

For example, did you know that in World War II, the average men's jacket size was 38, and the average men's shoe size was 6? Quite a change from today's youth! Now, if you consider that most soldiers carried between 75 and 100 pounds of field gear, you will begin to have a real appreciation for the generation that saved the world.

THE WORLD WAR II COHORT TODAY

In 2001, the World War II Cohort is 74–79 years old and its members (17 million of which are now living) are still bound together by the experiences of the war years. They are beginning to slow down with age, but a large number still remain active and involved, either through social groups, volunteer activities, or part-time jobs. See the Snapshot feature for a Multi-Dimensional Marketing™ overview of this cohort, which we developed using the Lifestage Analytic Matrix™.

The World War II Cohort is an excellent example of why there's a difference between a cohort and a generation. As noted in Chapter 1, "Toward a New Era of Marketing," a *generation* is a biological construct, demarcated by the time it takes to be born, become an adult, and have children of one's own. This is usually around 20–25 years. A *cohort,* on the other hand, is formed by momentous historical moments — defining events. Sometimes the defining moments are very sharply outlined (visualize the Alps mountain range — World War II was bounded by Alps on either end, and it defined the people who came of age during this time equally as sharply). Other times, the defining moments are more gradual. Anyone — male or female, whether in the service or working in the factories — who became an adult in America between 1940–1945 was profoundly influenced by the war in fundamental, value-forming ways that differ from those who came of age either before or after. The person who was 19 in 1935, and thus nearing 30 when the war ended, was undoubtedly influenced by the war, and possibly was in the service. But his core values were formed before the war started. As a result, his attitudes are very different from those of his brother who is five years younger.

As we will see in the next chapter, the converse holds for the Postwar Cohort. Between 1946 — the end of the war — and 1963, the assassination of President Kennedy, there were no "Alps." There were "hills," such as the Korean Conflict, the Civil Rights Movement, and the Cold War. But they were not sufficiently high and steep enough to separate one group's coming of age during that period from another. Thus the Postwar Cohort is the longest of this century — 17 years.

It's important to keep in mind that members of the World War II Cohort are the parents of the oldest Baby Boomers. They sacrificed so that their children would have a comfortable life. It's interesting, then, to note the huge gap in values that exists between these two groups. The World War II Cohort staked their lives on obedience, trusting authority, and honoring and fighting for institutions. But remember the "grand-father law" or the "cohort-skipping" effect — each cohort tends to rebel somewhat against the values of its parents. Thus, it's not surprising that those who so respected authority produced children who readily rallied around the adage "Don't Trust Anyone Over 30!"

TAPPING THE WWII COHORT MARKET

The World War II Cohort, while small, offers an underserved marketing opportunity (see Table 4.1). In retirement, they have experienced a higher level of well-being due to greater assets, pension, and Social Security than any previous cohort. And unlike younger generational cohorts, who are more likely to stretch their incomes among the needs of several family members and a large mortgage, the World War II Cohort has already put their children through school, and most own their own homes outright. With these major expenditures out of the way, even a small income translates into a tremendous amount of discretionary buying power.

TABLE 4.1: WWII COHORT MARKET POTENTIAL

	Age 65–74	Age 75+	Total Population
Median Net Worth (1995)	$106,900	$92,300	$55,600
Median Income (1999)	$28,928	$23,937	$43,951
Avg. Annual Expenditures (1999)	$29,864	$22,884	$36,995

Source: Consumer Expenditure Survey, 1999. Bureau of Labor Statistics

Name of cohort:	WWII
Born between:	1922–27
Coming of age:	1940–45
Age in 2001:	74–79
Population:	17 million ✦ 8%

Key cohort values and concerns:
- ✦ Patriotism
- ✦ Romance
- ✦ Self-reliance
- ✦ Respect for authority

Current and next lifestage:
- ✦ Retirement
- ✦ Post-retirement job
- ✦ Widowhood
- ✦ Grandparent and great-grandparent
- ✦ Adult day care

Emotions and affinities:
- ✦ Nostalgia
- ✦ Buy American
- ✦ Volunteerism
- ✦ Sexual ambivalence
- ✦ Convergence of male and female roles

Physiographic profile:
- ✦ Chronic conditions
- ✦ Cardiovascular problems
- ✦ Vision impairment
- ✦ Senility and Alzheimer's
- ✦ Constipation, incontinence, and erectile dysfunction

Social activities and lifestyles:
- ✦ Gardening
- ✦ Family and church
- ✦ Purchasing behavior
- ✦ Cautious savers and spenders

The Depression Cohort has many of these conditions, too — however, this is the cohort when they first become major drivers of attitudes and behavior.

STEP 1: LOOK AT KEY COHORT VALUES AND CONCERNS

It's not surprising that the World War II Cohort shares some common values with both the Depression Cohort (sacrifice for a common cause) and the Postwar Cohort (patriotism). But the cohorts differ, too, in that no cohort holds all these values collectively, and quite as strongly, as the World War II Cohort.

"BOOGIE WOOGIE BUGLE BOY" PATRIOTISM

Having fought in the war, worked in war industry plants, or given up possessions to further the war effort, Americans who came of age during World War II still remain one of the most patriotic of cohorts. This is partly because what they were fighting for was perceived in clearly defined black-and-white terms — to stop world domination by the forces of evil. The media did not question the simplistic approach offered by the government, and thus contributed to the good versus evil mind-set. Movies, such as *Thirty Seconds Over Tokyo,* a fictionalized account of Col. James Doolittle's daring 1942 bombing of Japan, glorified war heroes and boosted morale. In contrast, more recent wars, such as Vietnam, were mired in shades of gray as the media dug out inconsistencies in the government's story line, raising doubts in the minds of many Americans.

The World War II Cohort responds well to patriotic themes. Images that reflect those themes, such as the flag, stir deep emotions with this group. Tom Brokaw's bestselling book, *The Greatest Generation,* is filled with

Is This the Music You Love?

If these songs don't rekindle fond memories or bring a tear to your eye, then you likely did not come of age during World War II.

- "I'll Be With You in Apple Blossom Time," by the Andrews Sisters
- "I'm Making Believe," by the Ink Spots
- "Ole Buttermilk Sky," by Hoagy Carmichael
- "Temptation," by Perry Como
- "I'll Never Smile Again," by Frank Sinatra and the Pied Pipers
- "The Very Thought of You," by Vaughn Monroe
- "The White Cliffs of Dover," by Vera Lynn
- "Long Ago and Far Away," by Jo Stafford
- "I Left My Heart at the Stage Door Canteen," by Sammy Kaye
- "Elmer's Tune," by Glenn Miller
- "Take the A Train," by Duke Ellington

stories of members of this cohort. The book is peppered with accounts of World War II vets' always saluting the flag . . . even standing up, covering heart with hand and tearing up at the sight of the flag. Can you imagine this cohort's grandchildren following suit? Not really. That's because they are part of a completely different generational cohort with different defining moments and different values.

"YOU MADE ME LOVE YOU"

The 1940s were an intensely romantic period, as evidenced by the music, movies and books of the time. As loved ones shipped out, possibly never to be seen by their families again, tearful good-byes followed by years of worry were the only option. After Pearl Harbor, the marriage rate soared, as servicemen sought an emotional tie to home before going overseas.

In marketing to the World War II Cohort, romance can be a powerful sales tool. While the sexual intolerance of the Depression Cohort was relaxed with World War II, sexual mores were still more intact than we see today. Romantic settings of candlelight dinners, hand-holding, soft music, and champagne elicit strong feelings in this group. And they can provide a wonderful context for advertising messages, one that grabs attention. In ads for La-Z-Boy recliners, for example, the company uses a scene of a couple sitting on a wide porch of a Victorian-type home. The young man is dressed in clothes of the '40s, while the woman, clearly his sweetheart, is looking down demurely as he speaks to her. Older adults immediately relate to the ad, which goes on to emphasize how long the company has been in business — another strong selling feature for this cohort.

Many opportunities arise to target this cohort by means of romantic overtones. Certainly, the music of the era was romantic and can grab this cohort's attention when used today. Promotional activities can be developed to key on the romance of yesteryear. Ballroom dancing contests can be sponsored. Love letter writing and collages of pictures of couples in romantic settings during World War II could be the focus of other contests.

To show you just how romantic this group is, some members of the World War II Cohort are even using computers and the Internet to meet mates online. San Francisco-based SeniorNet provides an avenue for older adults to communicate, even though they may be located hundreds of miles apart. Older users jump online and chat about grandchildren, gardening, and play memory games like trying to remember the lines to songs from their coming-of-age years — "Button Up Your Overcoat," for example. SeniorNet fanciers can even log on to the Wednesday night "cocktail hour" and talk of love. Participants are finding that the Internet is an easy way for lonely seniors to socialize, and even meet the next love of a lifetime. What a wonderful outlet for those without companions.

SELF-RELIANCE AND RESPECT FOR AUTHORITY

This cohort faced very high odds, yet prevailed over Axis forces that, at least at the outset of the war, had both strategic surprise and a tactical preponderance of force on their side. Not only did they prevail against the enemy, but they overcame logistical hurdles that would have seemed impossible a decade earlier — such as the Lend-Lease Program that kept Russia in the war on the Allied side. Lend-Lease supplied Russia with tanks, combat aircraft, motor vehicles, 15 million combat boots, and a myriad of other war material, including enough food to supply 12 million soldiers — all with no strings attached. Other logistic miracles on a scale unprecedented until then included Operation Overlord (the D-Day invasion), and the entire war in the Pacific, which included supply lines and communication routes thousands of miles long. If they could do that, this cohort could do anything, a conviction embodied in the slogan of the SeaBees, the Navy's Engineers: "The difficult we do immediately; the impossible takes a little longer!"

Largely because of fear of defeat, people came to respect authority during the war in ways previously unheard of. In the military, following orders was a requirement, due to the strict discipline and chain of command of military life. On the home front, authority was respected and propaganda believed because of the perceived threat of enemy attack or infiltration. This had a lasting impact on the World War II Cohort, which they still carry with them today. Here's an example from the American Heroes Museum at the Ramada Express Hotel Casino in Laughlin, Nevada, that illustrates the role authority played at home:

> *The Jewel Tea Company became one of the largest suppliers of canned rations for the military. National security was a priority. Because of the fear of enemy infiltration, no talking was allowed in the production areas. The work was tedious, repetitive, and backbreaking. Women made up the largest sector of this labor force. The hours in silence and drudgery produced worried thoughts and concern for loved ones. Morale was low. Innovative management at the Jewel Tea Company instituted a social break twice a day. They brewed their own strong black coffee and allowed the workers to leave the production rooms and socialize for 10 minutes, morning and afternoon. Production shot up 20%! And security was not compromised. The Secretary of the Treasury recognized the Jewel Tea Company for its enormous contribution to the war effort. And, to this day, government contracts carry the stipulation of a coffee break, morning and afternoon.*

This cohort struggled at home and in the military for the greater good of the nation and the world. They share with the Depression Cohort the discipline needed to keep focused on a task and delay rewards indefinitely. They did without, and had the dignity and the integrity not to complain about it. The war galvanized this cohort's values to focus not on their petty wants and desires, but on the good of the group. Even today, they are proud of their self-reliance and the sacrifices they made during the war years.

Marketing can reflect these strong values in promotional campaigns. Using icons such as Rosie the Riveter, you can show how a brand can help them "do it yourself." "Mastery over your life" products can be positioned to help the World War II Cohort hold on to its independence and self-reliance. For example, a manufacturer of grab bars for bath tubs (offered in attractive enamels rather than institutional steel) could show consumers telling friends about how this product allows them to maintain their independence and still feel secure. Or, you could use a direct reference to the war effort: "We showed 'em we could do it in the '40s, we can still do it today." Or, financial institutions could offer "We can do it!" bond drives, which would encourage older people to set up bond accounts for grandchildren and great-grandchildren.

V-Mail, the High-Tech Communication of the '40s

Today, we have e-mail, but during the latter years of World War II, "V-Mail" was a popular way to correspond with a loved one serving overseas. V-Mail letters were written on forms that could be purchased at five-and-ten-cent stores or the post office. These special forms were photographed, put on film, flown across the world and then reproduced at the mail center closest to the recipient's position. The development of the V-Mail system reduced the time it took a soldier to receive a letter by a month — from six weeks by boat to twelve days or less by air. However, the main advantage of V-Mail was its compact nature. Reduction in the size and weight of the letters translated into more space for crucial military supplies on cargo planes. One advertisement explained that 1,700 V-Mail letters could fit in a cigarette packet, while reducing the weight of the letters in paper form by 98%. Transport of the letters by plane minimized the chances that the enemy would intercept the letters, although writers were reminded to delete any information that might prove useful to the enemy in case some V-Mail was captured.

Americans on the home front were encouraged by the government and private businesses to use V-Mail. Letters from home were compared to "a five-minute furlough," and advertisements that instructed how, when, and what to write in a V-Mail reached a peak in 1944. Letters were to be cheerful, short, and frequent. V-Mail made it possible for servicemen halfway across the world to hear news from home on a weekly basis.

STEP 2: ANALYZE CURRENT AND NEXT LIFESTAGE

The World War II Cohort has entered into what might be called a "life satisfaction" mode, in which they tend to worry less about the things that once concerned them (accumulating assets, their looks, and raising their children), and focus more on doing what they enjoy.

ENDING THE DAILY GRIND

Retirement has not been the huge worry for the World War II Cohort as it has been for younger groups. The GI Bill, plentiful jobs, Social Security, Medicare, and healthy company pensions have all contributed to a relatively comfortable retirement for this cohort. For the most part, they did not have to deal with downsizing or unemployment, like cohorts on either side of them. Having had time to adjust to retirement, they have remained active in various social groups, and many have kept in touch with old friends from World War II, holding reunions each year. Reminiscing about the past gives them a sense of purpose and a feeling of pride about their accomplishments and contributions.

Ralph E. Warner, author of *Get a Life: You Don't Need a Million to Retire Well,* suggests that challenging the brain is one of the best ways to stay happy while retired. Instead of focusing on finances, Warner recommends developing good health and fitness habits, strengthening ties with family and friends, and, most important of all, having a plate full of interesting things to do. "Accentuating the positive" is a welcome theme with the World War II Cohort and can be used to gain a marketing advantage with this group.[2]

Elderhostel, an educational travel program for people aged 55 and up, has benefited from this cohort's more active and adventurous retirees. Although Elderhostel offers a wide range of courses both in the United States and abroad, the three hottest categories are active outdoor, service, and intergenerational. These touch on values of importance not just to the World War II Cohort, but to younger groups, as well.

TAKING POST-RETIREMENT JOBS

Bored with retirement and looking for new challenges, many World War II Cohorts became the first of the "senior entrepreneurs," a group that is now growing in popularity among younger cohorts. Most work out of their homes as consultants, thriving on the flexibility and challenge such positions offer. Others have started full-fledged companies after retirement.

Although from an older cohort group, the late Harlan Sanders, better known as Colonel Sanders, is a good example of a successful senior entrepreneur. At age 65, he invested a $105 Social Security check and built the Kentucky Fried Chicken empire. He sold the franchise nine years later and made $2 million. Perhaps he could be an elderhero for this cohort.

Other seniors are taking jobs at fast-food restaurants or as greeters at discount stores, not just for financial reasons, but to remain active and to have a social outlet. McDonald's, Burger King and Wal-Mart are just a few of the companies that have welcomed and encouraged retiree employees. Research shows these older workers, compared to younger counterparts, tend to be on time more often, more reliable on the job, and less likely to complain. Sounds too good to be true! And with the current low unemployment rates, more companies are turning to older workers to fill their labor ranks. This accomplishes two tasks — older workers help fill the dwindling employee pool, and older customers feel welcome when seeing people closer to their own age.

WALKING ALONE IN WIDOWHOOD

Widowhood is an undesirable and often unanticipated change, and it can have immediate negative physical and emotional effects on the surviving spouse. In fact, studies have shown that widows and widowers face a higher risk of dying than people who have not lost a spouse. Women aged 75–84 make up 83% of all widows and widowers, and 65% of women in this same age group are widows. Men are seven times more likely to remarry after the death of a spouse, so widowhood has a much larger impact on women than it does on men.

For many older widows, the biggest challenge following the loss of a spouse is in managing household finances and developing their own credit history. Loneliness is another big problem. While many marketers prefer to avoid widows as a group, due to emotional sensitivities, others have come to realize that this lifestage represents a major change, and thus a potential marketing opportunity. For example, a lawn care company that offered widows free service for a couple of weeks could clean up on goodwill. Or how about financial assistance programs offered by local banks for helping in this transition?

Here's another good example — credit card companies have begun to transfer credit histories of deceased men to their surviving spouses. And many major cruise lines, including Royal Cruise Line, have run successful host programs, in which older men are given room, board and expenses in exchange for their services as on-board escorts, dance partners, and dinner companions for older widowed passengers. Instead of trying to avoid the reality of widowhood, these companies are taking a sensitive approach and meeting the needs of this growing market.

GRANDPARENTS AS HISTORIANS AND STORYTELLERS

Because of increased life expectancies, grandparenting is essentially a post–World War II phenomenon. In fact, great-grandparents are more common today than grandparents were in 1900. As a result, today's grandparent–grandchild relationship may last 30 years or more. Grandparents, even of the same age group, are not a homogeneous lot, though, and there are a variety of grandparenting styles (see feature below, "Grandparenting Styles"). Because they are not as vigorous as they once were, World War II Cohort grandparents these days have taken on a more formal role and tend to act as family historians and storytellers. They also tend to offer gifts of money rather than pursuing activities, such as traveling with their grandchildren, which requires greater mobility. This makes them a prime target for financial services, as they decide how to pass on their considerable wealth.

Our work with focus groups has shown that grandparents and great-grandparents show tremendous pride in their grandchildren. And, they love doing activities with them. But they sometimes also don't want these activities to go on too long. When we suggested a daylong bus trip, many thought this would be difficult for them to do, especially with smaller grandchildren. And this preference gets more profound as grandparents age.

That said, many possibilities for having fun abound. For example, local nurseries could sponsor a "Hold My Hand" program, where grandparents bring grandchildren to learn about flowers, shrubs, and trees. Shopping malls could sponsor arts and crafts activities explicitly for grandparents and their grandchildren. And retailers could co-sponsor birthday events for grandparents and their grandchildren at local restaurants.

Grandparenting Styles

✦ **Distant Figure:** Contact with grandchildren is quick and infrequent, and because of the remoteness, grandparents have little lasting impact on their grandchildren. Tends to be the style of the oldest cohorts, especially the Depression Cohort.

✦ **Formal:** Follow what they believe to be the proper and prescribed role for grandparents. Maintain a constant interest in grandchildren, but don't offer advice on childrearing. Most often the style of the World War II Cohort.

✦ **Reservoir of Family Wisdom:** Found most often in grandfathers, who impart special skills or information to grandchildren. Lines of authority are well-defined, and subordinate positions of grandchildren and their parents are acknowledged and accepted. This role seems to cut across cohorts; it has more to do with individual family lineage and traditions than cohort, per se.

✦ **Surrogate Parents:** Usually found in grand-mothers who are responsible for taking care of their grandchildren. This role is more common today, given the higher divorce rates of Baby Boomer parents.

ADULT DAY CARE, HOME-BASED SERVICES, AND ASSISTED LIVING

Americans are less likely to use a nursing home today than they were a decade ago, even though they're living longer, according to the U.S. Health & Human Services Department. Adult day care, home-based services, and assisted living communities have become popular alternatives to the dreaded nursing home. As a result, nursing homes are increasingly focusing on sicker patients.

Adult day care has boomed in recent years, particularly in the Sun Belt retirement communities. It provides active physical and mental stimulation for seniors, and helps to alleviate loneliness. By providing this kind of socialization, adult day-care centers can lessen the factors that lead to depression in the elderly.

The Miami Jewish Home & Hospital for the Aged finds that its day-care center provides a new form of medical treatment to participants — companionship. The 40 or so men and women who attend every day form a kind of support group for each other. The day begins at 10 a.m., after a light breakfast of toast and beverages. Light exercise classes give way to stringing beads and other crafts, but everybody's favorite is rehearsing for the annual musical, such as *The Sound of Music.*

Many successful marketers of home-based services, including healthcare, housework, lawn care, and computerized calling services that check on seniors, have found a burgeoning market with older adults, including the World War II Cohort. Home-based services help this cohort maintain its independence, while providing much-needed assistance.

Assisted-living communities are the fastest-growing segment of the eldercare market. And people aged 75–85 comprise the prime market. This group is active, but slowing down. Successful marketers point to an "active lifestyle," rather than a "nursing home" approach, even though access to medical care and security are prime concerns for this age group.

STEP 3: EXAMINE EMOTIONS AND AFFINITIES

This cohort is still very group-oriented and is very much interested in feeling a part of a community. Because the war aroused such intense emotions, nostalgia is a very useful tool for marketers to invoke. Patriotism, for obvious reasons, is also a strong motivator, as is invoking the sense of duty and of self-sacrifice for the common or greater good.

BEING "IN THE MOOD" FOR NOSTALGIA

Because romance played such an important role when they were coming of age, members of the World War II Cohort are some of the most nostalgic adults around. Marketers can tap into this affinity for nostalgia by using words, icons and music of the '40s. As evidenced by several recent examples, this approach can bring substantial rewards:

✦ For a direct marketing campaign designed to increase cable subscriptions among the World War II Cohort, one of our clients used postage stamp-sized pictures of Gen. Douglas MacArthur that were put on the corner of envelopes with the copy, "If you remember V-J Day, we've got some new programs you're going to love." This attention-getter immediately communicated that the envelope's contents were for members of the targeted cohort. With all other elements of the offer the same as previous mailings, subscription response rates surged from 1.5% to over 10%.

✦ Drug-maker GlaxoSmithKline promoted its multivitamin — Geritol Extend — with an ad campaign featuring the big-band classic, "In the Mood." It also held "Geritol Extend Big Band Bash" dance contests across the county in eight cities. A direct-mail campaign among 13 million households included a toll-free number for information about the contests and an offer of a free audiocassette. In addition to widespread publicity, this effort resulted in a 21% increase in sales.

✦ Vintage Air Tours now offers day trips from Orlando to the Florida Keys on two renovated World War II–era Douglas DC-3 aircraft. To the delight of passengers, stewardesses, wearing 1940s uniforms and seamed stockings, distribute old issues of popular magazines, such as *Life* and the *Saturday Evening Post*. They also serve champagne, juice, or soft drinks, while chatting about the war and other "current events" of the 1940s.

✦ In Florida, appreciative World War II and older cohorts packed audiences at Condo Circuit's auditorium and swooned while entertainer Buddy Greco, well into his 70s, belted out his hit "The Lady is a Tramp." Condo Circuit is a collection of about 20 retirement communities peppering Florida's east coast that banded together to offer retirees a nostalgic trip into the music of their past. Debbie Reynolds, Joel Grey, Ben Vereen, Jerry Vale, and Donald O'Connor are just a few of the old guard entertainers brought in to offer condominium owners an exclusive performance of their old hits, and take their smiling fans for a trip down memory lane.

BUYING AMERICAN IS LIKE MOM AND APPLE PIE

The World War II Cohort is fiercely patriotic, so they are big proponents of the "Made in the U.S.A." label. They are less likely than younger generational cohorts to buy foreign cars and other products, even if tests show them to be better or cheaper. Having lived through World War II, they still tend to be somewhat suspicious of foreign goods. As a result, marketers can use the "Made in the U.S.A." label as a selling point to this cohort. To them, "Buy American" is right up there with Mom and apple pie as a very American thing to do.

GIVING BACK TO SOCIETY THROUGH VOLUNTEERISM

Doing your civic duty has always been a part of the mind-set of this cohort. It all started with enlisting in the military during the war, and continued in the form of public service groups afterward. The Rotary Club, the Lions, the American Legion, the Veterans of Foreign Wars, and the various ladies' auxiliary groups that accompany these clubs, are just a few of the many volunteer groups — based on the war's popular theme of the need to contribute to the greater good of society — that gained prominence after the war. Now that they are in their 70s, members of the World War II Cohort still believe in the importance of volunteerism. Seventeen percent of the World War II Cohort do volunteer work. Twenty percent are in fraternal organizations — twice the national average. And, this cohort gives one third more to charities than the national average.

In an effort to tap into this affinity for volunteerism, one of our clients established a "Homework Helpers" program where older adults congregated at community centers and helped under-privileged students who were struggling in elementary and high school. The public relations value was outstanding. The same could work for your company or community. How about having a "community cruise director" assemble members of this cohort to "cruise" the local community and clean up parks and other public areas? It could be co-sponsored with a non-profit group, such as AMVETS. Or your company could coordinate with the American Legion and its auxiliary, or some other such organization, to start a victory garden with the produce going to feed the homeless. The opportunities are endless!

In Arizona, Sun City Grand, an active retirement community built by Del Webb, coordinated with a local retirement community to sponsor "Operation Start Write," a program in which retirees bought backpacks, notebooks, paper, crayons, pencils, pens, and other school supplies for needy elementary students. About 100 retirees took part, doing their own shopping and delivering the purchases to Sun City Grand offices.

"The City of Volunteers"

Over the years, Sun City, Arizona, has become known as "The City of Volunteers." This is largely due to the civic-mindedness of many older Americans, including members of the World War II Cohort, who have chosen to retire there.

For the city's 40th anniversary in 2000, a committee found out just how true the slogan really is. They discovered that Sun City volunteers logged nearly 3.5 million hours each year, a number that translated into more than $17.2 million in economic value to the county and its non-profit agencies.

MOVING FROM PIN-UPS TO FAMILY LIFE

In a way that parallels their feelings about money and spending and saving, this cohort is somewhat ambivalent about sex. The Depression was a sexually repressed time (just as it was financially depressed), and someone coming of age in the early 1940s had that as a backdrop. But World War II opened up a lot of sexual opportunities the Depression Cohort never had.

Men in particular experienced more chances for sexual exploration because the war took them to the far-flung corners of the world, away from the prying eyes of parents and family. Recently declassified Defense Department studies indicate that over 80% of servicemen had intercourse while serving overseas during the war years. Sexy pin-ups of favorite movie stars, such as Betty Grable and Rita Hayworth, were popular with soldiers, as they sought relief from the desperate realities of war.

At home, women were no longer cloistered in the home — they earned their own paycheck, they could go out unescorted, or on blind dates with lonely servicemen, or to USO dances unchaperoned. For both genders there was a certain *Carpe Diem* mentality, because one never knew when a romantic interest might be shipped far away, or even killed. Returning home after the war, both sexes settled into more predictable routines of marriage and family, but many felt some ambivalence about their sexual past.

Despite the fact that this cohort isn't as puritanical about sex as the Depression Cohort was, marketers would be well advised to focus on romance and avoid sexual themes in marketing to this group. They still tend to find overt sexual messages offensive.

"Behind" the Scenes

Did you know that the sexy pin-up shot of Betty Grable that was so popular with World War II soldiers was designed to hide, rather than to expose?

The GI's favorite pin-up was 6-months pregnant when the over-the-shoulder photo was taken. She didn't want to disappoint her many fans, so she agreed to the famous rearview shot.

CONVERGING MALE AND FEMALE PERSONALITY CHARACTERISTICS

It has long been observed that as people age, traditional male and female attitudes often switch or converge. Men become less aggressive and more compassionate, while women often become more independent and assertive. A number of reasons have been suggested to account for this, including:

+ **A change in life patterns.** The woman is freed of the responsibilities that accompany child rearing, the man less driven by the need to economically support the family. Said another way, she is no longer the "nest-keeper," he's no longer the "hunter."

+ **A change in hormone levels.** A drop in testosterone in males and a drop in estrogen in females results in a more equal balance for both.

+ **A clinically observed decrease in the axon density of the corpus callosum** (the link that connects the left and right cerebral hemispheres). This decreases the dominance of the left, or masculine, logical, deductive, aggressive hemisphere, and balances it more equally with the right — feminine, artistic, holistic and emotional — hemisphere.

Whatever the cause, the convergence of male and female personality characteristics is a real phenomenon that astute marketers can use to influence buying behavior of the World War II Cohort. For example in advertisements, show older men helping their wives with housework or grocery shopping, or portray older women trying new activities on their own.

STEP 4: BUILD A PHYSIOGRAPHIC PROFILE

In many ways, the World War II Cohort has a similar physiographic profile to that of the Depression Cohort. As a result, much of the same advice we outlined in Chapter 3, "The Depression Cohort," with regard to advertising type size, color schemes, lighting, and message content, also applies to the World War II Cohort. One of the main differences, however, is in the World War II Cohort's willingness to seek out information and to talk openly and frankly about potentially embarrassing health issues, such as impotence, incontinence, and constipation.

Marketers have been criticized for ignoring older consumers, for negatively stereotyping them, and for focusing on their disabilities rather than their strengths and abilities. There is some improvement in this neglect of the oldest cohorts, as the aging Boomer phenomenon starts to swing the spotlight in their direction, but neglect is still the norm. The aging process cannot be stopped, but accommodation can be made for the deficits that accompany it. The first step is to understand the physiological changes that come with growing older. Then, accommodations can be made that will help improve the standard of living for all of us as we age.

COPING WITH CHRONIC CONDITIONS "AS TIME GOES BY"

Chronic conditions, such as arthritis, osteoporosis, and high blood pressure are all just a part of every day life for the World War II Cohort. Products designed to compensate for these physical changes enhance the quality of life for those affected. Because the decrease in vision, hearing, and muscle strength are more socially visible than more private deficits in taste, smell, and touch sensitivity, attention to accommodation in these areas can have a sizable impact on older individuals' bodily image and life satisfaction.

DOING AEROBICS TO GLENN MILLER TUNES

Cardiovascular and strength problems are one of the main health issues for this cohort. More than 37% of those aged 75+ suffer from hypertension and need low-sodium products in their diet. Over 35% of the same group suffer from heart disease. Next to arthritis, which afflicts 55% of those over 75, heart problems are the leading chronic condition.

Many marketers, including makers of cereal and other "heart-smart" products, such as Total, Raisin Bran, and Quaker Oats, have successfully targeted the senior market with the pitch that their products are good for your cardiovascular system. Another example is Take Time Fitness Centers in Florida, which has built a thriving Sun-Belt chain. Instead of using the driving Top 40 music typical of most aerobic programs, Take Time offers exercise classes that include the more tranquil sounds of Glenn Miller and Guy Lombardo. The emphasis is on slow movements and dance, rather than vigorous exercise. Such approaches not only meet market demands, but also promote greater life satisfaction.

Grip strength also decreases about 10% per decade after age 40. To help combat this, Wilson Sporting Goods now offers a line of golf clubs with heads specially weighted to compensate for age changes affecting grip strength. And Procter & Gamble now offers Tide laundry detergent with snap-on lids, rather than the usual perforated flap, to accommodate for declining grip strength.

DEALING WITH "MISTY" VISION

From age 65–79, the eye lens begins to cloud, and older adults often need considerably more light to read or do work up close. Cataracts affect 11% of people aged 65–74 and 23% of people aged 75 and up. As with the Depression Cohort, the World War II Cohort is now beginning to have trouble distinguishing between the green/blue/violet end of the color spectrum, something almost no marketers (except our clients!) seem to have realized. Yet it's incumbent on marketers to find creative ways to meet the needs these changes create. Some are picking up the gauntlet. For example:

✦ *Reader's Digest* saw its large-type edition increase in sales by more than 100,000 copies from 1998–99. The magazine has also begun to attract advertisers, such as Pfizer, Johnson & Johnson, Miracle Ear, and Amtrak, who wish to target older audiences.

✦ Oversized print novels are the fastest growing segment for book publishers.

✦ Selchow & Righter Co. brought out a version of its popular Scrabble word game with letter tiles (and the letters themselves) 50% larger than normal.

Accommodating Changes Makes "Cents"

Many hotels and motels have begun to see the value in accommodating physiographic changes.

Choice Hotels' Rodeway Inns, for example, has retrofitted 25% of its rooms for senior guests. And instead of calling them senior rooms, they smartly named them "Choice rooms." The rooms include brighter lighting, clocks with larger numbers, telephones and remotes with bigger buttons, room service menus with larger type, and grab bars in the bathrooms.

Many hotels are finding that the changes originally geared for special-needs guests, such as wider doorways, are also popular with younger guests, who may be fumbling with briefcases or big suitcases.

And even though Baby Boomers don't like to acknowledge their failing eyesight and less-nimble fingers, they, too, are beneficiaries of these new features. Just in time, now that they are entering their 50s.

"THE FOG CREEPS IN . . .": FACING SENILITY

People are living longer, but that doesn't necessarily mean their mind can keep up with the rest of their body. In fact, as life expectancy has increased over the last century, so has the incidence of Alzheimer's, a devastating disease that slowly robs the elderly of their mental capacity. Alzheimer's becomes more prevalent after age 75. This makes it a major concern for the World War II Cohort.

Not every older person is destined to get Alzheimer's (and products for those who do should be marketed to their caregivers), but most begin to experience some memory loss or mild senility in their late 70s or 80s. Marketers need to keep this in mind when communicating with older audiences. For example, nonsense syllables should be avoided in brand or company names; with no point of reference, they are easily forgotten or confused. This is a mistake often made by new companies today. For example, Accenture is the new corporate name of Anderson consulting, Agilent is a spinoff from Hewlett Packard, Avaya was formerly a division of Lucent, and Acela is the new high-speed AmTrak train running between Boston and Washington. These are all difficult for older people to remember and relate to.

Information processing itself is sensitive to many factors. With aging, people experience a variety of deficiencies in their perceptual, learning, and memory processes. These deficits are:

- ✦ **Physical.** Eye impairments, for instance, inhibit perception of visual stimuli; the central nervous system also slows, affecting the speed with which stimuli are processed. Because of this, the pace of information delivery should be slowed. The vogue in television advertising today is to evoke the style of MTV, with as many as 50 cuts (scene changes) in a 30-second commercial. For this cohort, the messages and the images simply don't register.

   Other eye impairments include a loss of flexibility in the neck and eye muscles, which can be accommodated for by placing products at eye level, neither elevated nor near the floor. As for hearing, decreases in the ability to perceive the higher tonal frequencies make high-pitched voices hard to hear.

- ✦ **Psychological.** There is, for instance, an increase in cautiousness one seems to acquire to compensate for increased uncertainty about one's surroundings.

- ✦ **Social.** There's reduced interaction with family and friends due to self- or society-imposed withdrawal — or a shift in important values from lifelong achievement to quality of life. One way for marketers to overcome this is to depict older people interacting with younger ones in advertisements, not just with others of this cohort.

As a marketer, you must keep in mind that these changes affect how intended messages are transmitted and received, as well as the relevancy of your message.

ADVERTISING FORMERLY TABOO ISSUES

These are all topics most people would rather not deal with. But a few marketers are beginning to address these touchy health issues in hopes of cashing in on a previously unmet need.

In a departure from most pharmaceutical advertising, Pfizer succeeds in its efforts to raise awareness about erectile dysfunction (E.D.). In a television and print ad campaign clearly aimed at the World War II Cohort, Pfizer used former presidential candidate Bob Dole to talk about the sensitive subject of E.D., which is often a side effect following prostate surgery. Dole, who was wounded in World War II, was able to address this subject with dignity by invoking themes reminiscent of the war years: "It may take a little courage to ask your doctor about Erectile Dysfunction. But everything worthwhile usually does."

In a two-page *National Geographic* ad for Viagra™, Pfizer plays on the World War II Cohort's penchant for straightforward facts with this copy — "Seven more reasons to feel good about Viagra (plus one that everyone already knows)." The slogan for the drug, which improves erections in men, also touches a subtle romantic theme, avoiding seamier implications — "Love life again." This, of course, can be interpreted two ways.

STEP 5: UNDERSTAND SOCIAL ACTIVITIES AND LIFESTYLES

Research has shown that staying active is the key to long life. The World War II Cohort has always been group oriented, so it is natural for them to participate in social activities and to be involved with neighbors and their community.

CONTINUING TO CULTIVATE VICTORY GARDENS

During the war, gardening was not just a hobby but a necessity. Victory gardens sprang up wherever there was space to grow a few vegetables. This fresh produce helped to offset the limited supplies that could be purchased with ration stamps. Gardening is still a popular pastime among World War II Cohorts, showing that hobbies they developed when they were coming of age have stood the test of time. Younger cohorts are now getting into gardening, too, but they are more likely to enjoy the status and the idea of gardening, rather than the pure functionality of growing vegetables. Nevertheless, makers of gardening supplies, including nostalgia products and heirloom vegetables and flowers, may find a mass-market approach works well for a wide range of cohort groups, including the World War II Cohort.

PRAISING THE LORD AND PASSING THE AMMUNITION

As any generational cohort ages, family and church or synagogue often become the focus of social activity, as friends begin to pass away. This is particularly the case for the World War II Cohort. This cohort, like the Depression Cohort, holds strong religious values, and has found great personal peace in their faith in God. Religion was a strong source of comfort as they fought in combat, pulled together to support the war effort, and suffered through the difficulties of losing friends and loved ones. Their spiritual side kept them going.

The aging effect of wanting a "safe journey" to the other side after death is amplified for this cohort. They faced the death of young family members more than any cohort alive today, and stronger religious connections are the fallout. In marketing to this group, reflect their dedication to family and religion, showing them as having lived a good life that will be rewarded in the hereafter.

STEP 6: INVESTIGATE PURCHASING BEHAVIOR

When it comes to purchasing behavior, the World War II Cohort is more likely to spend more than the Depression Cohort did at the same age. Although the World War II Cohort remembers the Depression, the event did not affect the cohort to the extent that it did the Depression Cohort.

Lessons learned when we come of age last a lifetime. Look at the impact rationing and conservation has had on the World War II Cohort.

Even now, more than 50 years later, they are still very cautious when it comes to spending. They prefer to save a lot and spend a little. Value and quality are very important to this cohort, and in general, they are very brand loyal.

For example, when it comes to buying a car, the most critical factor in determining car owner loyalty is age, according to a survey by JD Power & Associates. Survey results found that the oldest customers are twice as loyal to the make as the youngest customers, and they also were more loyal to the salesman and dealership.

Because they have time to seek out the best deals, members of the World War II Cohort are active and demanding consumers. And they remember a time when customer service meant something. They want information about the real value of the products and services offered. Rebates, coupons, and various discounts are attractive incentives. However, flashy advertising campaigns that exaggerate or oversell offer little appeal to this group.

They read newspapers, magazines, and advertisements more thoroughly than most cohort groups and they prefer print media for information, turning to broadcast media for entertainment. Their families often recognize them as astute shoppers and their advice is frequently sought out. As a result, they can be a great source of referrals for others, both in their own and other cohort groups.

FUTURE OUTLOOK: COMFORT AND CONVENIENCE ARE KEY

Because the World War II Cohort is getting older, the future doesn't hold as much promise as it once did for this cohort. In fact, World War II veterans are dying at a rate of 1,500 a day — up from 32,000 deaths per month just a few years ago. This grim statistic is not meant to depress you, but to help you see the reality — and the opportunity — of their situation. In the very near future, this cohort will face the same lifestages as those now experienced by the Depression Cohort.

While not the greatest market to target, both the Depression and World War II Cohorts will continue to present a specific target for a wide range of organizations — churches, non-profit foundations, charities, and so forth. They will also offer many opportunities for things such as home-care products and services, nursing homes, assisted-living facilities, funeral pre-planning, financial services, nostalgia products, and more. So while they will never offer the numbers or the buying power of younger cohorts, they are not as tight with their money as the Depression Cohort, and they are more likely to pay for comfort and convenience in their golden years.

You First

Historically, the impetus for most national memorials, including the Washington Monument, the Lincoln Memorial, and the FDR Memorial, has come roughly 50 years after the event or the death of the individual to be honored.

But the Vietnam Memorial, which opened in 1982 in Washington, D.C., clearly broke with tradition. Not uncharacteristically, perhaps this cohort "wanted it now." After the Vietnam Memorial was built, the Korean War veterans began angling for their own memorial, and it was dedicated in 1995.

Only after that one was underway, did the World War II veterans speak up for theirs. This is just the kind of attitude and willingness to delay gratification that was so typical of this cohort in its coming-of-age years.

CONCLUSION: A LAST CHANCE AT IMMORTALITY

Although the World War II Cohort represents a small market, this group offers clear opportunities for marketers who are able to meet their needs. But keep in mind that with the right marketing approach, they are loyal customers — yours for the taking. The World War II group came from an era when sacrifice for the common good, patriotism, and loyalty to authority were encouraged — ideals that may seem like old-fashioned and outdated concepts to many marketers today. But to the World War II Cohort, these values and affinities are still cherished. Marketers who want to tap this market will be best served to acknowledge these values, and the tremendous sacrifices made by this group, and to try to take them back to a simpler time when they were just beginning to experience the world as young adults. In the end, this cohort just wants to feel that its contributions have not been forgotten, and that it still holds relevancy and commands respect in the fast-paced age we live in.

One of our clients, Stephen Winchell & Associates (SW&A), Inc., of Arlington, Virginia, used cohort marketing to do precisely this. They were hired by the American Battle Monuments Commission to help raise $12–$15 million of the $100 million needed to build a national World War II memorial in Washington, D.C. Not surprisingly, focus groups revealed that World War II veterans did not want their efforts to be forgotten by future generations, and they felt that if the memorial were not built soon, it would never happen.

SW&A developed a direct mail campaign targeting World War II veterans that played heavily on the romantic and patriotic themes of the '40s. They secured endorsements from former war correspondent and TV newscaster Walter Cronkite — "The Most Trusted Man in America" — and enlisted former Senator Bob Dole as the campaign chairman. SW&A also developed three direct mail packages that used larger typeface and included such World War II images as:

✦ Black and white battle photos.

✦ A Rosie the Riveter poster (the image, in this case, was used to evoke nostalgia).

✦ An autograph from the daughter of Rose Monroe, the real-life Rosie the Riveter.

✦ A personalized "Willie & Joe" cartoon, a popular World War II cartoon series by artist Bill Mauldin that first appeared in the Armed Forces newspaper *Stars and Stripes*.

✦ Recruitment posters.

✦ Commemorative war bonds.

The theme running through all of the packages included several emotional messages designed to appeal to this cohort:

✦ Our generation came together to save the world.

✦ It has been 50 years and we still don't have our memorial.

✦ Thirty thousand World War II vets are dying each month.

✦ We can't allow the next generation to forget what we did.

In short, the memorial was positioned as a last chance at immortality — a permanent and prominent reminder on the American landscape forever acknowledging the debt to a remarkable cohort.

The results have been fabulous and have exceeded all expectations! Although SW&A was given a five-year goal of raising $12–$15 million for the effort, more than $20 million was raised in the first three years alone. Nearly 400,000 donors responded with an average gift of $38 each.

By focusing on themes reminiscent of the war years, and taking into account other factors described by Multi-Dimensional Marketing and the Lifestage Analytic Matrix, SW&A developed a successful direct mail campaign that transported the aging vets back to the glory days of their youth.

TABLE 4.2: How to Tap the WWII Cohort Market

Cohort values	✦ Play off their strong sense of patriotism and love of the flag.
	✦ Play off their strong sense of romance and love.
	✦ Show a sense of gritty determination, a "can-do" sense of purpose.
	✦ Show respect for authority.
	✦ Evoke images of camaraderie.
	✦ Acknowledge past sacrifices and service.
Lifestages	✦ Reflect current lifestages — retirement, post-retirement jobs, widowhood, grandparenting and great-grandparenting, and adult day care.
	✦ Show intergenerational transfer of values to grandchildren.

Emotions and affinities	✦ Use nostalgia to remind them of their youth.
	✦ Emphasize charity and a giving back to society.
	✦ Reflect convergence of male and female roles.
	✦ Romance is good, but overt sexual references are not.
	✦ Show respect for people, authority, organizations, and institutions.
	✦ Focus on enjoyable activities, and don't depict situations that imply danger, harm, or risk.
	✦ Stress comfort and convenience and avoid creating hassles.
Physiographics	✦ Avoid nonsense syllables in brand or corporate names.
	✦ Slow the delivery of information.
	✦ Avoid use of high-pitched voices.
	✦ Position products in retail stores at eye level due to flexibility reduction.
	✦ Use positive images and younger people in advertisements.
Social activities and lifestyles	✦ Show them participating in group activities, civic clubs, gardening, and family and church activities.
Purchasing behavior	✦ Depict them as still saving, but spending more on comfort and convenience.

ENDNOTES

1. *Decade of Triumph: The '40s.* Time-Life Books, Alexandria, Virginia, 1999.

2. Ralph E. Warner, *Get a Life: You Don't Need a Million to Retire Well,* 3rd edition. Nolo Press, 2000.

CHAPTER 5

THE POSTWAR COHORT

From its earliest beginnings in 1946, The Vermont Country Store catalog recognized the power of nostalgia. The austere-looking, black-and-white catalog specialized in providing older customers with practical, hard-to-find products of yesteryear. More than 50 years later, the company still publishes the same catalog, called *The Voice of the Mountains*. It is still printed in black-and-white ink on inexpensive paper, giving it the look and feel of the old Sears & Roebuck catalogs most of its customers grew up with. And although aimed at an older demographic, it was not targeted to any specific cohort groups.

Nostalgia clearly is the bait that lets The Vermont Country Store ring up sales. Through careful, relentless attention to locating products and brands older Americans grew up with, the company has built a loyal following worthy of a standing ovation.

Among the cornucopia of unique products offered are Sifer's Valomilk Candies (since 1931, "When it runs down your chin, you know it's a Valomilk!"), Peanut Chews, coin-sorter wallets, Necco wafers, Lincoln Logs, double-edged safety razors, and the once-famous "502" full-figure bra. When was the last time you saw one of those in a retail store? Certainly not at Victoria's Secret. Some of you have probably never even *heard* of some of these products. As you might expect, the vast majority of sales come from customers over the age of 50, with those over 65 being a major subgroup.

We at Lifestage Matrix Marketing were asked to help the Vermont Country Store develop a new approach that would allow the company to tap the "younger" end of the mature market. The Postwar Cohort was clearly in their sights as a kind of dress rehearsal for the Baby Boomers.

First, we segmented their customers into generational cohort groups, and the company began building catalogs featuring products from the coming-of-age years of its cohort-driven mailing list. Included in the postwar catalog were products such as manual "push" lawnmowers complete with grass catchers, old-fashioned parlor fans, real latex rubber swim caps, and a black tabletop telephone with a rotary dial. Through the artful use of pictures and copy, the store called out to the Postwar Cohort with language, icons, and memories specific to them. For example, one page shows a black-and-white photograph of two well-dressed 1950s housewives investigating a washing machine, while a suited salesman points out how it works. The copy reads:

> *No matter how fondly we remember our youth, few of us would trade our washing machines and vacuum cleaners for the devices our parents made do with. My mother's wringer washer was a labor-saving device in 1950, but it sure wouldn't be by today's standards.*
>
> *Still, many things our parents and grandparents relied on work wonderfully well even now. No dryer dries clothes as gently as a wooden drying rack. And a wool dust mop is indisputably more efficient in many instances than a turbo-powered vacuum cleaner.*
>
> *We're lucky to live in an age of conveniences, but so many long-lived products still make so much sense, we wonder why they have all but disappeared.*

BIRTH OF THE MIDDLE CLASS

Often, the postwar era is generically referred to as "The '50s." That's because that decade brings to mind a mood that typified the feel-good postwar era. In reality, the postwar era lasted 17 years. It officially began after the end of World War II in 1945 and lasted through 1962, until the assassination of John F. Kennedy.

In many ways, it was an ambiguous time. On one hand, economic prosperity reigned as Americans had money to spend for the first time since before the Depression. They moved to the suburbs in droves, bought cars, and filled their new homes with all the latest consumer goods. On the other hand, the threat of nuclear war loomed large, and a fear of communism spread like wildfire across the country.

Nostalgia — How Sweet It Is

Here are just a few of the nostalgic vignettes used by the Vermont Country Store in its catalog geared toward the Postwar Cohort:

"When I was young, I knew kids who were allowed in their living rooms only on special occasions — and usually under adult supervision."

"It used to be assumed that no bed was properly made until it was topped off with a bedspread. I belong to that old school."

"Memory tells us that the days when no woman ventured out without first donning hat and gloves were simpler."

Each catalog is peppered with 8–10 such vignettes that tug at the heartstrings and nostalgic memories of readers, and clearly motivate purchases. Not surprisingly, Postwar Cohort sales are significantly better from the new Postwar-targeted catalog than from the long-standing *Voice of the Mountains* book. Segmenting the company's mailing list into generational cohorts and directing specific "books" to each has helped to fine-tune the Vermont Country Stores' mail-order business and significantly increase sales.

This contributed to a tacit uneasiness about being singled out as different. Life in the postwar era was largely about fitting in, going with the flow, and not rocking the boat.

Postwar Cohort Defining Moments

The end of World War II was the defining moment that kicked off a series of events that shaped members of the Postwar Cohort and still influence them today:

✦ End of World War II

✦ Good economic times

✦ Moving to the suburbs

✦ Cold War

✦ Korean War (or "Korean Conflict")

✦ McCarthyism

✦ Emergence of rock 'n' roll

✦ Civil Rights movement

CONSUMERISM AND SUBURBIA

Following the war, the switch from wartime production of bombers and military supplies to automobiles and consumer goods didn't happen overnight. Jobs and houses were hard to come by at first, and prices of food, clothing, and other consumer products skyrocketed with the pent-up demand. But by 1947, an economic boom was underway. So was the biggest surge in births in the country's history — what we now call the Baby Boom. Times were good, and Americans were buying new homes in the suburbs faster than builders could produce them. And they needed washing machines, televisions, and furniture to fill those homes, and automobiles to get to and from work, and toys for the children, and on and on. Consumerism and "keeping up with the Joneses" became the national pastime. Consumer product companies stepped in to fill the void with slick advertising campaigns that insinuated, "Don't you want to be part of the crowd?" Buying was such an integral part of the suburban lifestyle that Postwar Cohort members still carry that attitude with them today. So you can see why companies that mix nostalgia with purchasing, such as The Vermont Country Store, have such a stronghold on this cohort. They provide the link to the wonderful days of the past.

Don't expect this attitude on keeping pace with peers to change as this generational cohort moves into old age. They will want to conform then as they do now. Retirement communities, for example, will be able to offer cookie cutter condominiums and standardized meal plans because "being like the others" is more than just okay, it's a way of life.

MAYBELLENE IN A COUPE DE VILLE

Having suffered through the Depression and the war years with worn-out jalopies or no car at all, by 1950, many Americans suddenly found new cars within reach. Cars became an integral part of the status-driven, suburban lifestyle — the ultimate symbol of success. For the first time, automobiles were not just a means of transportation to and from work and for the occasional Sunday drive, but a way for owners to express their own individual tastes and unique personalities. We call them *necktie products,* because like neckties (and like other products, such as beer and cigarettes) they are a form of self-expression as much as a way to deliver some functional benefit. Fancy front grilles and sweeping airplane fins in back gave a new look to cars of the '50s. And bright new colors, such as Tampa Turquoise, Emberglow, Chiffon Green, Tango Red and Fantasy Yellow, replaced the staid colors of yesteryear. Advertising entered a new era during this time, too, as achieving just the right image suddenly became a top priority for middle-class Americans.

Suddenly people wanted to do everything in their cars. Drive-in restaurants, movies, banks, and laundry services sprang up all over the United States to accommodate the growing number of drivers. Going on vacation by car became a practical reality as many Americans set out on Route 66 to "See the USA in Your Chevrolet." The car culture was also reflected in the music and movies of the time — Chuck Berry's hit song "Maybellene" and James Dean's drag race in the motion picture *Rebel Without a Cause.* Route 66 even became the focus of a popular television program.

Also for the first time, many teenagers had regular access to cars. This gave them more privacy in dating and contributed to a higher level of sexual freedom than teens had known previously. They weren't anywhere close to the free love of the late '60s and '70s, but they did give a whole new meaning to the phrase "in the backseat."

EVERYBODY LOVES LUCY

Also in the postwar era, television entered what many have termed its "golden age" — a time of tremendous growth and excitement about the new medium. Variety shows, beginning with Milton Berle's *Texaco Star Theater* in 1948, were a big hit with viewers. By the early '50s, television had such a hold on the American public that when Lucille Ball, the star of the ever popular *I Love Lucy* show, became pregnant, two-thirds of TV sets in the country tuned in to watch the previously filmed arrival of Little Ricky on January 19, 1953. It was the highest rating to date for television, surpassing even the inauguration of President Dwight D. Eisenhower. *I Love Lucy* mirrored typical middle-class life in the '50s — upholding the traditional roles for men and women, children and family, moving to the suburbs, and keeping up appearances. Other popular TV shows of the time (see "Popular Postwar TV Shows") echoed similar themes.

TV had a tremendous impact on everyday life. Surveys at the time showed that Americans were staying up later, eating fewer meals together at the table, and had even begun to time their trips to the bathroom with commercial breaks — all as a result of TV. In 1954, Swanson introduced the "TV Dinner," a cheap and easy way for busy women to feed their families' appetite for TV *and* a hot meal . . . often on a TV tray.

Popular Postwar TV Shows

I Love Lucy

Milton Berle's Texaco Star Theater

The Colgate Comedy Hour

Gunsmoke

The $64,000 Question

The Honeymooners

Our Miss Brooks

The Adventures of Superman

The Adventures of Ozzie and Harriett

Leave It to Beaver

Father Knows Best

Dragnet

Alfred Hitchcock Presents

The Flintstones

My Three Sons

The Andy Griffith Show

The Dick Van Dyke Show

Bonanza

"SHAKE, RATTLE, AND ROLL"

Popular music of the late '40s and early '50s included light, upbeat songs by clean-cut singers, such as "Come On-a My House," by Rosemary Clooney, and romantic ballads, like "Mona Lisa" by Nat King Cole. But by the mid-'50s, Americans got their first taste of rock 'n' roll — a new sound that had its roots in black rhythm and blues. Bill Haley's 1954 hit, "Shake, Rattle, and Roll," marked the beginning of this new era in music.

When Elvis Presley appeared on the *Ed Sullivan Show* in 1956, he became rock 'n' roll's new superstar. His trademark pelvic thrusts and gyrations set off alarm bells with conservatives. Parents and critics labeled him a "sex maniac." But teens loved Elvis, and millions of girls swooned at the thought of him. The Beach Boys' 1961 hit "Surfin' USA" was another new sound for rock 'n' roll that drove teens wild.

A PLACE IN THE SUN AND OTHER POPULAR MOVIES

With television becoming a standard fixture in American living rooms, movie ticket sales dropped off precipitously in the '50s. To compete with TV, movie producers focused on making high quality classics, such as *Rear Window* and *A Streetcar Named Desire,* and epic films, such as *Ben-Hur* and *Spartacus,* which accentuated the movie industry's obvious advantage over TV — the big screen.

Hollywood also pursued technological advances, such as improved color and wide-screen formats (Cinemascope), to help lure audiences away from the flickering tube in their living rooms and out to the theater. In addition, movies became more permissive as actors and actresses joked about such scandalous topics as adultery and pregnancy on screen. Marilyn Monroe (*Some Like It Hot*), Brigitte Bardot (*And God Created Woman*), and Jane Russell (*The French Line*) also set new standards for female sex appeal.

DUCK AND COVER

Hanging over this rosy picture of American prosperity was a growing threat of communism and nuclear war. After World War II, tensions between the West and the Soviet Union intensified as the Soviets continued their expansionist policies and seized power in Eastern Europe. In

**Icons of the
Post-war Era**

Elvis Presley

James Dean

Marilyn Monroe

Grace Kelly

Elizabeth Taylor

Marlon Brando

Audrey Hepburn

Katharine Hepburn

Humphrey Bogart

Frank Sinatra

Lucille Ball

Yogi Berra

Hank Aaron

Mickey Mantle

Chuck Berry

The Beach Boys

1953, when the Soviets exploded their first atomic bomb, the United States realized its nuclear dominance was a thing of the past. The Soviets posed a new threat not just to Western democracy, but to world peace. The threat of communism wasn't limited to Europe and the West, though. In 1949, communists gained control in China as Mao Tse-tung rose to power. And in 1950, communist forces from North Korea attacked South Korea, precipitating the Korean War (or "Korean Conflict").

In 1957, the success of the Soviet satellite Sputnik launched a new international competition in space exploration and missile technology. It pitted the communists against the capitalists in a race that would continue until the end of the Cold War in 1989. This ongoing international tension left many Americans fearful and uncertain about the future.

Schools instituted civil defense drills and taught students to "duck and cover." Americans were also encouraged to build underground bomb shelters as a way to survive a nuclear attack. In her book, *The Fifties: A Women's Oral History,* Brett Harvey describes the decade as one of searching for stability:

> *The future seemed, at one and the same time, full of promise and hedged about by Cold War fears of the atom bomb, an aggressive Russia, and the insidious peril of creeping communism. What better bulwark against these dangers and uncertainties than the warm, enveloping security of the family? A 1959 Life magazine cover story showed a newlywed couple spending their honeymoon in their own bomb shelter, surrounded by canned goods, water, supplies, and*

generators: a perfect metaphor for marriage as a self-contained world — secure, private, surrounded by consumer goods.[1]

When John F. Kennedy took office in 1961, Cold War anxiety reached new heights. With the construction of the Berlin Wall and the Bay of Pigs fiasco in 1961, and the Cuban Missile Crisis in 1962, Americans grew more fearful of a nuclear attack.

THE COMMUNIST SCARE

Following World War II, in an attempt to stop communist infiltration, the U.S. House of Representatives conducted a highly publicized investigation of the entertainment industry in 1947. The investigation led to prison sentences for contempt for a group of witnesses known as the "Hollywood Ten" and blacklisting of others accused of fraternizing with known communists. The House Un-American Activities Committee, which ran the investigation, used scare tactics and pressured witnesses to name former associates. A series of high-profile cases added fuel to the fire:

✦ Alger Hiss, a former State Department official, was accused of Soviet espionage, and was convicted of perjury in 1950 and sent to prison.

✦ Republican Sen. Joseph McCarthy received national attention in 1950 when he alleged that communists had infiltrated the U.S. State Department. Although a Senate investigation cleared the department of any wrongdoing, McCarthy continued to repeat the accusations during several radio and television appearances.

✦ Julius and Ethel Rosenberg were convicted of espionage for passing A-bomb secrets to the Soviets, and were put to death in the electric chair in 1953.

In 1953, with the Republicans in control of Congress, McCarthy launched a nationwide witch-hunt to rid the country of communists. His Senate hearings, some of which were broadcast on TV, relied on unidentified informers and unsubstantiated accusations. McCarthy's investigations ruined numerous lives and contributed to the widespread feelings of fear and suspicion that plagued the '50s. Finally, in 1954, the Senate condemned McCarthy for his unethical handling of the investigation and hearings. Nevertheless, McCarthy made his mark on the American psyche.

THE CIVIL RIGHTS MOVEMENT

During the '50s, blacks began to mount legal challenges to long-held practices of segregation. Particularly in the South, whites opposed integrating schools and getting rid of Jim Crow laws that called for "separate but equal" facilities for blacks. Martin Luther King, Jr., a Memphis preacher, emerged as the new leader of the Civil Rights movement during the Montgomery bus boycott in 1955. He preached nonviolence and urged blacks to "meet hate with love."

Despite King's call for peaceful change, angry confrontations over school desegregation followed. But the effort persisted, and by the end of the next decade, blacks had gained equal access to schools, lunch counters, buses, and other public places. What would be far more difficult was changing long-held attitudes about race.

THE POSTWAR COHORT TODAY

The first key to understanding the mature market is to realize that it is not a homogeneous mass. Far from being undifferentiated, we all grow more disparate as we age, not more alike. Therefore, to talk about the 35-year span of the "50+ market" as an entity is in most cases meaningless, just as the "15-to-50-year-old segment" would be of little use to most marketers.

In 2001, the Postwar Cohort is 56–73 years old, and in 2000, represented about 21% (47 million) of the U.S. population. This cohort covers a 17-year time span, encompassing the longest time frame of any generational cohort group. For this reason, there are very real differences between the oldest and youngest members of the Postwar Cohort. Even when this cohort was being formed, those coming of age between 1946–1954 were a bit different from those coming of age between 1955–1963, although not different enough to be classified as separate cohorts. This can be seen in their musical preferences — the older

Postwars came of age with the relatively bland, upbeat music of Patti Page and Rosemary Clooney, and echoes of the Big Band era (Lawrence Welk). In some ways they reflect many of the values of the World War II Cohort that preceded them. The younger Postwars experienced early rock 'n' roll and have started to exhibit a few of the tendencies of the Boomers who followed them. To use the cohort cartography analogy, there's perhaps a small hill in the middle of the Postwar Cohort, not enough to divide them, but enough to give a different flavor to certain characteristics.

Postwar Civil Rights Timeline

+ **1954:** Supreme Court strikes down "separate but equal" segregation practices in Brown vs. the Board of Education of Topeka, Kansas.

+ **1955:** Rosa Parks refuses to give up her seat, sparking the Montgomery bus boycott; Martin Luther King emerges as civil rights leader.

+ **1956:** Supreme Court affirms lower court ruling calling bus segregation unconstitutional.

+ **1957:** Eisenhower federalizes the Arkansas National Guard to allow nine black students to attend Central High School in Little Rock Arkansas.

+ **1961:** First Freedom Riders go to the south to challenge segregation.

Today, the lifestages of the two tend to be different because of the length of the cohort, and the corresponding difference in ages of the oldest and youngest members. The younger Postwars are active and looking forward to retirement and pursuing their own interests. They have begun to feel the renewed sense of freedom that comes with being an empty-nester. Older Postwars, meanwhile, have begun to slow down a bit, but they too are much more active than their predecessors were even 10 years ago.

SNAPSHOT OF THE POSTWAR COHORT

Name of cohort:	Postwar
Born between:	1928–45
Coming of age:	1946–63
Age in 2001:	56–73
Population:	47 million ✦ 21%

Key cohort values and concerns:

- ✦ The American Dream
- ✦ Conformity
- ✦ Stability
- ✦ Family
- ✦ Self-fulfillment

Current and next lifestage:

- ✦ Divorce and remarriage for some
- ✦ Empty-nesting
- ✦ Grandparenting
- ✦ Eldercare
- ✦ Retirement
- ✦ Retirement communities

Emotions and affinities:

- ✦ Desire experiences, not things
- ✦ Enjoying life
- ✦ Changing roles for women
- ✦ Nostalgic
- ✦ Sexually repressed

Physiographic profile:

- ✦ Chronic medical conditions
- ✦ Aches and pains
- ✦ Changing body structure
- ✦ Vision and hearing loss
- ✦ Memory loss
- ✦ From looking good to feeling good

Social Activities and Lifestyles:

- ✦ Travel
- ✦ Family and grandchildren
- ✦ Volunteerism

Purchasing behavior:

- ✦ Spend some, save some
- ✦ Internet

As a group, most Postwars are either retired, or will be soon. Some have no plans to retire, or are exploring new opportunities to start their own businesses from home. They have come to accept gray hair and the aches and pains of age as part of the game, but do not like the negative connotations of terms such as "seniors." Their focus has shifted away from acquiring material objects, and is more centered on sharing experiences with their spouses, families and friends. The Snapshot feature shows a Multi-Dimensional Marketing™ overview of the Postwar Cohort, which we developed using the Lifestage Analytic Matrix™.

Some have called this cohort group the "Eisenhower Generation," "The Silent Generation," the "Bridge Generation," or even a "window on the Baby Boom." As described earlier in this chapter, the Postwar Cohort experienced the beginnings of the social revolution that began in the mid-1950s and caught fire in the 1960s. Now that their children have left the nest, the Postwars largely see this time in their lives as a second childhood. They are interested in enjoying life and fulfilling their dreams. They are unique in that they share characteristics with both their Depression-era parents (conservative with money, but they like to splurge now and then) and their Baby Boomer and Generation-X children (more liberal than their own parents). They are not as indulgent as the Boomers or Xers, but they clearly have been influenced by them.

Because of the GI Bill and the prosperity of the Postwar era, members of this cohort are more likely than previous cohorts to have a college education, although those with college degrees are still very much in the minority. Many also have large savings accounts, healthy retirement pensions, and sizable home equity. They are not only well off, but they are living longer and healthier lives than previous cohorts. This makes them a powerful new force in the market for products not previously purchased by older adults, such as roller blades, hiking gear, and high-tech equipment.

TAPPING THE POSTWAR COHORT MARKET

The Postwar Cohort offers significant market potential. According to Census figures, the 55–64 age group has the highest net worth of any age group (see Table 5.1). Second in line is the 65–74 age group. The

Postwar Cohort cuts right across these breakdowns, so you can see what a gold mine this segment offers. This cohort came of age when what you bought defined who you were, so they are not afraid to spend money. It was also when the use of credit — "buying on time" — first became widespread. Postwars are active adults who are rediscovering their own interests. This group has considerable wealth and responds well to upbeat marketing messages that show them as active, involved, and "with it."

TABLE 5.1: POSTWAR MARKET POTENTIAL

	Age 55–64	Age 65–74	Total population
Median net worth (1995)	$111,300	$106,900	$55,600
Median income (1999)	$49,430	$28,928	$43,951
Avg. annual expenditures (1999)	$39,394	$29,864	$36,995

Source: Consumer Expenditure Survey, 1999, Bureau of Labor Statistics

In the past, the older demographic segment was looked on as more likely to be a burden than a bonanza; however, the Postwar Cohort today has enormous buying power, particularly in the financial services sector, and also in clothing, recreational travel, and housing. Although the statistic includes the World War II and Depression Cohorts as well, the 55+ segment today controls 77% of the total assets of the United States. The Postwars are helping to fashion the mature market as a powerful force in marketing.

STEP 1: LOOK AT KEY COHORT VALUES AND CONCERNS

Compared to Baby Boomers, Postwars tend to be much more conservative and group-oriented. They are optimistic about the future and value family above all else. These values, described in this section, were shaped by the defining moments of their coming-of-age years.

REALIZING THE AMERICAN DREAM

Thinking back on their coming-of-age years, members of the Postwar Cohort often describe feeling as if "the world was our oyster." The possibilities and opportunities seemed endless. The first key to success was being in the right place at the right time: a real-estate company, advertising agency or practically any business starting up in the late 1940s and early 1950s was "doomed to succeed." The second key seemed to be in having the right attitude. This group made Norman Vincent Peale's *The Power of Positive Thinking* a popular self-help reference.

Unlike some younger generational cohorts, especially Generation X, this cohort is a big believer in the American Dream. After all, they are living proof that it *does* exist. Or at least it *did*. Many started out with nothing and achieved a level of success unmatched by their parents. And the oldest of this group gave their Baby Boomer children all the toys and material possessions money could buy. This gave Boomers an expectation of entitlement that they still carry with them today.

Marketers who appeal to this group's belief in the American Dream and its optimism about the future are likely to find their own dreams suddenly coming true. Marketing communications to this cohort should express a positive view of the world and the future — the opposite of the "edgy" approach that appeals to Gen-Xers.

GRAY FLANNEL SUITS FOR EVERYONE

Sloan Wilson's *The Man in the Gray Flannel Suit* was a popular novel of the '50s. It chronicled the new suburban lifestyle in which men effectively aspired to be exactly alike. Cookie-cutter housing developments, such as Levittown, Pennsylvania, sprang up after the war. The homes in these neighborhoods were so alike, kids playing at their friends' houses never needed to ask where the bathroom was. The '50s bred conformity like no other time in history. Mass production of consumer goods allowed more and more people to become more and more alike. Membership in country clubs and other social clubs increased along with the rise of the middle class. For some people, the sameness that permeated middle-class society was comforting. To others, it was oppressive. But this conformity laid very definite social lines, leaving little doubt about where one stood. In marketing to the Postwar Cohort, keep in mind that messages that emphasize fitting in and joining the club ring very true to this age group.

In the future, we can expect this generational cohort to appreciate being in special clubs or organizations that have a common goal. Supermarkets, for example, can cater to retirees by offering special club memberships and by providing value-added activities on-site, club shuttle service to the store, and related nutrition seminars co-sponsored by local healthcare providers. This cohort is particularly open to the many possibilities for clever marketing.

"STAND BY ME"

Because of the uncertainty that overshadowed their coming-of-age years with the Cold War and the prospect of nuclear war, stability is still highly prized by the older members of the Postwar Cohort.

Financial services is one sector that can benefit from this message. Scudder Kemper Investments' Guide to the Generations — The 1999 Study," found that Postwars believe that a financially secure retirement is their generation's biggest concern. Emphasizing how long your company has been in business, for example, goes a long way to assure the Postwars that you will be there in the future. Of course, as the mutual fund disclaimers say, "past performance doesn't guarantee future success." But to the Postwars, longevity is one reassuring sign of stability.

"FATHER KNOWS BEST"

This cohort married earlier, had babies earlier, had more babies per capita, and had less time between babies than previous cohorts. By 1959, 47% of all brides were married before the age of 19, and two-thirds of women who entered college never finished — usually dropping out to get married. Some have called the '50s "an all-out embrace of domesticity." Everything was centered on the family. And believe it or not, college-educated women had the highest birthrate of all.

Given these facts, it's no surprise that the Postwar Cohort values family. Even now, this cohort tends to be family-oriented and somewhat conservative in its thinking about what constitutes a family. They are very much into their grandchildren, and as you'll see later in this chapter, spending on grandchildren has more than doubled during the last decade. Of course it has! After all, the oldest Postwars are the parents of the Baby Boomers. Postwars indulged their children, and they are doing the same with their grandchildren, too. It helps, too, that the largest cohorts to date — the Leading-Edge and Trailing-Edge Boomers — are the ones having the grandchildren.

"THE SILENT MAJORITY"

The Postwar Cohort suffers from being in the shadows of other cohorts. The Depression Cohort rebuilt America, the World War II Cohort saved the world, and the Leading-Edge Boomers bore the brunt of the Vietnam burden and protested against authority. But Postwars have no such significant contributions to point to. They are sometimes referred to as "silent" because they hold this transitional position in American society.

As a result, this age group has been overlooked and underpublicized. Little has been written about them. As we pointed out in earlier chapters, many generational cohort values emerge from a state of lacking — what was missing during the coming-of-age years creates needs and preferences that last a lifetime. Symptomatic of this, this cohort hasn't yet produced a president, and the odds are getting slimmer all the time. It did, however, give us Jesse Jackson, Ralph Nader, Gloria Steinem, Muhammad Ali, and other societal movers and shakers — yet they all chose to basically work within the institutions they were trying to change, and did not try to change them from the outside. These people didn't achieve the true leadership status of older or younger cohorts.

Marketers can profit by making the Postwar Cohort feel better about themselves. They were the first group to be acquainted with computers. They brought us rock 'n' roll. And let's not forget that this group is actually a frontier cohort: defining retirement rights and opportunities and setting the stage for the Baby Boomers behind them. There is much to this cohort's credit that can be played up in marketing campaigns.

There is also a lot that can be done to give Postwar Cohort members a sense of fulfillment. Offer them adventure events that display their strengths. Banks, stores, and healthcare providers might sponsor running and bicycle races and other contests for special Postwar Cohort classes. Prizes for winners in the Postwar class could be nostalgic — a complete set of Elvis recordings or a set of videotapes of hit movies of the postwar era, such as *Gidget, Gigi, A Summer Place,* and *To Kill a Mockingbird.* In short, make them feel special as part of your offering.

STEP 2: ANALYZE CURRENT AND NEXT LIFESTAGE

People often find that their 50s can be the most turbulent period in their lives. Divorce, children leaving home, retirement, remarriage, illness, children returning to the nest (or even being born!), and children leaving grandchildren in the nest are all common. These lifestage changes can be traumatic, but for you as a marketer, they can also lead to shifts in buying patterns. While Postwars continue to buy lots of things for grandchildren, they also are becoming more interested in fulfilling their own desires. As a result, adventure travel, outdoor sports, and the Internet are becoming popular activities for those aged 56–73. This is opening up brand-new markets to older consumers.

DIVORCE AND REMARRIAGE FOR SOME

Because reliable birth control was not available and premarital sex was taboo during the Postwar years, many couples rushed into marriage out of sexual frustration. Many of these ill-fated marriages eventually ended in divorce 7, 14, even 20 years later. Now, second, and third marriages are not uncommon for this group. Unfortunately, research shows that second and third marriages don't have any higher success rate than first marriages. And even though it is kind of late in the game, some Postwar men are now starting new families. It just shows you how much times have changed. You can see how the divorce and remarriage lifestage can easily spark a chain reaction of other lifestages that would have been rare for this age group just 10–20 years ago.

As this group moves into the 65–82 age brackets over the next decade, we can expect fewer marital separations due to divorce. At the same time, look for those in this generational cohort who are separated due to breakups or death to seek companionship in others of the opposite sex. Sexual activity between these older singles will increasingly take the form of affectionate caressing and romantic hand-holding rather than sexual intercourse. Marketers that reflect such sentimental sexuality in promotional programs will be right on target. Romance should be depicted as "back in style" — at least for this cohort.

"FREE AT LAST" EMPTY-NESTERS

The departure of the last child from the nest is a time filled with both anxiety and anticipation. It marks the end of day-to-day child-rearing activities, freeing up parents from many personal and financial demands. Spending on leisure activities and items, such as vacations, vacation homes, boats, golf club memberships, and luxury cars, typically soar during this lifestage.

For most people, the empty-nesting lifestage is a happy one. Mothers, in particular, see this time as a chance for greater freedom.

However, some women (usually those who have devoted themselves solely to raising children) experience overwhelming sadness and depression at the sudden loss of identity. But in time this usually passes.

From a marketing perspective, this lifestage offers some very real opportunities. As you saw earlier in this chapter, Postwars mostly have the biggest nest eggs of any cohort. As a result, they are generally less concerned about finances than younger cohorts, such as the Boomers. They saved when they were younger and have put money aside for retirement. Now, they have money to burn, and they are looking for exciting new activities and products to challenge and entice them. That's where you come in. Some hot markets for empty-nesters include gourmet foods, high-quality fresh foods, take-out meals from restaurants and supermarkets, household furnishings, luxury cars, and financial services. A number of adventure travel companies, such as Discovery Cruise Lines emphasize this theme: "Now you have the freedom — both financial and familial — to explore the Galapagos."

Benefits of an Empty Nest

Marketers can tap the potential of the empty-nest lifestage by showing the following kinds of fulfillment and satisfaction in their marketing messages:

+ Increased personal freedom
+ Sense of accomplishment
+ Discovery of adult child as a social resource
+ Increased spending money

FUN-SEEKING GRANDPARENTING

Healthier, more active, and better-educated, today's Postwar grandparents have taken on a role with new dimensions. The majority can best be characterized as desiring a "fun-seeking" role with their grandchildren. Grandparents are "good pals," and the more they become distanced from the authoritarian aspects of parenting, the more desirable they find this warm, indulgent role to be.

Grandparents can function as mentors, caretakers, mediators between child and parents, role models, teachers, nurturers, family historians, and problem-solvers. They also can serve as surrogate parents, as dual parental careers create the need for child supervision during the workday. Marketers can exploit each of these high-involvement roles in promotional campaigns.

The teaching role, for example, offers a prime opportunity to encourage product usage. Grandparents provide an intergenerational bridge for the transfer of many activities and products. Ads could depict grandfather and grandson sharing a lesson in fly-casting and enjoying your product, like the grandchild's first Oreo cookie or Lifesavers candy, along the way. Or, you could structure contests in which grandparents could win exotic, yet educational vacations — such as safaris into deepest Africa, tours of the Holy Land, or walks along the Great Wall of China — for themselves and their grandchildren.

While the travel industry seems to be getting the picture, many sectors continue to ignore the very real sales opportunities grandparents represent. Research shows that cash makes up about 60% of gifts given by seniors. Experts believe shopping frustration plays a large role in this.

Toy stores, for example, are so focused on capturing the young parent market that they ignore the fact that spending by grandparents is on the rise. According to the polling and market research firm Roper Starch Worldwide, spending by grandparents on their grandchildren more than doubled from 1988–1998 (from $250 to $505 a year). What's more, with Baby Boomers now becoming grandparents, a grandparent boom is just about to explode. And longer lives and second marriages mean grandchildren have more grandparents these days, making grandparents a growing market for children's toys and other gifts.

While the aggressive pricing strategies and limited sales support of toy superstores may appeal to busy parents, they have just the opposite effect with Grandma and Grandpa, who value service and convenience. Having a knowledgeable sales staff, who can answer questions about the latest toys and assist Grandma and Grandpa in finding that special gift will bring big returns for marketers willing to invest in providing exemplary service. Houseware retailers know that cash-strapped parents often won't pay the extra money for frilly baby linens and dust ruffles. But this is exactly the kind of thing grandmothers *love* to buy. So why not make it easy for them?

Latching on to this principle, Genesis Direct of Secaucus, New Jersey, began marketing a catalog called *Gifts for Grandkids*. Between 1995–1998, Genesis Direct's customer base tripled to 95,000 and sales soared four times to over $5 million. The company provides a quarterly newsletter that offers tips to help grandparents carry out their roles. It provides a birthday club that acts like a personal shopper for the grandparent. Products included in the catalog clearly aim to attract younger Postwar and Boomer grandparents: golf clubs, tennis paraphernalia, as well as a special potato-race sack for grandparent–grandchild competitions.

Financial services is another sector with tremendous grandparent appeal. Because some Boomers have not bothered to set money aside for their kid's education, more and more Postwar grandparents are footing the bill for college. This, too, opens up a market for educational IRAs and trusts targeting older adults.

Although many older adults don't like the idea of getting old, most do like the idea of being grandparents. As a result, the grandparenting relationship is one of the most positive messages marketers can use in tapping this segment. Hoover, GlaxoSmithKline, and Merck are just a few of the companies using the grandparenting lifestage in their ads to bond with seniors. This makes good marketing sense.

Postwars put a premium on "family values," as do their older counterparts. We can expect an almost tunnel vision from this generational cohort on ensuring the intergenerational transfer of family values. Postwars want their grandchildren to know the importance of being honest, responsible, and working hard at one's job. And they will fret if their children do not respect these wishes. As usual, such an understanding provides opportunities for successful marketing. Marketers should offer contests that help deliver such values to Postwars' grandchildren. For example, the contest prize won by Postwars could be a week for the grandchildren at a spa-like site where "finishing school" behavior is taught to grandchildren — along with fun events, too.

ELDERCARE: "THE OLD LADY AND THE SHOE"

As it turns out, empty-nesters tend to provide more assistance to elderly relatives than their siblings who still have children at home. Time and other family obligations are a key determinant in taking on the role of caregiver. An estimated 80% of disabled older people who need care receive it at home from a family member. In most cases, the primary caregivers are women — wives, daughters, daughters-in-law, or nieces. As a result, the average American woman spends 17 years raising children and 18 years helping aging parents or relatives. This should make eldercare quite an important lifestage for marketers.

The Postwar Cohort covers a large enough age span that many younger members of this cohort are often on the giving end of eldercare, while some of the oldest members just now are beginning to be on the receiving end. This lifestage includes a lot of emotional stress for caregivers, as they begin to see their parents as frail and vulnerable for the first time. But this lifestage can also contribute to an improved sense of self-worth from helping a parent or relative who needs assistance. Here, family values come to the surface again.

Boomers are largely driving the increase in eldercare services, but Postwars are benefiting also. They are not as willing as Boomers to "hire-out" the care of Mom or Dad on a regular basis, but they do appreciate having help now and then. Financial services, home health-care, meals on wheels, lawn care, grocery shopping, and errand services are just a few of the many opportunities for marketing intervention — aimed at the caregiver, not the cared-for — that this lifestage offers.

TO WORK, OR NOT TO WORK?

Retirement is one of the most significant transitions in adult life. Despite an increasing number of females in the work force, retirement still remains a predominantly male role because the current crop of retirees does not yet include large numbers of women. But that will change as Boomers start to retire. The average male today retires between 61–62 years of age. And the latest research suggests that while Boomers generally would like to retire even earlier, they are realizing that they will more likely work well into their 60s.

With the newly signed Senior Citizens Freedom to Work Act of 2000, Social Security recipients aged 65 and over can collect full federal benefits, ending caps on how much they could earn without having their Social Security benefits cut. This could have a lasting impact on older workers, allowing them to work as long as they want to, or feel they need to.

Because of their age and large salaries, some younger members of the Postwar Cohort are falling victim to downsizing and early retirement. For those looking to retire, these compensation packages can be a great deal. But for those who don't have the financial resources to quit working, finding a new job at age 55+ can be a real challenge. Plus, early retirement packages are growing increasingly skimpy as corporations look to trim the fat. Being forced to take an early retirement package can cause a tremendous loss of identity and self-esteem.

Although retirement often symbolizes the loss of personal identity and status, the degree of stress that accompanies its arrival depends on the perception of loss and a person's ability to find other sources of meaning. Studies show the greatest retirement concerns of workers aged 40 and older are having sufficient money, maintaining good health, being able to help others, being productive, and maintaining good relationships with family. The first two offer clear opportunities for financial institutions, insurance companies, and healthcare providers. Being actively productive is crucial to a positive self-image and quality of life in retirement. This can be encouraged through partnerships with nonprofit groups, churches, senior centers, and so on.

Marketers can build a bond with this cohort by helping alleviate retirees' achievement anxiety. Diversions to help fill free time might include hospitals or wellness centers where ballroom dance contests could be staged, or seminars that focus on an array of wellness-promoting activities could be sponsored. Landscape nurseries could bring together retirees to rake leaves in public areas in the fall or start a garden with the produce going to feed the homeless. Remember how we just noted how important building membership clubs will be in the future? We helped one of our clients, Friendly's, an Eastern restaurant chain, design a membership club for retirees. Called Friends of Friendly's, the club promotions never mentioned an age requirement but the benefits subtly attracted those in the retirement lifestage. Discounts were given for meals taken between 2 and 5 p.m. in the afternoon when non-retirees were at work. Day trips were organized and some even offered engaging games and activities. In one case, a train trip took members to a charming Vermont town in the magnificent Green Mountains for lunch and then returned before dinner. Along the way, participants played a challenging Murder on the Orient Express mystery game with prizes for the winners.

FINDING HOME, SWEET HOME IN RETIREMENT COMMUNITIES

Rather than the cramped efficiency apartments or tract home developments of yesteryear, today retirement community developers focus on providing active lifestyle communities complete with state-of-the-art wellness programs and workout rooms, as well as roomy master suites. These communities often provide large rooms where residents can entertain children and grandchildren, especially during the holidays. Developers are creating a country club atmosphere where championship golf courses, tennis courts, and walking paths dot the community.

At the same time, many emphasize intergenerational communities that support a variety of ages. Age-restricted communities are not popular with this cohort. And as residents age, they will want assisted living nearby and even more specialized care, such as Alzheimer's housing. These are the kinds of features preferred by the oldest members of the Postwar Cohort today. The concept for the communities seems to be to build in levels of care throughout their lives so that residents never have to move again.

Postwars are very much into an active lifestyle. They don't want to play shuffleboard or checkers all afternoon. They are more likely to want to take a computer course, finish a college degree, volunteer for a good cause, or take a day trip with friends. This shift in attitude is changing the face of retirement communities forever — and none too soon, with the Boomers fast on the heels of the Postwar Cohort.

During the 1990s, over 30 retirement housing communities were built near college campuses. Among them were Swarthmore, Bryn Mawr, the University of Vermont, Denison University in Ohio, William and Mary, Notre Dame, Dartmouth, and Northwestern University. These schools added value to housing options by offering a host of special perks to senior residents, including discounts on tuition, free library passes, and lower prices on sporting events, concerts, special lectures, and plays. And they often throw in free computer Internet hookups. In turn, the residents are often guest lecturers, on-campus tutors, and part-time helpers on the campus. Keep in mind that going to college falls dead center in the coming-of-age years. And many colleges and universities are just beginning to realize the important role they have played — and continue to play — in various cohorts' defining years. Tapping into a cohort's coming-of-age experience on campus is certainly a powerful marketing technique. Look for other similarly unique forms of retirement communities to emerge in the future.

Our work with developers suggests that moving to communities of any form is not in the cross-hairs of most people until they reach retirement — and retirement is where even the youngest Postwars will be heading over the next decade. But right now, these young Postwars are looking to stay where they are as they contemplate stopping working; so, our prediction is that the mass exodus to Florida and Arizona will abate, and there will be much more of an "aging-in-place" phenomenon.

STEP 3: EXAMINE EMOTIONS AND AFFINITIES

Certain emotions and affinities become much stronger as we age. The Postwar Cohort is now transitioning into many new lifestages, many of which prompt emotional thoughts about their life's accomplishments and goals with respect to career, family, and friends. For younger Postwars, this results in a mid-life crisis. For older Postwars, it motivates them to value their time more deeply and to try to find greater meaning in their daily lives. These emotional touchstones, if understood and acknowledged by marketers, can tap deep motivational pools.

DESIRING EXPERIENCES, NOT THINGS

Most Postwars have passed through the acquisitive stage of life, and are no longer seeking a lot of additional possessions. It's true that some are building and decorating their long-awaited dream homes, or upgrading their furniture now that the kids are gone, but most are looking for something else. As a group, Postwars tend to more highly value their time, and what they do with it, than do younger generational cohorts. They are looking for enjoyable and enriching experiences with friends and family that they can savor for years to come. As a result, travel (adventure and otherwise), volunteer activities, and hobbies that are geared to this cohort are all excellent ways to tap into their yearning for new and meaningful experiences.

LETTING THE GOOD TIMES ROLL!

There's a reason why men and women aged 55 and over make up the primary market for casinos. It's because they have time to spare, they're looking for fun activities to do with their friends, and they want to enjoy life and let the good times roll. Many hope to strike it rich. The oldest Postwars, in particular, like having their transportation (bus tours), meals, and entertainment all coordinated through one provider. It takes away the hassle and allows them to enjoy themselves without worry.

Unlike their parents, the Postwar Cohort is very willing to enjoy life and spend at least some, if not all, of their children's inheritance. Their parents experienced the Depression, and felt an obligation to ensure that "my offspring will never have to go through what I did." The Postwars grew up during the greatest economic boom of the twentieth century — their expectation is that times will mostly be good in the future, so why not enjoy the present a little bit now? This "live-life-to-the-fullest" attitude has helped improve the market for new financial products, such as reverse mortgages. These mortgages allow cash-strapped homeowners to realize some of the equity from their houses without having to pay a monthly payment to the bank. Borrowers can receive either a lump sum or a fixed monthly payment for life, even if they outlive their home's appraised value. The mortgage is not paid until the homeowner dies or moves. This allows people to spend their money on themselves, not save it for their children to inherit. Look for new and different financial vehicles to emerge to allow utilization of accumulated assets.

Do You Remember . . .? Postwars Certainly Do

+ Blackjack chewing gum
+ Wax, Coke-shaped bottles filled with colored sugar water
+ Candy cigarettes
+ Soda pop machines that dispensed bottles
+ Home milk delivery in glass bottles with cardboard stoppers
+ Party lines
+ Newsreels before the movie
+ P.F. Flyers
+ Butch wax
+ S&H Green Stamps

REPRESSING THE BIRDS AND THE BEES

With little reliable birth control to depend on, most members of the Postwar Cohort came to think of premarital sex as tantalizing, but dangerous. Particularly for women, fear of pregnancy or a ruined reputation convinced many to delay sex until after marriage. For those who did get pregnant, hasty marriages, illegal abortions, or going to an unwed mothers' home (where babies were put up for adoption), were the norm. This mind-set may seem foreign to younger cohorts, who came of age when birth control pills and legalized abortion were readily available and helped to separate sex from reproduction. Unlike today, however, having a baby out of wedlock in the postwar era was one of the worst disgraces a woman could suffer. It meant a loss of reputation—and in the Postwar era, a woman's reputation was her most valuable asset.

Because their coming-of-age years were fraught with sexual tension, the Postwars still carry some of these same repressed attitudes about sex with them today. They are titillated by sexual innuendoes and subtleties. Why do you think Elvis and his provocative hip thrusts were so popular?

Or Marilyn Monroe and her billowy, low-cut dresses? Or Brigitte Bardot — Hollywood's "sex kitten"? Their popularity was all about the *suggestion* of forbidden pleasure that lurked beneath the surface.

You can use sexual innuendo to tap this cohort, but don't take it too far. *Playboy* was designed for this cohort; *Hustler* wasn't. This is not a group that will respond well to over-the-top sexual content.

"Condominium Casanovas" Contribute to Increase in AIDS Among Matures

Did you know that older adults are one of the fastest-growing HIV-infected populations in the United States? Seems unbelievable to younger cohorts, but it's true. And while of little marketing potential in itself, this phenomenon shows the folly of stereotyping the elderly as frail and sexless, and of grouping the "50+" into one huge undifferentiated mass.

In fact, promiscuity is common at many senior centers, where women outnumber men by 7 to 1. Pregnancy is no longer a concern, so many seniors no longer feel the need to take precautions and use condoms. So-called "Condominium Casanovas" go from one woman to the next, sometimes passing on AIDS or other sexually transmitted diseases in the process.

Health officials assumed that seniors weren't at risk for AIDS because (as younger cohorts always thought) older people don't have sex. But obviously that's not the case.

To help educate seniors, AARP has produced an AIDS-prevention video called *It Could Happen to Me*. The video is distributed to seniors nationwide. Meanwhile, in Florida and other states with high concentrations of seniors, public health officials are handing out condoms at senior complexes, offering free HIV tests, and training older counselors to educate their peers about the dangers of unsafe sex.

CHANGING ROLES FOR WOMEN

Women of the Postwar era came of age when roles for women were largely limited to that of wife and mother. Even college-educated women were expected to give up aspirations of a career once they got married and had children.

Many found raising babies and doing housework mundane and unfulfilling, but there was social pressure not to complain or want more out of life. In addition, a woman who left college before finishing to get married and have a family was ill-prepared, economically or in self-esteem, to fend for herself if divorce occurred. Betty Friedan's 1963 book, *The Feminine Mystique,* helped to give a voice to millions of frustrated housewives. It sparked the women's rights movement, which picked up momentum in the '60s and '70s.

Postwar women were on the leading edge of this trend. These days, they are very supportive of strong roles for women; however, many still feel that women have an obligation to their family first. In marketing to this group, portray women as competent and intelligent, but with a commitment to family.

Marabel Morgan wrote a controversial but popular book in the 1960s titled *The Total Woman.* The theme was that it is a woman's place to serve her man — in short, the antithesis of women's liberation. Many women, feeling the traditional perception of the family role of women, embraced this philosophy as a safety net for their preference for the past.

NOSTALGIA AND THE "YOUNG AT HEART"

Even people who didn't come of age in the Postwar era often think of that time as somehow more idyllic and innocent than the current age in which we live. School shootings, terrorist bombings, and drug addiction were practically unheard of. So you can imagine the fond feelings the Postwar Cohort holds toward the late '40s, '50s and early '60s. The passage of time has softened the rough spots, and allowed them to romanticize their coming-of-age experience. Nostalgia becomes more important as people age, and they begin to define themselves based on the memorable experiences of the past.

Smart marketers can tap into these feelings and win big. For example, General Motors has brought back the Impala, a popular model first introduced in the '50s. In television ads, GM casts the new Impala as a sleek, sporty sedan, but uses a Chevrolet slogan from the '50s to boldly embrace the Postwar Cohort: "See the U.S.A. in your Chevrolet." This immediately takes Postwars back to the car mania of their youth when the slogan was first developed. As with other older cohorts, nostalgia is a good way to help the Postwars feel young again. This is the clear strategic intent behind Chrysler's hot rod–looking PT Cruiser.

To mark the 45th anniversary of the TV dinner, Swanson used nostalgia to launch a comeback campaign for its frozen meals in 1999. During a special anniversary sweepstakes promotion, it brought back its famous aluminum tray and the words "TV Dinner" for a special, limited-edition package. This revived many fond memories for the Postwar Cohort, who came of age eating these dinners in front of their television sets, and contributed to a 20+% increase in sales for a time.

End of Olds Brand Reflects Changing Cohort Values

General Motors' plan to discontinue its Oldsmobile line — the oldest brand in U.S. automotive history — is a move that clearly reflects changing cohort values in the marketplace.

In the '50s, the Oldsmobile brand was a symbol of American prosperity and dependability, and it was all the rage among Postwars and older cohorts. This loyalty continued into the '80s. But as time went on, the brand picked up a stodgy image and was never able to attract younger consumers. Oldsmobile's high point was 1985, but since then, it has been in a decline.

As Baby Boomers reached middle age, they shunned the Olds brand, seeing it as the kind of car their aging parents drove. Boomers, instead, preferred sportier, sleeker models, such as the Mazda Miata or SUVs, which better helped them project an image of youth and vitality. "Father's Oldsmobile" was clearly not for them.

STEP 4: BUILD A PHYSIOGRAPHIC PROFILE

When it comes to physiographics, there is quite a difference between the youngest Postwars and the oldest. Unless they have a serious disease, such as cancer, those in their 50s and early 60s generally feel pretty good physically. Of course, they have gray hair and wrinkles, and their skin is drier than it used to be, but they have come to accept these changes as a natural part of the aging process. They have excellent mobility, which allows them to travel and enjoy outdoor activities. Beginning about age 65, however, the aches and pains begin to increase, and it becomes harder to recover from minor physical problems. Also during this time of life, people begin to think about their own mortality, as peers begin to die or experience serious ailments.

Over the next 10 years, because the range of the Postwar Cohort is so large, we will witness a wide range of physical changes across this age group. Their physiological profile will take on that of their predecessors — the Depression and World War II Cohorts. And the youngest members will assume that of the currently oldest Postwars.

My aching back and other chronic conditions

Chronic medical conditions, such as high blood pressure, high cholesterol, arthritis, diabetes, constipation, and heart disease, increase with age, so it is no surprise the Postwars are often affected. Doctor visits and annual exams have become part of their regular routine. Because this cohort is acutely aware of their health, they tend to be more health conscious than younger groups. This makes them a prime target for low-fat foods (such as oatmeal and prepared salads) that can help lower cholesterol levels.

Marketers are also beginning to accommodate these physical changes — with fantastic response from older consumers. Women are two times more likely than men to suffer from arthritis; therefore, in an effort to accommodate this market, housewares manufacturers, including Oxo and Libman, have come out with ergonomically designed kitchen utensils, such as can openers and carrot peelers. These utensils have larger handles than normal, which allow people with declining grip strength to grasp them more easily.

The spirit is willing, but the flesh is weak

Understanding the less obvious nuances of aging provides unique opportunities to create competitive advantages to various age segments. For example think of the difficulty a 70-year-old would have in climbing into Ford Motor Co.'s oversized SUV, the Excursion. But automotive supplier Lear Corporation worked three years on adjustments that will make today's and tomorrow's older adults entry and exit a lot easier. In focus groups and surveys of drivers age 55–70, Lear found ease of entry and exit were the biggest problem these people faced. So its designers raced to the drawing board and came up with the TransG design, for transgenerational. The vehicle, a cross between a car and a truck, was set lower to the ground for accessibility. Designers gave it power rotation seats that swivel outward 45 degrees and have leather trim to allow easier sliding in and out. They gave it a four-point seat-belt system that would not require the passenger to reach over their shoulders, and the seat and door armrests are positioned higher for greater comfort. Unfortunately, given the long tooling lead times required in the automotive industry, the TransG design has yet to appear in the marketplace.

Common Chronic Conditions

Most Americans who are 65 or older have at least one chronic condition, if not more. The most common are shown in the chart below.

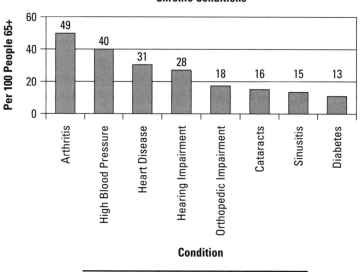

Chronic Conditions

While Lear had aging Baby Boomers in mind because of their numbers, these alterations reflect aging effects, not cohort effects. Postwars and older cohorts are the first to benefit. With the coming wave of aging Boomers, however, more and more companies will be attending to bodily changes. And you should, too. A good design is a good design, regardless of the age profile it happens to be targeted for.

Top 10 Reasons to Anticipate Getting Older

✦ Finally, you can eat dinner at 4 p.m.

✦ Your investment in health insurance is finally beginning to pay off.

✦ People no longer view you as a hypochondriac.

✦ Your secrets are safe with your friends because they can't remember them either.

✦ Your supply of brain cells is finally down to a manageable size.

✦ Your eyes won't get much worse.

✦ Things you buy now won't wear out.

✦ There's nothing left to learn the hard way.

✦ Your joints are more accurate than the National Weather Service.

✦ In a hostage situation, you are likely to be released first.

A SHIFT TO THE MIDDLE OF THE BODY

Women over time tend to gather weight around their hips while men tend to gain weight around their waist. Finding stylish clothes that fit can be a real chore for older adults, but clothing makers, such as Levi Strauss and JC Penney, are making inroads into this growing market. We worked with Levi Strauss to bring out its line of Slates slacks (and reconfigure its ActionSlacks line) targeted at older male adults partly by accommodating for changes in body structure. As an example, very few retailers stock men's pants with waist sizes 36" and over and inseams 30" and less, presumably because store buyers and pants manufacturers are younger, taller, slimmer people themselves. This makes pant shopping very tedious for Postwar Cohort men, simply because it's so hard to find something that fits older, shorter heavier people. In our focus groups, a common occurrence would be to have an older man recount how he sometimes bought six pairs of slacks at one time, in a variety of colors — not because he really loved the brand, but because he was finally able to find them in his size! What a marketing opportunity!

Especially for women 60 or older, osteoporosis becomes prevalent, a silent disease that can lead to broken bones and a curved spine. It, too, can lead to changes in body shape. In an ad encouraging older readers to get a bone density test to detect the presence of osteoporosis, pharmaceutical maker Merck tastefully addresses this health issue. The ad shows an attractive gray-haired woman undressed except for a robe modestly covering the front of her body. The copy asks, "See how beautiful 60 can look? See how invisible osteoporosis can be?" The ad shows the Postwar group in a way that is positive, not lewd or offensive, while encouraging them to take charge of their own health.

BIGGER AND LOWER IS BETTER FOR SEEING AND HEARING

Most people start to notice vision impairments in their 40s. But the situation continues to worsen in the 50s and the 60s. Many marketers are picking up the gauntlet, though, and are beginning to accommodate these changes. At the former Shearson Lehman Hutton, Inc. (now part of Solomon Smith Barney), the average investor was 53 years old just a few years ago, and the average age of its high-net-worth trust investor was 59, six years older. Valuing the trillions of dollars of wealth held by its older market members, Shearson printed its prospectus for investment products in type that was one-third larger than usual to compensate for declines in vision. They found that it only increased the size of the prospectus from 24 pages to 26 — a very minimal increase in cost when you consider the potential returns.

Probably the most noticeable change for people in their late 50s is loss of hearing. Men are two times more likely to be affected than women, and it often contributes to greater isolation from family and friends. As hearing starts to falter, the solution is not to raise up the intensity of the sound. The problem is one of frequency of sound. Higher pitches are not heard as clearly. Hence, marketers should use spokespersons with lower pitched voices when using radio or TV to reach this age segment. Because women generally have higher pitched voices, care must be exercised in using female communicators.

KEEPING THOSE MEMORY SYNAPSES FIRING

Beginning as early as our 30s, synaptic neural transmissions in our brains can begin to slow, resulting in some loss of memory and forgetfulness. As we age, the situation tends to get worse.

Doctors say passivity contributes to loss of memory and senility. To improve memory, doctors recommend keeping neural synapses firing by learning new information — pursuing new interests, such as tap dancing or bridge, which build creativity and encourage the brain to form meaningful new connections. Physical exercise is another way to improve mental function.

Marketers can help to accommodate this change by encouraging Postwars to participate in stimulating activities, such as educational seminars and non-stressful sporting events, such as golf, croquet or horseshoes.

SWITCHING FROM LOOKING GOOD TO FEELING GOOD

Postwars have come to accept the fact that they are past their physical peak. With this realization comes less emphasis on weight-watching for physical appearance, and more of an internal focus on overall health. There is a very real shift in mind-set here — from looking good, to feeling good. Extending longevity becomes a top priority.

Hoping to tap into this affinity, Clinique ran a campaign targeting older women that proclaimed, "Beauty isn't about looking young." Not your typical cosmetics ad, but it hit home with Postwars, who are going through an attitude adjustment about aging. They are letting go of the insecurities of youth and focusing more on inner health rather than outward appearance. We are not privy to the sales response to this campaign, but it played very well in our focus groups.

The Postwar Cohort eats healthy foods, such as Quaker Oats, fruits, vegetables, and Healthy Choice frozen dinners, not because they are dieting, but because these foods are low in fat and believed to help reduce cholesterol. This kind of "good for you" positioning works wonders with this cohort because they have begun to think about their own mortality. For this group, the days of greasy cheeseburgers, French fries, and chocolate malts at the drive-in are over.

Since far-sightedness is often a problem for people over 55, marketers need to make it easy for older consumers to read their packaging and buy their products. This includes using larger type, and avoiding colors in the gray-blue-violet spectrum, which are harder to see.

Moderate exercise is another popular activity, with walking and golf being two of the most popular for this age group. Shopping malls have gotten the picture by encouraging "mall walking" by older adults before regular hours. This activity not only encourages physical activity and good health, it also promotes sales, as mall walkers become window shoppers and ultimately customers of mall shops. Subtle, but very effective.

STEP 5: UNDERSTAND SOCIAL ACTIVITIES AND LIFESTYLES

Not surprisingly, the Postwar Cohort is drawn to social activities that are group-oriented, such as cocktail parties, RV camping, and so on. This is largely a throwback to their coming-of-age years, when group activities were prized above all else. But these days, Postwars are also looking to try new things and indulge themselves a bit.

THE SKY'S THE LIMIT FOR TRAVEL

Older travelers (those 55+) make up about $60 billion of the $293.7 billion travel industry. Overall, this market travels more frequently, for longer periods of time, and spends more than younger Americans. And among this group, adventure travel is H-O-T. Adventure travel excursions include everything from helicopter tours, hiking the Pacific Crest Trail, bicycling through Holland, whitewater rafting down Idaho's Salmon River, horseback trips through the Rocky Mountains, and an 18-day voyage to the North Pole aboard a Russian icebreaker.

Why are Postwars so interested in adventure travel? Because they have the time and the money, they are generally in good health, and many have already visited more mainstream destinations. Younger members of the Postwar Cohort are also looking for something unique and exciting in part because their coming-of-age years were relatively quiet and predictable. Remember, each cohort seeks what it most lacked when coming of age. These days, Postwar travelers want more activities and more exotic destinations than even their younger Boomer counterparts. Ecotourism to places such as Costa Rica, Trinidad, and Ecuador are now the latest rage among the 55+ set.

Hard-to-Read Packaging

For one of our clients, we did a comparison of two frozen dinner brands positioned squarely at health-conscious Postwars and Baby Boomers — ConAgra's Healthy Choice Country Glazed Chicken and Stouffer's Lean Cuisine Chicken a l'Orange. In analyzing the packaging, here's what we found:

ConAgra's Healthy Choice

✦ Healthy Choice uses black, 8-point type for "Keep Frozen" and the color choice for the front facing is black on very dark green — very hard for older eyes to read.

✦ The endorsement of the American Heart Association is hidden on the side where the pull-tab would obscure it once open.

✦ Microwaving and conventional oven cooking directions uses yellow and white on a very dark green background (a reasonable contrast), but type size is abysmally small.

As a result, spending on trips and equipment for adventure travel has leapt from about $130 billion annually a decade ago to $220 billion today, and older travelers account for about half of that spending.

For the less adventurous, group travel packages are another popular way to travel. Senior centers and community groups have partnered with the travel industry to provide full-service tours that include airfare, hotel, meals, and tips. Popular travel destinations include historical sites, natural wonders, seashores, special events, and festivals.

For those 55 and over, Elderhostel is another popular travel and educational option. Each year, thousands of older Americans, aged 55 to over 90, travel to more than 60 college campuses in the United States and abroad to take courses on everything from history to archeology. This program provides a mind-expanding sense of purpose by offering leisure activities, classroom instruction, and travel, such as rafting and camping in the Grand Canyon, and sailing and living aboard a 101-foot schooner in Puget Sound, Washington. Responding to pressure from

- ✦ The ingredients, an important element for many older consumers, are hardly readable because of small type size.

- ✦ The use of a green background offers less contrast than Lean Cuisine, making the picture less eye-catching.

- ✦ Glare is caused by the use of a glossy matte finish.

- ✦ The underside of the package is printed in too small type, yet the black type provides good contrast against a soft yellow background.

Stouffer's Lean Cuisine

- ✦ Lean Cuisine beats Healthy Choice hands-down on color contrast with a vivid product picture set on a white background.

- ✦ The use of orange and green print on the package offers good contrast also, although the glossy finish creates glare.

- ✦ The ingredients are much easier to read: black on white. But the type size is still too small.

participants and would-be participants, Elderhostel recently lowered the age of eligibility for its educational adventures from 60 to 55.

Traveling with grandchildren is another popular form of travel. Grandtravel, of Chevy Chase, Maryland, focuses exclusively on grandparent–grandchild travel. In 1999, Grandtravel offered 19 world-wide destinations, with tours targeting grandparents with grandchildren aged 7–17. One was a trip to understand Native American culture. It included visiting reservations in Utah, Colorado, Arizona, and New Mexico, and provided horseback rides, a "slow version" white water raft expedition, a train trip, and an all-terrain vehicle ride to the top of Red Mountain Pass in Telluride, Colorado. But while grandparents want to be with their grandchildren, our research tells us they don't want to be with them constantly and for an extended time period. The "24-7" for them will not work. Such travel marketers should build in outlets for the grandparents to have a respite from their grandkids. This preference will only increase as Postwar grandparents age physically and find it more difficult to keep up with the children.

INDULGING GRANDCHILDREN

Postwars indulged their children, so of course they are going to indulge their grandchildren, too. They enjoy spending time with their children and grandchildren, and many make it a priority to visit often.

One of the most popular activities for grandparents and their grandchildren is talking on the telephone, and this opens up many new opportunities for phone companies and phone card providers, who could market a special rate phone card just for grandkids to call their grandparents.

LET'S ALL PITCH IN AND HELP!

Because the Postwar Cohort is so group-oriented, they are particularly active as volunteers. They want to help others and continue to feel like contributing members of society. In Los Angeles, for example, a senior center started a senior mentor program, which matches seniors with at-risk youth. The mentors share their life experiences and help nurture the youth. The youth, meanwhile, allow the seniors to make valuable contributions to the community and remain active and involved.

By showing older volunteers in a positive light, or by partnering with older volunteers for community-based projects, your marketing can transcend the routine and help a good cause at the same time. One upscale retirement complex in Michigan, for example, partnered with a local animal rescue group to hold pet adopt-a-thons. Residents were encouraged to invite friends and family to the monthly events, which were held in the complex's activity room. The events served three purposes — they provided a wonderful intergenerational social outlet for the residents, offered them a volunteer opportunity, and helped find good homes for homeless cats and dogs.

STEP 6: INVESTIGATE PURCHASING BEHAVIOR

This cohort is conservative when it comes to money and purchases, but not nearly so much as older cohorts. Postwars want to indulge themselves a bit, and they have the means to do just that. They have the money — peak earning years are not far behind them, and they are past major expenses, such as college tuition and home mortgage payments. They have the time — many are retired, or partly so. And they have the freedom, without ties to home and hearth, as they become empty-nesters.

SPENDING SOME, SAVING SOME

Like other older generational cohorts, members of this group see themselves as 10–15 years younger than they really are. As a result, they don't like the label "senior" and they avoid most products that are targeted for "old people." So tread cautiously when trying to target this group. Use subtleties, like music, movies and messages from the Postwar era, to hint "This product is for you!"

The Home Shopping Network (HSN) and other television retailers have the right idea. HSN has signed Postwar stars, including actress Connie Stevens and '50s music heartthrob Frankie Avalon, to hawk products on their popular shopping network. Viewers, many of whom are members of the Postwar Cohort, have a comfort level with these old-timers, and they show it by supporting their products. Stevens sells about $50 million each year in clay masks and her Forever Spring skin creams on HSN, while Avalon sells about $10 million a year in tanning products, painkillers and vitamins. It's a far cry from the top of the music charts (Avalon sang the 1959 hit song "Venus"), but what better proof that nostalgia sells?

SURF'S UP FOR 55+ ONLINE

The Postwar Cohort has a wide range of interests and economic circumstances, as well as widely varying expertise in technology. In addition to sharing many of the same coming-of-age experiences, and other factors described in this chapter, they also share a key characteristic that makes them pure gold to marketers — they have the time to explore their interests. And they are using the Internet in growing numbers to do precisely that. Grandchildren are largely responsible for getting their grandparents on the Internet, and the Web opens up a whole new area of opportunity for marketing to grandparents.

Given the diversity of older adults online, Web sites should avoid appealing to "seniors" or other terms that imply "old people," and focus instead on lifestage topics, such as retirement and estate planning, social activities, such as adventure travel, or physiographic changes, such as high cholesterol and arthritis. But keep in mind that age often has nothing to do with the sites online seniors visit.

In an effort to tap into this growing market, PC makers, software developers, and website marketers are scrambling to donate computers to senior centers, set up training programs, forge partnerships with groups such as AARP, and offer discounts to seniors.

San Francisco-based ThirdAge Media, which runs a site targeting empty-nesters and retirees, has had considerable success in the online senior market. The company arranged for Quaker Oats Co. to host its Heart Smart Challenge on ThirdAge.com. The company offered 1,500 ThirdAgers a free bowl of oatmeal every day for a month in exchange for information about their cholesterol levels. Quaker had previously done a similar study of a small town with excellent results, but the online event had the added benefit of generating lots of discussion in the site's chat rooms. Other ThirdAge sponsors, including E*Trade, Merrill Lynch & Co. Inc., General Mills, Inc., and Procter & Gamble Co., are now wanting to get in on the action and host their own online events.

Online shopping is another emerging market. Watch for an explosion in the next 10 years. Some Postwars see the Internet as a way to avoid the chaos of the shopping mall, particularly at the holiday season. Yahoo! ran a series of radio commercials citing "Gina, Tina, and Staci with an i" as really good reasons to avoid the mall. In many ways, online shopping has the same advantages as the catalog shopping favored by some Postwars. Plus, it eliminates driving in heavy traffic and cuts down on time spent walking around the mall. But many of the oldest Postwar consumers, particularly those who are retired, still prefer shopping in stores. After all, it is an excuse to get out of the house, get a little bit of exercise, and socialize. Also, members of this cohort are particularly likely to fear that their credit card numbers will be stolen if they give them out over the Internet. Prominent messages that they "are entering a secure site" when they get to that screen can help them overcome this fear.

FUTURE OUTLOOK: ACCOMMODATE PHYSIOGRAPHIC CHANGES

This generational cohort covers the longest time span of any cohort we have discovered. The older end of this cohort — those 73 in 2001 — will advance to 83 over the coming decade. They will bring their values to these new ages but, overall, they will be hampered by new physical challenges. They will forever embrace family values and stability; they will forever be saddened by family breakups of their children and grand-children; they will forever want order in their lives; and, they will be centered on the "Big Two" — deteriorating physical health and outliving their financial resources. Any products and services that marketers can design to reduce these concerns will be met with great applause. The future holds widowhood, some dating and romance with an older age theme, and concern for estate planning to ensure their children and grandchildren receive at least some of their assets.

The younger end of this cohort will move from the 56–66 age category into the 66–76 category. This subgroup will enjoy a much more optimistic outlook and a more active lifestyle. They are the OPALs (Older People, Active Lifestyle) that we see portrayed in so many advertisements today — by Centrum, Zantac, Fidelity, and the like. This subgroup will look for more excitement in retirement and will crave new means for gaining recognition as a group. Successful marketers will continue to tell them how important their contributions to the world have been and are. They will increasingly face the declines of aging, which will provide pharmaceutical and healthcare companies with huge opportunities. This younger Postwar segment will increasingly have the time and discretionary money to be the darlings of the market-place. Marketers must change their focus away from youth if they want to tap into this mother lode. Give them great experiences that make them feel great about themselves!

CONCLUSION: ONE LAST DRESS REHEARSAL

The Postwar Cohort is leading the mature market in the trend toward a more active lifestyle. They are not content to sit back in their rocking chairs and watch the world go by. Instead, they are looking to trek through rain forests or take a class to learn the history of the Oregon trail. Having set aside money when they were younger, this group is — for the most part — comfortably well off. They are not the freewheeling spenders that younger cohorts are. But they aren't afraid to buy nice things and indulge themselves a bit either.

With their net worth at its peak, mortgages paid off or nearly so, and kids gone from the nest, Postwars suddenly have extra cash just waiting to be spent. As a marketer, it's up to you to help them find a way to spend it. It's a difficult job, but someone has to do it. Table 5.2 offers some practical tips on how to do this.

If you haven't done so already, we recommend that you use the Postwar Cohort as a kind of test case to introduce yourself to cohort marketing and ease into the mature market before the Boomers arrive. You'll be glad you did. While Postwars are a sizable segment in and of themselves, the Boomers will always be the stars of the show. We like to think of the Postwars as the last dress rehearsal before the Boomers make their grand entrance onto the stage of the mature market. We only hope you'll be ready for them when the curtain goes up.

TABLE 5.2: HOW TO TAP THE POSTWAR COHORT MARKET

Cohort values
+ Characterize them as believing in the American Dream.
+ Stress conformity and being pro-business.
+ Stress "don't rock the boat" work ethic.
+ Emphasize institutional stability and familiar social structures.
+ Sense of neighborhood community.
+ Show them in positive economic circumstances.
+ Make them feel special in buying and using your products.

Lifestages
+ Recognize that divorce and remarriage are not uncommon.
+ Portray freedom of the empty nest.
+ Emphasize their role as grandparents.
+ Acknowledge role as caregivers, retirees, and part-time employees.

Emotions and affinities
+ Appeal to sense of "safe adventure."
+ Depict them as enjoying life to the fullest, having fun.
+ Emphasize a relaxation of physical appearance.
+ Suggest *mild* naughtiness (double entendres, etc.).
+ Show them as having a sense of fulfillment.
+ Use nostalgia appeals, without explicitly invoking age ("seniors", etc.).

Physiographics	✦ Avoid high-pitched voices in communications.
	✦ Use sharp contrast in packaging, advertisements, and other communications.
	✦ Avoid colors in the cool end of the color spectrum (gray, blue, and violet).
	✦ Use models 10–15 years younger than this cohort.
	✦ Show a greater concern for health and healthy food.
	✦ Acknowledge mild but chronic aches and pains, to show you "understand."
Social activities and lifestyle	✦ Show them as active and looking for adventure.
	✦ Show them spending quality time with grandchildren and other family.
	✦ Depict older volunteers in a positive light.
Purchasing behavior	✦ Show them spending a little, saving a little.
	✦ Show them spending on health, travel, entertainment, and grandchildren.
	✦ Depict online shopping as a viable purchasing alternative.

ENDNOTES

1. Brett, Harvey. *The Fifties: A Women's Oral History.* New York: HarperCollins, 1993.

CHAPTER 6

THE LEADING-EDGE BABY BOOMER COHORT

Picture this: Row after dusty row of plum trees (the fruit source of prunes) reaching into the sky as far as the eye can see. A few weeds poke out of the dry ground. A magpie calls. Otherwise, silence. No one tends these trees or picks the fruit because no one wants it. It is left to shrivel and rot in the sun. Why? What went wrong?

WRINKLED FRUIT, WRINKLED PEOPLE, RIGHT? . . . WRONG!

What kind of people eat prunes? Older people, right?

Which age segment of the U.S. population is growing faster than any other? You guessed it — older people.

It didn't take a rocket scientist for the California Prune Board to conclude that older people's affinity for prunes coupled with Baby Boomers turning 50 could mean big bucks for plum growers in the coming years. It seemed to make perfect sense — more older people, more prunes. The prune board encouraged its growers to plant additional plum trees to meet the coming demand for prunes expected as Baby Boomers begin entering their twilight years. And grow more plums they did.

Unfortunately, the prune board's predictions didn't hold and prune consumption has continued to decline. They approached us at Lifestage Matrix Marketing to find out why.

What we learned was not good news for the prune board: The 50+ age group, particularly those over 65, *used to* eat a lot of prunes. But people who are now hitting 50 — the Baby Boomers — have never liked them. What's worse, the dried fruits run counter to the youth culture Boomers created in the '60s and '70s. Prunes have an ageist stigma: If you eat prunes, you must be constipated, and if you're constipated, you must be old. I'm not old and constipated, they rationalize, and therefore I don't eat prunes. In fact, prunes reflect the generational cohort preferences of their parents — the same parents Boomers rebelled against in the '60s. It's a cohort thing.

You Might Be a Leading-Edge Boomer if . . .

1. You sat on the edge of the runway when the Jefferson Airplane took off, and now have begun to notice your hearing isn't what it used to be.

2. You tend to not trust people under 30.

3. You refuse to admit to yourself that the "body-slimmer" you bought is really a girdle.

4. Your teenager's questions about what you did in the '60s give you the cold sweats.

5. You have a well-worn copy of Dr. Victor Strasburger's 1993 book, *Getting Your Kids to Say "No" in the Nineties When You Said "Yes" in the Sixties.*

6. You're planning on a big inheritance from your parents as your main source of retirement income.

AS SEXY AS A . . . PRUNE?

We recommended an approach that required the prune board to radically reposition their product to capitalize on Boomer self-gratification and their love affair with their youth. From our research, we learned that prunes are second only to dehydrated blueberries as the best fruit source of the element boron, a chemical that, unlike synthetic supplements, such as DHEA, naturally stimulates the body's production of estrogen and testosterone. These hormones, in turn, increase muscle mass, strength, and sexual performance — all youthful results. In other words, "prunes equal better sex." (But not too many prunes! Eating more than five prunes at a time does tend to promote laxation, a bodily function that unfortunately takes precedence over sexual arousal.) This is just the type of positioning that would appeal to aging Boomers. Plus, it opened a lot of creative possibilities for radio and television ads. (*Note:* As we go to press, the Prune Board has just received permission from the Department of Agriculture to relabel prunes "dried plums." We think this is a positive move, and we recommended it some years ago, but it's too soon to know if it will have a big effect on consumption.)

A NEW TRUTH ABOUT MARKETING

The prune board found out the hard way a new truth about marketing — simply assuming that tomorrow's seniors will respond to marketing in ways similar to today's seniors could lead to disastrous results. What worked in the past won't necessarily work today, especially when you're talking about Baby Boomers. Once again, it's a generational cohort effect. Marketers must develop entirely new approaches to appeal to Boomers as they enter new lifestages and begin to face the one thing that now scares them the most — growing older.

Prunes are not the only product facing a drop in the market because of resistance from Baby Boomers. In fact, many products and brands that appeal to older generational cohorts are finding just this kind of opposition from Boomers today. For example:

+ Whiskey sales have plummeted as middle-aged Baby Boomers have turned instead to lighter wines and microbrewed beers.

✦ Station wagons have all but disappeared, replaced by SUVs and minivans as the vehicles of choice for shuttling the kids to soccer and ballet.

✦ Per capita coffee consumption continues to decline despite the "Starbucks" phenomenon. Consumption indexes are precisely and inversely correlated with age.

✦ "Casual Fridays" have turned into "Casual Everyday" in many companies, as relaxed Boomers have risen to positions of power (see Chapter 1, "Toward a New Era of Marketing"). This has caused major headaches for traditional clothing makers (and big smiles for the Gap). The *Wall Street Journal* reports that for women, the power suit has gone the way of the corset. In 1997, a survey of 1,400 career women by Liz Claiborne found that only 19% wore a suit to work every day, compared to 36% in 1995.[1]

Many social values are coming under the gun, too. Cohort values, attitudes, and preferences drive the behaviors of different age cohorts, and no cohort has turned societal values on their ear like the Baby Boomers. Consider these examples:

✦ Organized religion has taken a big hit in membership in recent years, particularly the Catholic Church, which does not embrace contemporary Boomer values of self-indulgence, birth control, feminism, and abortion. Not only has membership in the Catholic Church fallen among Boomers, but there's also a shortage of priests and nuns, which reflects the church's inability to entice Boomers to take up ecumenical vocations during the sexual revolution of the '60s and '70s. A recent study of Boomers showed a scant 47% regularly attend church services, while, seemingly contradictory, 92% believed themselves religious. This shows Boomers' affinity for spirituality outside the bounds of the church establishment. In addition, some churches have turned to nontraditional services, held at different hours (such as 6 p.m. Sundays) and often in unusual places (coffeehouses, movie theaters, and dinner theaters) to entice Baby Boomers and younger cohorts.

✦ Country club membership has declined since the 1940s, when "the club" was the apex of social activity for affluent families. The group mentality and social mores represented by country clubs have all but lost their meaning for Boomers. The same tended to be true for fraternities and sororities when the Boomers were in college — it's interesting to note that those institutions are currently undergoing a resurgence, driven by the institutionally-accepting N-Gen Cohort (see Chapter 9, "The N Generation Cohort").

IF YOU'VE SEEN ONE BOOMER, YOU'VE SEEN THEM ALL — NOT!

The Baby Boom is usually defined as the 76 million people born between 1946–1964, since this is indeed when the annual birthrate bulged to over 4 million per year. The growing-up and coming-of-age experiences of this group cover a broad patchwork of history: the tranquil '50s, the turbulent '60s, the cynical '70s, and part of the materialistic '80s. The huge swings in social attitudes and economics during these times make it impossible to group the Baby Boomers into a single cohort. Rather, we think the Baby Boomers really include two distinct generational cohort groups: the Leading-Edge Boomers, who came of age between 1963–1972, and the Trailing-Edge Boomers, who came of age between 1973–1983. That's why we have separated them and given each their own chapter.

The events that separate the Leading-Edge Boomers from the Trailing-Edge Boomers were less jagged, less dramatic, than events like The Depression or World War II, but they were just as real. They included the end of the Vietnam War, the end of the draft, Watergate (the final nail in the coffin for institutions and the establishment), and the end of a decade of prosperity — the Standard and Poor's 500 lost 40% of its value from 1973–1975, ending a stream of economic gains that had continued largely uninterrupted since 1945.

Here are some other distinguishing factors of Leading-Edge Boomers:

✦ More idealistic than Trailing-Edge Boomers.

✦ Grew up during idyllic times, while Trailing-Edge Boomers remember assassinations and Vietnam during childhood.

✦ Unlikely to switch brands for price, whereas Trailing-Edge Boomers are more likely to seek out a good price than a specific brand.

✦ Willingly accept debt (unlike older cohorts), but don't actively embrace it to support an otherwise totally unaffordable lifestyle like the Trailing-Edge Boomers.

✦ More likely to want to return to the lifestyle of their childhood when they retire.

"WE'RE SPECIAL, OH SO SPECIAL"

Due to their numbers, Leading-Edge Boomers have always thought of themselves as special, and they are used to being catered to. In fact, they are part of the most marketed-to group of all time:

✦ When they were babies, their parents made Dr. Benjamin Spock's *Infant and Childrearing* the second bestselling book in the history of the world, after the Bible.

✦ As pre-teens, they dominated the media in shows such as *Leave It to Beaver* and in merchandising with fads such as Davy Crockett caps and hula hoops.

✦ As teens, they propelled Coca-Cola, Pepsi, McDonald's, and Motown into corporate giants, and made the inventor of Clearasil rich.

THE "BOOB TUBE" AS SURROGATE MOTHER

Beginning in the mid-'50s, the Leading-Edge Boomers were the first cohort group united by a technological and communication phenomenon unprecedented in the history of the world: television.

Television's enormous power profoundly influenced this group. Because they were the *first* to experience it as a uniquely pervasive influence on styles, language, aspirations, and even family dining patterns (the TV dinner), they are forever *separated* by it from the cohorts that preceded and followed them.

Leading-Edge Boomer Quiz

What events do you remember from your formative years? Here's a short quiz to test your memory:

1. When did the one-night "baby boomlet" from an East Coast power outage occur?

2. When did Star Trek debut?

3. Super Bowl I: Who played, who won, and in what year?

4. Who first walked on the moon, and when?

5. When did Archie Bunker first utter the nickname "meathead"?

6. Who said, "Tune in, turn on, drop out"?

7. What was the Beach Boys' first hit?

8. When did the Beatles break up?

Answers

1. The tremendous blackout of the Northeast started at 5:16 p.m. on November 9, 1965.

2. *Star Trek* debuted on September 8, 1966.

3. On January 15, 1967, the Green Bay Packers beat the Kansas City Chiefs in Super Bowl I, 35–10.

4. Neil Armstrong set foot on the moon at 10:56pm (ET) on July 20, 1969.

5. *All in the Family* debuted on January 12, 1971.

6. Timothy Leary

7. "Surfin' USA"

8. 1970

The immense impact of first-time television immersion as a social norm can be seen in the former U.S.S.R. The "Evil Empire" fell not from threat of destruction, but from television shows like *Dallas,* beamed for the first time into the homes of a populace who till then had not the slightest conception of the riches that Capitalism offered.

DEFINING MOMENTS: "JOHNNY, WE HARDLY KNEW YE"

The Leading-Edge Boomers began coming of age in 1963, the year John F. Kennedy was assassinated. It marked a turning point, a bold departure from the security and trust of childhood, and the start of a period of profound dislocations that still haunt our society today. And as we saw in Chapter 2, "What Makes Us Tick: Using the Lifestage Analytic Matrix™," new cohorts often form with an earth-shattering defining moment.

Where Were You When . . . ?

Do you remember where you were when you first heard about the shooting of JFK in Dallas? For truly defining moments, most who were in their coming-of-age years remember what they were doing with crystal clarity.

Consistently, Leading-Edge Boomers remember where they were when JFK was killed. It was an ultimate defining moment.

The Kennedy presidency had seemed like the natural extension of continued good times, of economic growth, domestic stability, and a liberated and early transfer of power from an older cohort to a much younger one. Kennedy's assassination in 1963, followed by Robert F. Kennedy's in 1968, and Martin Luther King Jr.'s in 1969, signaled an end to the status quo, and galvanized a very large Boomer Cohort just entering its formative years. Suddenly the leadership was no longer theirs, neither was the war, and authority and the establishment that had been the bedrock of earlier cohorts disintegrated in the melee of the 1968 Democratic National Convention in Chicago. The Vietnam War was a rallying point for the nation's youth. Many saw it as a needless sacrifice of American and Vietnamese lives.

Leading-Edge Boomers: Defining Moments

✦ Assassination of John F. Kennedy (1963)

✦ Vietnam War (~1964–1973)

✦ Assassination of Robert F. Kennedy (1968)

✦ Assassination of Martin Luther King, Jr. (1968)

✦ First man on the moon (1969)

Despite the social turmoil of the '60s, the Standard & Poor's 500 index continued an upward climb, and Leading-Edge Boomers continued to experience good economic times. Neil Armstrong's 1969 walk on the moon embodied much of the optimism and the feeling of technological superiority that many Americans felt at the time. In fact, economic prosperity and a low unemployment rate helped fuel the carefree attitudes and experimental nature of the '60s. Leading-Edge Boomers wanted a lifestyle at least as good as they had experienced as children in the '50s, and with nearly 20 years of steady economic growth on record, they had no reason to expect that would change.

Beginning around 1965, however, psychologists began to notice a shift in patterns of human behavior — the site of concern suddenly moved from outside the self to within the self. "The Age of the Individual," as Ronald Reagan later put it, was born. It's not surprising that this paradigm shift occurred when Leading-Edge Boomers were coming of age. According to psychologist Martin E. P. Seligman, at least four historical factors came together to make this happen:[2]

"THE AGE OF THE INDIVIDUAL"

✦ Rise of "personalized" mass production

✦ General prosperity

✦ Assassinations of public leaders

✦ Loss of faith in God and the family

The first two factors exalted the self, while the last two weakened commitment to larger social institutions, Seligman argues. The result was a significant increase in depression across the country. This shift contributed in large part to the popularity of psychotherapy beginning in the late '60s, and also gave rise to the self-help movement ("I'm OK — You're OK") of the '70s and '80s.

TODAY'S LEADING-EDGE BOOMERS BEGIN TO WORRY . . . JUST A LITTLE

MAD magazine's mascot Alfred E. Neuman and his famous quote, "What? Me worry?" epitomize the carefree attitude of this cohort's coming-of-age experience. This attitude has begun to change as Leading-Edge Boomers break the mid-century mark. In their youth, they could afford to mock authority, fight the establishment, and champion causes. They were looking for something to push against, and their parents and other authority figures were an easy target. Now, their parents are older and need assistance, not resistance. And Boomer priorities are beginning to shift. The self is still of prime importance, but there are other considerations to add to the mix — eldercare, children heading off to college, job insecurities, and retirement just around the corner.

Using the Lifestage Analytic Matrix™ (see chapter 2), we have developed a Multi-Dimensional Marketing™ snapshot of today's Leading-Edge Boomer (see Snapshot feature). It is largely a picture of middle-aged men and women trying to do their own thing, while the ball and chain of family responsibilities keep them from it. There are a lot of inner conflicts here:

✦ Family responsibilities versus their own protected individualism

✦ Empty-nesting and growing older versus the youth culture they created in the '60s

✦ A middle-aged conservative outlook versus the anti-establishment views they held in their youth

SNAPSHOT OF THE LEADING-EDGE BOOMER COHORT

Name of cohort:	Leading-Edge Boomer
Born between:	1946–54
Coming of age:	1963–72
Age in 2001:	47–55
Population:	31 million ✦ 14%

Key cohort values and concerns:
- ✦ Personal and social expression
- ✦ Protected individualism
- ✦ Youth
- ✦ Health and wellness

Current and next lifestage:
- ✦ Empty-nesting
- ✦ Childrearing
- ✦ Some grandparenting
- ✦ Second career
- ✦ Divorce

Emotions and affinities:
- ✦ Nostalgia
- ✦ Rebellious
- ✦ Social justice
- ✦ Sexually experimental
- ✦ Generational community

Physiographic profile:
- ✦ Vision problems
- ✦ Weight changes
- ✦ Hypertension
- ✦ Arthritis
- ✦ Gray hair and hair loss
- ✦ Menopause

Social activities and lifestyles:
- ✦ Exercise
- ✦ Leisure a necessity

Purchasing behavior:
- ✦ Plastic surgery
- ✦ Big spenders
- ✦ Convenience is key

In her 1993 book, *The Master Trend: How the Baby Boom Generation Is Remaking America,* demographer Cheryl Russell writes that the responsibilities of middle age often conflict with the free agent mentality of Boomers.[3] Leading-Edge Boomers have tempered the egocentricity of their youth in part by getting married, having families, and taking on greater responsibility at work. But they still aren't quite comfortable with the role. It runs counter to the message they grew up with: "We're special. We come first."

In many ways, Bill Clinton is the quintessential Leading-Edge Boomer. He is highly educated; came of age during the '60s; avoided the Vietnam War; smoked marijuana (although he says he didn't inhale); married a working woman; has one child; has strayed from the bonds of marriage; keeps his eyes open for new sexual experiences; and always seems willing to renegotiate his commitments. For him, truth may be optional, but expedience is mandatory. As Russell points out, he is like a character out of the Boomer nostalgia movie, *The Big Chill.*

It's ironic that in the 2000 presidential race, George W. Bush and Al Gore, both Leading-Edge Baby Boomers, spent considerable time trying to distance themselves from the Boomer liberalism of their youth. Bush refused to answer questions about his alleged cocaine use, and Gore tried to downplay the fact that he smoked a few marijuana joints while in Vietnam.

The point often overlooked about Leading-Edge Boomers is that their tastes and affinities really haven't changed much in 30 years. Sure, they have evolved to survive and thrive in the capitalist society in which we live, and the expression of their values sometimes shifts, but their basic tendencies remain the same. They are still focused on self-gratification, personal fulfillment, and new experiences. It's up to marketers to position their products in ways that tap into these latent feelings and offer Boomers the self-indulgence they feel they deserve.

TAPPING THE LEADING-EDGE BOOMER MARKET

Since they first came on the scene, the Baby Boomers have driven everything in American marketing. Early on, marketers recognized the value of treating the Boomers differently. Even as babies, they had their own distinct market segment. As they grew up, this phenomenon only intensified. Over the years, Boomers have continued to wield tremendous influence on social attitudes, styles, and fashions purely because of their sheer numbers. Marketers have had no choice but to listen.

Census statistics show Leading-Edge Boomers have the highest income and highest average annual expenditures of any generational cohort group (see Table 6.1). They outspend other cohorts in virtually every category from food away from home, apparel, services, transportation, and entertainment. This makes them a prime target for many marketers.

TABLE 6.1: LEADING-EDGE BOOMER MARKET POTENTIAL

	Age 45–54	Total population
Median net worth (1995)	$90,600	$55,600
Median income (1997)	$59,822	$43,951
Avg. annual expenditures (1997)	$46,511	$36,995

Source: Consumer Expenditure Survey, 1999, Bureau of Labor Statistics

There's no question that the Boomers have money to spend, and they have proven they are not afraid to spend it. The trick is to devise marketing strategies and tactics that allow you to tap this valuable segment. Multi-Dimensional Marketing offers valuable clues about how to do this.

STEP 1: LOOK AT KEY COHORT VALUES AND CONCERNS

Cohort defining moments create the personal values that stay relatively unchanged as we move through life. These values are central to creating the common bond that makes each cohort a viable market segment. No other generational cohort has shown the dramatic shift in values from its preceding cohort that we find with the Baby Boomers. Using our "cohort cartography" analogy, the assassination of JFK created a defining moment that represented a spike the size of the Matterhorn — a huge, extremely sharp divide that separated Leading-Edge Boomer values in major ways from those of the latter end of the Postwar Cohort.

"DO YOUR OWN THING, MAN"

Personal and social expression are part of the Boomer's "Do-your-own-thing" attitude. Now, however, they are more focused on personal, rather than social, expression. Members of the Postwar Cohort thrived on being conformists. Businessmen wore the archetypal gray flannel suit, white shirt, and felt hat to the office. Few deviated from the standards set by their peers. It was part of the "Don't-rock-the-boat" mentality of that cohort's time.

But then along came the "Counterculture Revolution," complete with its tie-dyed shirts, blue jeans, sandals, long hair and beards. Suddenly, there was a 180-degree turnaround in appearance and attitude. The "I-Gotta-Be-Me" Boomers were present and accounted for. These individualistic values still remain, only today they are found in the "Casual Friday" at the office, brought to you by Boomers now in the ranks of management.

If ever there was a product with individualist Boomers clearly in the cross hairs, it was the Saab. From the mid-1980s until 1993, Saab's quirky 900 Series was the embodiment of individuality — and Boomers loved it. In the mid-1990s, the average age of the 900 owner was 42, at that time right in the middle of the Leading-Edge Boomer Cohort. The average age of Saab's up-market 9000 series was 49 — squarely at the upper end of the Boomer Cohort and at their peak income stage.

To capture awareness and sales from this cohort, Saab sent out a wave of advertising to the tune of $50 million. The "Find-Your-Own-Road" brand campaign used an artist's drawing of executives shedding and shredding their corporate suits, jumping into their Saab 900 convertibles and heading off for the great outdoors. The car was shown as a facilitator of freedom and independence — just what a Boomer dreams of. Saab used outdoor, television, and print advertisements and captured a 30% explosion in brand awareness. Sales of Saabs surged. But by 1999, Saab decided to scrap the campaign.

To grab even greater sales, they felt they needed to broaden their appeal with a mass-marketing approach. The new campaign focused on Saab's engine performance — a topic that put Boomers right to sleep. This highly forgettable campaign was scrapped as well, and the company made the conscious decision to go with a global campaign. What came out — "Saab vs. Descartes" with a play on the phrase, *cogito, ergo sum* ("I think, therefore I am") and the implication that *feeling* driving out-competes *thinking* driving, and "Saab vs. Vivaldi," with the reference to Saab being "a car for all seasons" (the composer Vivaldi wrote *The Four Seasons*) — both left Boomers cold. In a heartbeat, Saab Cars USA forgot its loyal market. It stopped talking directly to Boomers. In crossing cohort lines, it lost its distinctive edge, and no longer touched the soul of the Leading-Edge Baby Boomer — or any other cohort for that matter.

What Saab should have executed was a campaign that spoke to its loyal market with other Boomer values, such as youthfulness or skepticism. Or, rather than try to duplicate the look of other successful cars, such as Nissan or Mazda, it should redesign its car first, then its message, to bring back its individuality.

LOOKING OUT FOR NUMBER ONE

Protected individualism is an important part of the Boomer mentality. Unlike their parents, Boomers *won't be coerced into doing things out of guilt,* or for the greater good of the group. As a result, voting is at an all-time low, and civic groups such as the Lions Club and the Rotary Club — once an important social mainstay for suburban America — are seeing huge declines in their membership. The reason? Time. When you factor in dual-income families, organized after-school activities for the kids, and the regular routine of meals, housework, and yard work, there's just no time left for anything else. As a result, civic duty has gone out the window, at least until the Leading-Edge Boomers become empty-nesters or hit retirement.

YOUTH: DON'T TRUST ANYONE OVER 30

Although young Boomers warned each other, "Don't trust anyone over 30," when they started to turn 30 themselves, the realities of life began to sink in. Suddenly there were family responsibilities, jobs, house payments, and so on. Boomers adapted, but they never quite forgot their obsession with youth. This is evident in the way middle-aged Boomers are gobbling up low-fat food, buying hair dyes, and getting plastic surgery to look a few years younger. They are redefining what it means to be middle-aged. No longer is it "over the hill." Now, it's a new opportunity to do what you want to do, when you want to do it. It's their second chance to relive their youth.

An early sign of the coming "gray is cool" phenomenon is the recent batch of "gray" movies released by the major studios. *Space Cowboys* stars James Garner, Clint Eastwood — both in their 70s — and

Tommy Lee Jones — in his 50s. Harrison Ford, who was recently voted "The Sexiest Man Alive" at age 56 by *People* magazine, is planning to appear as the hero in the latest proposed installment of the Indiana Jones action-thriller series. Arnold Schwarzenegger stars in the action-adventure movie *The 6th Day,* and *Driven,* an auto-racing thriller, features Sylvester Stallone. Both Schwarzenegger and Stallone are also in their 50s. Some relatively older women are also cast as sexy stars, albeit less often. Susan Sarandon, in her 50s, is a perennial mega-star.

Obviously, these are not movies of the *Grumpy Old Men, Cocoon,* or *On Golden Pond* variety — these are action flicks, full of bravado and steamy romance. Boomers wouldn't have put up with 50+ action heroes 20 years ago, but they seem to like them now. We can expect to find increasingly more markers of "hip" aging in future movies, television programming, and advertisements as Boomers make their way into older age.

BOOMER, HEAL THYSELF!

Boomers are taking an active role in their own health and wellness. This is a switch from previous cohorts, who trusted that "doctor knows best." Skeptical and distrustful of authority, Boomers are more likely than other cohorts to seek out alternative remedies for health problems. According to supplement maker Nature's Bounty, for example, customers over 50 are the biggest vitamin users and the most likely to try the wealth of new herbal supplements on the market. Although the 50+ demographic currently includes only six years worth of Boomers, it's gaining another big chunk every year. Take a walk through your local pharmacy, and you'll see entire walls devoted to nothing but vitamins and herbal supplements.

You can reap major rewards by tying your product to health and wellness values. Retailers can joint-venture with hospitals to offer on-site health seminars — this is particularly appropriate for supermarket chains — that have a direct nutritional link to providing health and wellness. Offering tips in newsletters on health and fitness is another avenue to enhance satisfaction. Financial institutions should consider designing financial instruments (like the "Christmas Club") that promote saving strictly for health, wellness, and fitness purposes. For example, a "plastic" passbook could be used explicitly for cosmetic surgery. It may sound silly at first, but to connect with Boomers, you really have to start thinking "outside the box."

STEP 2: ANALYZE CURRENT AND NEXT LIFESTAGE

In the old days, youth was dedicated to education and job preparation, early adulthood to parenthood and career formation, and late adulthood to retirement. Growth periods in life took place in the first half of life and the second half was relegated to decline. This was the linear life path. Today the progression from one lifestage to the next is more cyclic. Second marriages, second families, second careers, and so on, happen in various sequences and with less regard to age than in the past.

In fact, Leading-Edge Boomers run the gamut when it comes to lifestages. From children still at home to second careers to grandparenting, Leading-Edge Boomers have the most lifestage options of any generational cohort. And how these lifestages are played out is a reflection of cohort values. Let's look at some of the current most common Boomer lifestages.

TESTING THE EMPTY-NESTING WINGS

In the old days, mothers devoted their entire lives to raising their children. When it came time for the children to leave the nest, mothers often experienced a sudden loss of identity. They were "empty-nesters," a term that implied that parents' roles had suddenly become obsolete. These days, however, as the kids leave home and eventually graduate from college, Leading-Edge Boomer parents are ecstatic. To them, the empty nest represents a lessening of their family responsibilities and opens new opportunities to focus on self-fulfillment and self-gratification. As the financial obligations to children diminish, Boomers are beginning to see disposable income "bonuses" of $5,000–$10,000 each year. But don't expect Boomers to necessarily save this money for retirement. They are more likely to use the money to buy a sports car or build their dream house. While the parents of Boomers looked to simplify their lives, downsize their homes, and retire to Florida after their children left home, Boomers are going in the opposite direction. They're building bigger, more luxurious homes with hot tubs and multimedia rooms. You can expect them to shun retiring in Arizona and Florida, too. We are already seeing the rise of retirement in colder (but less developed and less "senior") locales such as Ketchum, Idaho; York, Maine; and Charlevoix, Michigan.

As we saw in chapter 1, Mazda found out just how different Boomers are when they first introduced the Miata. It originally was conceived as an entry-level vehicle, a sports car affordable enough for 20-somethings. The first advertising reflected this, with young people frolicking on the beach. But two years later, the average age of the Miata buyer turned out to be 42! The Boomer empty-nesters were satisfying the sports car craving they had never been able to indulge before instead of purchasing the four-door sedan middle-aged people were supposed to buy. Mazda changed the advertising to say "Here's the sports car you've always dreamed about," and set those words over a musical bed themed from the Boomer coming-of-age '60s. This shift in cohort targeting has been an unprecedented automotive marketing success.

As the children of the Boomers become young adults themselves, the Boomers are increasingly coming to regard their children not as children, but as friends — social companions who they enjoy being with and doing things with. This is something Boomers and their parents would not have considered 30 years ago. But today's middle-agers are a different cohort — and so are their children. In part, this is due to 50-something Boomers trying to hold on to the last vestiges of their youth. They are not content to settle into sedentary middle-aged pursuits the way their parents did. Instead, they want to continue rock-climbing, biking, windsurfing, and rollerblading with their kids and other young people. In the future, as now, products, sales promotions, and advertising should reflect this ongoing love affair with youth and keeping fit. For example, "Walkabout" excursions are now catching on. These tours involve walking the length of Cape Cod, from the bridge to Provincetown, or walking the Greek island of Crete, with its fabulous Minoan artifacts and reconstructions. These new offerings create dramatic corporate promotional opportunities as well, as more Boomers will take to the pavement in their walking shoes.

CHILDREARING FOR HEY, HEY MAMAS (AND PAPAS)

Studies have shown that the huge generation gap that existed between Boomers and their parents has shrunk considerably between Boomers and their own kids. Openness with kids is now in style, and many Boomer parents have developed a closer relationship with their own kids than they ever had with their parents. This chumminess, though, has made it harder than ever for Boomers to say no to the kids and impose discipline. Boomer parents also are grappling with how to answer questions from their teenage children about their own behavior during the '60s. Some have decided to come clean with their kids.

Others walk a slippery slope, trying to justify lying in the name of a greater good. But overall, Baby Boomers support the "Just Say No!" line of reasoning. Boomer parents, by and large, understand the harm that the "sex, drugs, and rock 'n' roll" value system created.

Second families are also a part of the Boomers at middle age and beyond. When the "successful" Boomer acquires the "trophy wife" some 20 years his junior (or "upgrades," as they put it in Silicon Valley), the result is often offspring. We're just starting to see this emerge as a significant phenomenon, but it will be interesting to watch how it plays out when Boomer daddies have to change diapers at 55, or are in their 70s when their child enters college. But this is what the future holds. You can expect to find future promotional campaigns keying on the issues inherent in these revisited lifestages, and products and services arising to meet the problems faced by these new role enactments.

GRANDPARENTING FOR THOSE WHO THINK THEY'RE TOO YOUNG FOR THIS!

Even though many Boomers don't think they have reached the age or maturity level to be grandparents, some are part of the first wave of a grandparent boom that's already begun. In 2001, half of all grandparents were Boomers. This is sure to revolutionize the whole concept. As a group, Boomer grandparents have so far not become big spenders on their grandchildren. While they might like the idea of spending lavishly on the grandkids, they still need the money for their own immediate needs. Other Boomer grandparents are finding grandparenting to be a frustrating déjà vu experience: The same anxieties and guilt feelings they felt about not having enough time to spend with their own kids are all coming back.

Today's 50-something grandparents are indeed different from the grandparent stereotype of old. They tend to be far more friendly companions than strict mentors. But when the Boomer turns 75, a new grandparent model will emerge: the sage, or elder imparting wisdom to callow youth. We believe that the mellow, "Grandpa Windsong" image will turn far sterner, imparting a moral message along with wisdom and worldly advice. The very people who rebelled against authority of any kind in their own youth will now *be* the authorities — and they will revel in the role. But remember, they are the ones who created the latchkey child. We believe they will carry this in to grandparenting as well, preferring to keep at a safe distance so as not to infringe on their own free time.

"Grandma Starshine, Tell Us Another Story from Woodstock!"

Gramma. Gran. Nana. Grandmere. Regardless of the name, the image of "grandmother" is firmly fixed in our society. She's the kindly little old lady, white hair in a bun, a shawl over her print dress, knitting as she rocks, with a batch of cookies in the oven — sort of a Mrs. Claus doting on the grandelves.

But consider this: While the government doesn't collect data on grandparenting, per se, it does track "age at first birth." These data show that the Leading-Edge Baby Boomers typically had their first baby at age 22. So a woman born in 1955 would have had her first child around 1977. These children born in 1977 had their own first child at an average age of 24, or around 2001. Thus, this year, **the "average" woman became a grandmother at age 46** — the sum of her and her daughter's average ages when the daughter's first baby was born.

Is she frail and white-haired? Granny's response to that would likely be "Are you kiddin' me?!" And if there

---

Think of the marketing possibilities here, though. Purchases of toys, college savings funds, even childcare should dramatically increase as Boomer grandparents alleviate any vestige of guilt about their "me" decision. Contemplate one-to-one marketing that retrieves product preferences from grandchildren and translates that into online automatic purchases by grandparents to celebrate birthdays, graduations, and other important events. Couple it with personalized greeting cards, again, automatically (yet impersonally) generated, and you have generated a remarkable marketing machine!

What's more, an increase in direct buying from catalogs can be expected as being a "distant" grandparent no longer means "emotionally distant," but rather "geographically distant." Shopping this way allows Boomers to relax about their obligations and continue to pursue their own interests — things like traveling, spending more time at their vacation home, or keeping fit and healthy at the day spa.

were any cookies around, she'd be working them off at aerobics or jazzercise rather than baking them. Today's Boomer grandmother is a babe (although wearing bifocal contacts to combat presbyopia) who illustrates how the grandparenting lifestage is radically changing as we move into the new millennium.

The Baby Boom cohort has changed everything in its path, and there's no reason to think they won't change the grandparenting role, too. The roles of distant, formal, and authoritative grandparenting are more likely to be replaced with a companionate, "Let's-have-fun" role, but one defined to allow grandparents to continue their self-indulgence.

In dealing with the conflict typical of grandparents today (I love my new-found independence . . . but, wait a minute, shouldn't I be a surrogate parent and stand in for my dual-career children?), we would bet that Boomer grandparents will easily choose to serve themselves. They have indulged themselves all along, so why not in grandparenting?

Lifestage Matrix Marketing's unofficial motto — "50 ain't what it used to be" — is equally true of grandparenting. The old image of Grandma is of a little old lady in a rocking chair. The *new* image of Grandma is just as likely to be Priscilla Presley, twice a grandparent. This means Grandpa could be Elvis.

When looking at the fast-changing lifestage of grandparenting, don't assume old stereotypes still hold. "Grandparenting ain't what it used to be" either, a point that should always be kept in mind.

STARTING NEW CAREERS AT 50

The corporate downsizing of the '90s left a bad taste in the mouth of working Americans, and it is largely responsible for the weakened job loyalty that we see in the United States today. Workers have led the charge to redefine the workplace, rallying around everything from relaxed dress codes to a new emphasis on balancing work and home life.

Suddenly, climbing the corporate ladder is out and satisfying your inner needs is in. A case in point is how different generational cohorts respond to being "downsized." The Postwar and older cohorts reacted in shock and horror: "How could you do this to me? I've been a loyal worker for the company for 20 years!" In contrast, the downsized Boomer is more likely to say, "I should have quit this Mickey Mouse company years ago! I'm going to start doing things my way for a change."

Telecommuting is at an all-time high as Boomers use the latest technology tools to break new ground and work from home. Part-time work, job-sharing, and entrepreneurship are expected to flourish as Boomers look for new ways to find fulfillment in their lives. Mid-life career redirection will become even more commonplace as Boomers admit that the career path they chose at 20 doesn't necessarily match their needs at 50. Second careers are just another way for Boomers to redefine middle age and start over. They also offer a marketing opportunity for investment firms with suggestions for how to best invest an IRA rollover or lump-sum severance package.

DIVORCING BECAUSE YOUR PERSONAL NEEDS CHANGED

Since the '70s, the divorce rate in the United States has soared, with 50% of marriages over the past 20 years ending in divorce. This has been blamed largely on Boomers' self-interest and lack of commitment. And it has its good side: Men and women no longer need to suffer in one-sided, unhappy, or dysfunctional marriages. But the downside is that divorce has forever scarred the landscape of the American family, leaving many unresolved issues boiling beneath the surface. Single-parent homes and blended families are fast becoming the norm as mom and dad shuck one spouse for another, oftentimes leaving the children to fend for themselves in free-form families. In the 1990s, only 61% of children lived with both of their biological parents.

The number of third marriages (the kind that the 50ish Boomer is more apt to face) is, in fact, on the rise. In 1970, only 4.1% of women were getting married for the third time, and 3.8% of men. By 1990, those numbers had more than doubled, to 8.7% for women and 8.5% for men. Some of these three-timers shrug and say, "My personal needs and desires changed as life evolved." Some smart vacation companies have capitalized on this trend by packaging "Third-time-around honeymoon vacations!"

STEP 3: EXAMINE EMOTIONS AND AFFINITIES

Another result of defining moments is the shaping of how cohort members carry out their lifestyle, view others in their lives, and put new importance on different interests and wants. Each generational cohort also develops a set of desires that is unique to them and different from other cohorts.

TAKING ME BACK TO WHERE I ONCE BELONGED

Nostalgia is the yearning to return to the past, the pleasure we get from reliving fond memories. But we usually sanitize these memories, often making them more vivid and positive than they were when we actually lived them. Nostalgia is really an emotional state — and one that Leading-Edge Boomers really love. While older generational cohorts also love to reminisce, Boomers are making nostalgia a key marketing tool.

Scents have been shown to be the quickest route to a nostalgic remembrance. Dr. Alan Hirsch of Chicago's Smell and Taste Treatment and Research Foundation has found that the following odors bring immediate recollections of childhood: baking bread or cookies, baby powder, and parents' cologne and perfume. These odors work for all cohorts. Interestingly, some odors follow a distinct cohort pattern. Older cohorts, such as the Depression and World War II Cohorts, find that smells associated with nature — pine, sea air, horses, hay, and meadows — bring on wonderful childhood memories. Boomers, however, are more reminded of childhood by artificial odors, such as Play-Doh, plastics, scented markers, Sweet Tarts, and vapor rub. This clearly relates back to the odors they encountered as they grew up and came of age.

Dr. Hirsch also found that the smell of cut grass elicited a positive smell from generational cohorts older than Baby Boomers. Boomers, in a perfect reflection of their values, found that smell quite negative. It was associated with the weekly lawn mowing, Dr. Hirsch found, which was a chore the establishment (their parents) forced on them. So it is clear that the smell of cut grass will definitely not entice Boomers (at least, not the kind of "grass" grown in most lawns . . .). To help marketers tap the market, Dr. Hirsch has developed an odor machine that disperses various odors into the air in stores and other facilities to create a pleasant, nostalgic atmosphere.

Could That Be Nostalgia Tugging at Your Purse Strings?

There's nothing quite like Boomer nostalgia — those fond images, icons, symbols, and music of the '60s — to tug at our heart strings. Or, our purse strings.

Now that the Boomers have begun to move into their 50s, an age when we start to reminisce about the past like never before, nostalgia marketing is suddenly big business. No matter what our age, nostalgia takes us back to simpler times and makes us feel good. But for Boomers, who never really wanted to grow up in the first place, nostalgia has proven to be a very powerful tonic.

In a 1998 issue devoted to nostalgia marketing, *Business Week* said Americans are overwhelmed by the breakneck speed of the Information Age, with its high-speed modems, cellular phones, and pagers. It seems at times that things are out of control, especially to Boomers who are sandwiched between aging parents, kids still at home, and mounting job pressures. "We are creating a new culture, and we don't know what's going to happen," said futurist Watts Wacker. "So we need some warm fuzzies from our past."

That's where nostalgia comes in. It's those warm fuzzies that take us back to simpler times, and are so powerful as a marketing tool. Look at the return of the Volkswagen Beetle with its retro positioning: "Less

---

Nostalgia is a strong attention-getting device, but its use must directly relate to the values being targeted. Otherwise, it has no lasting effect. It may catch the eye of Boomers, but it won't necessarily result in a sale.

CHALLENGING AUTHORITY

The civil rights, anti-war, women's rights, nuclear power, and environmental protests of the '60s and '70s solidified a blatant disrespect for

Flower. More Power." The original Beetle was cheap to own, easy to fix, and fun to drive, and it personified an era of rebellion against conventions.

Then there's Ben and Jerry's ice cream, which hired social activists from the '60s — including Bobby Seale, the national organizer and co-founder of the Black Panther Party; Dolores Huerta, co-founder (with Cesar Chavez) of the United Farm Workers of America; folk singer Pete Seeger; and others — to promote its new line of smooth, no-chunks ice cream.

And there are myriad examples of companies using Boomer nostalgia music in hopes of pushing the right buttons. Here are just a few:

- Janis Joplin and Mercedes Benz ("Mercedes Benz")
- The Who and Nissan ("Won't Get Fooled Again")
- Elton John and AT&T ("Rocket Man")
- The Rolling Stones and Microsoft ("Start Me Up")

As many companies have learned, nostalgia helps to stir emotions like no other technique and helps people — particularly youth-oriented Boomers — return to the simplicity of their youth. Even if it only lasts 30 seconds, Boomers are finding nostalgia marketing well worth the trip.

authority that Boomers still carry with them today — but with a new twist. Gone are the vocal protests against the government. These days, aging hippies are more apt to take on corporate retailers, such as Wal-Mart, to preserve their own neighborhoods, rather than save the world. Using chants reminiscent of the anti-war years, they shout, "One, two, three, four — we don't want your Wal-Mart store!"

Boomers have aged, but because core cohort values don't change, they still challenge authority, especially when their own self-interests are at stake. Take consumer products, for example. Studies have shown that

Boomers are more likely than other cohort groups to research new products on their own, rather than rely on the authority of a sales clerk or slick marketing materials. Boomers are the most educated cohort ever. They demand information about product claims, ingredients, you name it. *Consumer Reports* and the Internet are just a few of the tools they use to gather this information. As Boomers reach their golden years, this penchant for challenging authority will no doubt carry over into investigating the best medical treatments and healthcare services.

OVERCOMING INJUSTICE . . . IF THERE'S TIME

Social justice was a buzzword of the '60s and '70s, but it fell out of vogue when Boomers finally joined the ranks of the employed and started their climb up the corporate ladder. In no time flat, social justice gave way to capitalistic pursuits.

But Boomers haven't completely turned their back on all of the causes they championed as young adults. Studies have shown that Boomers are the most likely of any cohort group to donate to charity. As they have grown more affluent and gotten busier, money has become an acceptable substitute for time spent protesting. The core values haven't changed, even if the expression of those values has.

As the Boomers age, their political leanings will change, too. The manifestation of their core values will become part of a political orientation that is both more liberal and more conservative, depending on the topic. Boomers have always been social liberals, and we predict they will become even more so as they get older, favoring, for example, help for the homeless, mentally ill, immigrants, and disadvantaged children. As they reach the empty-nest and eventually the retirement lifestage and thus have more discretionary time, the Leading-Edge Boomers will reenter the ranks of volunteers with a vengeance, augmenting their monetary activism.

At the same time, however, Boomers' traditional emphasis on individualism and distrust of authority — and the fact that their higher incomes make them a major segment of the tax base — will lead them to turn away from trying to solve social problems with more government spending. Their presumption will be that individuals acting in their own and societies' interest will allocate resources better than any government bureaucracy.

The official platforms of the major parties currently don't reflect this seeming dichotomy. The Democrats, generally pro-choice, pro-welfare and social liberals, often see the solution to social ills in centralized governmental regulation and spending. And the Republicans, while proposing tax cuts and reduced government spending, remain stubbornly conservative on social issues. We predict that the party that reflects social liberalism *and* fiscal conservatism will prevail in the future — whether that be one of the two major parties, or a brand new party.

SEX AND THE UNSQUARE OVAL OFFICE

Despite their advancing age, Boomers still see themselves as sexually tolerant and experimental. They are still looking to try new things. Bill Clinton's compulsion for new sexual experiences and his willingness to lie about them resulted in his impeachment. He saw Monica Lewinsky's star-struck compliance as something to be indulged in. It didn't deter him that she was a White House intern and a young, impressionable woman half his age. Because of the Boomers, Victorian attitudes about sex have been replaced with more openness in all age brackets — which we view as good in the abstract, even if occasionally reprehensible in the specific. Lovemaking isn't just for the young. Now, middle-age and older couples can admit that they enjoy sex, too.

In Finland, for example, the village of Kutemajarvi (which literally translates into "spawn lake" — no resemblance to Tchaikovsky's ballet intended) hosts an annual sex fair for people age 45 and up. The event is tied to the United Nations' designating 1999 as the International Year of Older Persons. To that end, the fair is aimed at creating the atmosphere for these older adults to explore the joy of sex. A trail stretching through forests and meadows is marked with detours for the ardent. And for couples interested in a "roll in the hay," barns complete with fresh, aromatic hay are also available. In typical Scandinavian style, gays are welcome, but on-lookers are not.

GENERATIONAL COMMUNITY BONDING

Literally from the start, Boomers knew they were part of something big. After World War II, suddenly everyone was having babies, homes were being built, and jobs were plentiful; life was good. Because they represented the largest increase in the birthrate in the history of the United States, Baby Boomers got used to marketers catering to their every whim. With all of the social upheaval of the '60s, Boomers felt an even greater sense of connectedness to their cohort group. In fact, they created their own youth subculture. It was us against them — us being the Boomers, them being anyone older than 30. This feeling of being a part of a larger group still remains with the Boomers today (even if "them" now includes anyone older or younger than they are). For example, the "oldies but goodies" radio format can quite explicitly reference "tunes of the times when the Boomers were growing up!" Unlike "seniors" who tend to resent being grouped in any way, the Boomers don't seem to mind the classification. In fact, it has always come with a lot of advantages.

Step 4: Build a physiographic profile

No one needs to be reminded that as we age, we undergo physical changes. How we handle these alterations can be dependent upon generational cohort values. For instance, we can be sure that, like the Oil of Olay ad, Boomers will fight aging all the way.

Beware, the hands of time

First, you start to gain a few extra pounds around the middle. Then, you notice a few gray hairs at the temples, and you have trouble reading the fine print on the cereal box. The next thing you know, you're stiff and sore when you've done no exercise at all. Or it's a cool day and you're suddenly so hot you want to scream. And then, all of a sudden, the doctor is telling you to watch your blood pressure and cholesterol. The dreaded disease has crept up on you without you realizing it — you've come down with a classic case of middle age.

But take heart. Chronological age isn't necessarily a good indicator of biological age. Good nutrition and regular exercise can go a long way to slow the biological clock. This is music to the ears of Boomers, who wish they could stay young forever. Eventually, though, the signs of aging will creep up. Table 6.2 shows a physiological profile of middle age. Vision problems, weight changes, hypertension, arthritis, gray hair, hair loss, and menopause are just a few of the physiographic changes now taking place with the Boomers.

TABLE 6.2: THE BIOLOGICAL CLOCK IS TICK, TICK, TICKING

Vision	The lenses of your eyes continue losing elasticity. The fine print grows finer, and finer, and finer.
Bones	Bone breaks take longer to mend; you notice stiffness in joints; 2% bone mass shrinkage per decade occurs after age 20. Arthritis can begin to affect joints.
Muscles	Muscle strength peaks at about 30, then drops slowly until 50, then drops fairly rapidly.
Digestion	Cutbacks in gastric-acid production slow down digestion, leaving you feeling fuller.
Lungs	Lung function peaks at about 20, then declines about 1% per year.
Heart	If you're healthy and fit, aging causes no noticeable change in your heart's ability to pump blood while at rest. However, high-blood pressure (hypertension) can start to become a problem for some.
Hair	Hair shaft size shrinks; men experience male pattern baldness; graying around the edges.
Skin	Skin loses its elasticity and wrinkles develop around the eyes, mouth, and forehead from common facial expressions.
Sex	For men, it takes longer to become aroused; more rest needed between orgasms. Somewhere between the mid-40s and mid-50s, most women undergo menopause.
Weight	Weight gain of about a pound a year between 20 and 50 is an indicator of good health and longevity.

As a flood of Boomers continues to reach their 50th birthdays, experts predict that menopause and other problems of middle-age will begin to receive more serious attention from the medical community, the popular press — and consumer product manufacturers and their advertising agencies. One example is a product called "Testosterol," heavily advertised on radio as a aid to sexual performance and lean muscle mass — sort of a Viagra for the aging Boomers, who may not yet fall into the primary Viagra age bracket.

IT'S NOT THE LEGS THAT GO FIRST

At about age 45, most people begin to experience one of the first signs of aging — farsightedness. It gets harder and harder to read newspapers and other small print. The human eye is optimal at age 8. Then it's downhill from there. The deterioration doesn't usually become obvious until about age 45–50. The doctor may prescribe bifocals to correct the problem, but now and then you may forget your glasses. You may go to the grocery store, for example, and if you are a Boomer dedicated to health and wellness, you want to read the ingredients and nutritional information on packages. But it many cases it's impossible because the type used is very small. The next time you are at the supermarket, examine the packaging and see how many marketers help you in your quest. We've done it for clients, and the answer is not many.

After a number of consulting engagements for various food companies, we at Lifestage have developed a long list of packaging and product principles to be followed in meeting the vision needs of middle-agers and up. Here are just a few:

- Employ at least 12-point type, but preferably 13-point or larger.

- Use high contrast in lettering and background (black on yellow is best, followed by black on white).

- Avoid glossy stock which creates glare; glare is increasingly difficult to process as we get older.

- Use colors that are in sharp contrast.

- Avoid colors in the blue, gray, violet end of the color spectrum because they often look the same to older eyes.

STEP 5: UNDERSTAND SOCIAL ACTIVITIES AND LIFESTYLES

Boomers are excited about their quality of life. In fact, quality of life is more important than their work life. Here are some ways that they spend their free time.

LESS IS MORE WHEN IT COMES TO EXERCISE

Health club memberships are down for the over-45 crowd, as Boomers reject the all-or-nothing fitness messages of the late '80s and early '90s. The popularity of walking, gardening, golf, outdoor activities, and yoga represent a lifestyle shift as Boomers seek the best payback for their limited leisure time. But again, Boomers are making their own mark, turning quiet pursuits such as gardening into a new status game with sculpted topiaries, fish ponds, and chic garden-wear. "Gardeners today want it big and they want it now," says home and garden guru Martha Stewart. This opens a wide range of opportunities for marketers both now and in the future.

WELCOME TO BEER CAMP AND ASSISTED BACKPACKING

With Boomers, leisure isn't an option, it's a necessity. When it comes to travel, Boomers aren't interested in the ho-hum family vacation package. They want adventure! Excitement! Fun for the whole family! This has opened up a whole new market for hotels and resorts. And active Baby Boomers who want unique vacation experiences are now checking out camps geared specifically for adults. For example:

- ✦ A California company now offers "Active Sampler" weeks to its regular bike trips. Campers sample rock-climbing, mountain biking, kayaking, aerobics, weight lifting, sail boarding, water biking, and tennis.

- ✦ A Kentucky company offers Beer Camp, where campers listen to talks and sample 276 different beers.

- ✦ Several Rocky Mountain dude ranches set aside entire weeks for adult camps.

Although energetic activities occupy Boomer leisure time now, in a few years their joints and muscles will begin to dictate active, but somewhat less vigorous, pursuits. As youths, the Boomer idealism translated into the fervent espousal of group causes, from anti-war to save the whales. As they enter late middle age, we believe this idealism will turn inward, leading to a surge in contemplative, introspective, low-impact individual leisure activities — things such as sailing, canoeing, fly-fishing, amateur astronomy, painting, and music. We also see a surge in new pursuits such as "assisted backpacking," where you're out in the wild, but you've gotten some help getting there from a water-taxi to a trailhead that *starts* five miles into the wilderness. In the High Sierras, some of the most popular outfitters offer llamas or donkeys to carry the tent and the packs, as well as the cooler and ice for the beer. (Perhaps it's a beer you first sampled when you went to beer camp!)

STEP 6: INVESTIGATE PURCHASING BEHAVIOR

Over the last 50 years, the purchasing behavior of Americans has gone through a radical shift. Once upon a time, buying on credit was something to avoid and bankruptcy was taboo. Those old-fashioned concepts have all been replaced with a "buy now — pay later" mind-set, where bankruptcy is the quick and painless remedy for financial problems.

A NIP AND A TUCK AND YOU'RE ON YOUR WAY

Aging Boomers are helping to make plastic surgery one of the fastest growing medical specialties in the United States. Since 1992, the number of cosmetic-surgery procedures performed by certified plastic surgeons has increased 153% to more than 1 million in 1999. For Boomers, who account for more than 40% of the market, liposuction and eyelifts have become accepted as a kind of middle-age rite of passage. More and more men are jumping on the bandwagon, too. They currently make up about 9% of all cosmetic surgery patients, and male liposuction has increased more than 200% since 1992. Some of this emphasis on looking young has to do with competitiveness in the job market. Youth equals success, and Boomers don't want to get caught with their wrinkles or gray hair showing.

The *New York Times* has called this an era of "faux fitness," where looking thinner and feeling great comes without any of the hard work or exercise. Bodyslimmers, hair coloring for men and women, and anti-aging creams and cosmetics are flying off the shelves. Day spas, where you can relax and have yourself made over from head to toe, are the latest rage. A person who feels young, they argue, shouldn't have to look old.

"OH LORD, WON'T YOU BUY ME A MERCEDES BENZ . . . "

The classical model of consumer behavior says that as people age, consumption declines and savings increase as they prepare for retirement. Unfortunately, the facts don't support this theory when it comes to the Boomers. Savings rates in the United States are at an all-time low, while consumer debt (credit card debt, mortgage debt, and personal property debt) are at all-time highs and getting higher. The economists are confounded. A huge population mass is turning 50 — historically when savings behavior kicks in — and it just isn't happening. Why? Because *Boomers have never saved, and they never will.* Again, it's a cohort thing. Their cohort values don't include a saving component, especially when the '90s booming stock market and inflated home values made them feel relatively secure.

Adding to the disinclination to save, Boomers have always felt they deserve the best of everything. Even though they may be on the verge of an empty nest, many aren't looking to downsize like their parents did. Housing surveys show that Boomers are more likely to buy the same size house, if not a larger one, when their kids leave home. They are looking for luxurious dream homes — with custom-designs and flexible spaces for entertaining — not retirement condos or ranches in Arizona and Florida.

There are several reasons for this. Family obligations top the list. Boomers started families later, and some have second families now, so many Boomers still have children at home. Also, their parents' invest-ment in higher education paid off in the form of higher paying jobs for Boomers. Combine this with the increase in dual-income families, and a picture of affluent, middle-aged Americans who want to satisfy their every desire comes into focus.

Housing developers have had a tough time trying to predict what the Boomers are going to do next. In one generation, the average house size has grown by 50%. New homes these days have 2.5 or 3 baths, and 16% of homes have a three-car garage, a figure that is expected to climb in the near future. In Tucson, Arizona, for example, builders have begun to offer five- and six-car garage options in some new subdivisions. Suddenly space is an "affordable luxury."

But as they become full-fledged empty-nesters, we see the Leading-Edge Boomers moving toward smaller, more efficient, easier-to-care-for houses. This is in keeping with their more contemplative natures, which will lead them to turn ever more inward as they age. In this regard, we think the Leading-Edge Boomers will be in marked contrast to the Trailing-Edge Boomers, who currently are driving the trend for 6,000+ square-foot suburban mansions. Always more materialistic and suffi-ciently insecure to need to show their affluence when they possess it, Trailing-Edge Boomers will continue to covet ever-larger edifices well into the future.

CONVENIENCE IS KEY AND TIME IS MONEY

The stress of juggling dual careers with family obligations, and the ever-increasing pressure to do more in less time has Boomers feeling overwhelmed. Recent studies show that 39% of all 45–54 year-olds feel rushed. They are at their peak in terms of responsibility — to their jobs, their children, and their parents. There's no time left for them.

Many Boomers are now paying others to cook, clean, mow the yard, pull weeds, drive, take care of the kids, and check in on their parents. In 1998, the number of servant-type jobs — nannies, maids, gardeners, pool cleaners, butlers, cooks, and the like — grew 8% to almost 1.8 million, more than five times the rate of overall job growth, according to the Bureau of Labor Statistics. This shows that Boomers are willing to pay big for services that make their lives easier. Consider these facts:

+ *Advertising Age* calls the restaurant industry a "'90s wet nurse for consumers too busy to prepare cozy family meals." Recent studies show that people aged 30–49 eat out more often than the average American.

+ Adult day care is booming. In 1978, there were 300 adult day-care centers in the country. In 1997, there were about 4,000, and that number is expected to grow, according to the National Adult Day Services Association.

FUTURE OUTLOOK: A NEW BREED OF OLDER AMERICAN

The radical changes already taking place in the demographics of the 50+ market have opened up a whole new opportunity for companies savvy enough to question successful marketing methods that worked in the past. Dusting off the same tired approaches year after year isn't going to work, especially with the Boomers. To be successful in the aging Boomer market, you must reposition your products with an eye toward a new breed of older American — those who see themselves as forever young in thought, looks, and lifestyle.

Whatever the future holds, there's no reason to think Leading-Edge Boomers will sit idly by and accept growing older as quietly and as sedately as their parents did. That's simply out of the question. They will fight it kicking and screaming every step of the way — until they reach the point when it simply can't be denied any longer, and then they just may be the first cohort group in which aging will be considered "cool."

BOOMERS DETERMINE WHAT'S HOT AND WHAT'S NOT

Just as they always have, Leading-Edge Boomers will continue to determine what's hot and what's not with each new lifestage they enter. As Boomers begin to tip the population balance to the gray side and reach their peak earning potential, a golden age of opportunity is about to dawn for marketers. Get ready to reap the profits.

But if you're suddenly mentally picturing a movie of yourself leisurely harvesting the aging Boomer market like a bunch of plump berries ready to fall from the vine, think again. Boomers will not be easy pickings. Capturing this market will require finesse, stamina, hard work, and a willingness to reinvent your marketing strategy.

The Lifestage Analytic Matrix and Multi-Dimensional Marketing provide a comprehensive way to keep track of the various and sometimes conflicting factors that impact buying decisions during different lifestages. The matrix helps you to recognize the diversity of lifestage alternatives today, and not to pigeonhole a particular group on the basis of age or demographics. Every time a person moves from one lifestage to another, there is a change in behavior. And as a marketer, such changes translate into very real marketing opportunities.

CONCLUSION: FOCUS ON KEY COHORT VALUES

Now you have seen what to do to appeal to those much-sought-after Leading-Edge Baby Boomers. Table 6.3 provides you with a summary of the key principles. Armed with this knowledge, we hope you'll do well. But even some of the best in the business can stumble. For example, the American Association of Retired Persons (AARP) — an organization serving over 30 million members — is struggling with how to appeal to Boomers.

In 1999, for example, the non-profit lobbying organization changed its name to just simply the acronym AARP—no more use of or reference to "retired." Over the years, the group has successfully positioned itself as being for retirees. Now it is trying to undo overnight what it has spent years doing. AARP maintains that it is not abandoning its traditional retiree members who want the insurance and service benefits it has offered for years. But the organization now has committees exploring new services and benefits that would appeal to Boomers.

AARP has even refocused its *Modern Maturity* magazine in its effort to cross-market to Baby Boomers. With over 37 million circulation, it is the most widely distributed magazine in America. Here's an example that demonstrates its new approach: In 1998, it featured 77-year-old Betty White on its cover with the headline, "Betty White, on Life, Loss, and Laughter." One year later, the magazine featured 52-year-old Susan Sarandon with this headline, "Great Sex — What's Age Got to Do With It?" and "Who's Sexy Now?" Talk about a shift in focus.

So tricky is it to envision a cross-marketed *Modern Maturity* magazine that even comedian Jay Leno has poked fun at the idea. He produced a fictional edition for Boomers with a cover that featured 50-something Boomer Mick Jagger with the headlines, "From Rolling Stones to Kidney Stones," and "Can't Get No Satisfaction? Try Bran Muffins."

Can the cosmetic and superficial changes made by AARP rope in Baby Boomers? We certainly don't think so. The cohort that created the youth culture has moved into their 50s, and they don't want to be lumped in with the same people they didn't trust 30 years ago. We believe AARP will go the way of the station wagon. What is needed is a sportier "SUV" organization that fully embraces the values of this target market: youth, individuality, health and fitness, quality of life, empowerment, choice, information, and so on. The superficial changes being undertaken at AARP miss the insights that you now have about the Leading-Edge Boomers. We hope you won't make the same mistake.

TABLE 6.3: HOW TO TAP THE LEADING-EDGE BABY BOOMER MARKET

Cohort values	✦ Avoid broad, cross-cohort contexts. ✦ Show them as "free spirits" avoiding responsibilities. ✦ Build indulgences into products and reflect self-gratification in advertising. ✦ Stress their desire for "being *me*" — place a strong emphasis on individualism. ✦ Show them as skeptical, questioning everything. ✦ Characterize them as holding on to their youth through exercise, eating healthy, and plastic surgery.
Lifestages	✦ Key into both new lifestages and repeat life stages: empty-nesting, divorce, second marriages, second families, and early grandparenting. ✦ Provide outlets for Boomer grandparents to diminish guilt for being distant grandparents.
Emotions and affinities	✦ Use nostalgia to gain attention: focus on images, icons, symbols and music of Boomer youth (most nostalgic of all cohorts). ✦ Appeal to sex and sensuality (more overtly than to Postwar and older cohorts). ✦ Show a positive sexual excitement and capability. ✦ Appeal to sense of cohort community: "We're the biggest and the best." ✦ Promote a positive self-image and feeling of attractiveness.
Physiographics	✦ Look for ways to build in health and fitness to products. ✦ Provide product features that will enhance body appearance (weight, muscle tone, hair color, and other aging effects). ✦ Use larger print in advertisements, labels, and other reading material. ✦ Build accommodation for reduced night vision and glare problems into appropriate products. ✦ Slow the presentation of visuals in advertising to accommodate a slowing of image tracking and a slowing of reaction time. ✦ Develop and promote products that can help alleviate the symptoms of menopause — such as soy-rich foods containing phytoestrogens.

TABLE 6.3 (CONT.)

Social activities and lifestyles	✦ Focus on quality of personal life versus work life. ✦ Show exercise and leisure as priorities.
Purchasing behavior	✦ Keep in mind that youth sells with this group. ✦ Play up high-end image that your product conveys to others. ✦ Cater to need for convenience.

ENDNOTES

1. Teri Agins, "The Power Suit Languishes as More Women Go Casual." *The Wall Street Journal Interactive Edition,* 26 August, 1999.

2. Martin E. P. Seligman, "Boomer Blues." *Psychology Today* (October 1988): 51.

3. Cheryl Russell, *The Master Trend: How the Baby Boom Generation Is Remaking America.* Perseus, 1993.

CHAPTER 7

THE TRAILING-EDGE BABY BOOMER COHORT

Imagine that you came of age during the late '60s, when young adults were thumbing their noses at the powers that be and banding together to right social wrongs through sit-ins and other protests. How do you think these events would shape your values and your outlook toward the future? If you were like most young adults of that era, you would come away with a sense of idealism and optimism about the future, even if you always remained suspicious of the establishment.

Now switch gears for a moment, and imagine that you came of age during the '70s, a time when the previously strong economy tanked, inflation spiraled out of control, the oil crisis caused a nationwide panic, and the president resigned under a cloud of scandal. How would these events shape your values? No doubt, you would not be at all optimistic about the future, and you would probably tend to feel cheated by events that were beyond your control.

The Baby Boom is typically defined as people born between 1946–1965. But this example shows just how different the attitudes are between the first wave of the Baby Boom and the second. That's why we have divided this 19-year group into two distinct generational cohorts. As you read in Chapter 6, "The Leading-Edge Baby Boomer Cohort," the Leading-Edge Boomers (those born from 1946–1954) came of age during good economic times, and were full of idealism and hope for the future. The Trailing-Edge Boomers (those born from 1955–1965) came of age during a time when chaos reigned and people turned inward to focus on the one thing that was within their control — themselves. That's why we have split them into two distinct cohorts. We call the first group the Leading-Edge Baby Boomers. The later group, we refer to as the Trailing-Edge Baby Boomers, or "Generation Jones."

Author Jonathan Pontell is credited with coining the "Generation Jones" label. His book by the same name (not yet in print) seeks to call attention to this overlooked group, often lost between the Boomers and the Xers, and to help build a common cohort identity. "Why Jones?" you ask. Because, like Smith or Doe, it conveys the idea of a large, anonymous generation. Plus, according to Pontell, "jonesin'" is a hip, passionate slang word of the '70s that means a strong craving for something or someone:

> Our generation has the jones. As children of the '60s, at the absolute height of American's post–World War II affluence and confidence, Jonesers were promised the moon. Then, in the '70s, as the nation's mood turned from hope to fear, we were abandoned. While Boomers began with big expectations that were often realized, and Xers were never given much of anything to expect, it was our generation that was filled with the highest hopes and then confronted with the most dramatically different reality. Huge expectations left unfulfilled have deeply entrenched a jonesin' in us. This jonesin' has made us strikingly driven and persevering, and has given our generation a certain non-committal, pending flavor as we've continued to hold out for our original dreams.[1]

Jonesers are not as idealistic as the Leading-Edge Boomers, and they are not as cynical as Generation X. They are somewhere in between. Pontell writes that Jonesers are more likely to seek out what he calls "practical solutions to fixable problems." And we agree. This group is unique in the way it tempers Leading-Edge Boomer idealism with Gen-X cynicism.

Overshadowed by Boomers, Eclipsed by Xers

"While the Boomer and Xer choruses resulted in media feeding frenzies, our attempts to assert our collective identity were largely ignored. As early as 1972, The New York Times Magazine ran a cover story written by 18-year-old Joyce Maynard in which she proclaimed that she and her peers were the leading edge of a new generation, one qualitatively different than the Woodstock Generation. Her voice, like the others that followed in the mid-70s, weren't heard by a nation that wasn't ready to deal with a new generation. But for many of us in that new generation, it was a joke that we were being lumped in with the Boomers. It was obvious to us that we were a different generation."

Source: Jonathan Pontell. "Arguments for our existence."
GenerationJones.com

FROM SOCIAL JUSTICE TO . . . ME

Generation Jones came of age from 1973–1983, during a decade of crisis and lost confidence in government and other institutions. At the brink of adulthood, this cohort witnessed the Watergate scandal, the fall of Vietnam, and President Richard Nixon's resignation. These public failures coupled with the energy crisis, raging inflation, and a dismal economy led this cohort to be less optimistic about the future than the Leading-Edge Boomers before them. This younger group shunned the outward activism of their older Boomer brothers and sisters and shifted their focus to within. They sought self-fulfillment, cosmic awareness, and inner peace. Encounter groups sprang up around the country, physical fitness offered a new kind of natural high, and health food stores saw business grow faster than a bean sprout under a grow light. Writer Tom Wolfe called the '70s the "Me Decade." It aptly described the nation's new absorption with "self."

Generational Cohort Political Cues

This table shows how the experiences, fads, and mind-sets of Jonesers differ from those of cohorts on either side of them.

	Leading-Edge Boomers	Jonesers	Gen X
Slogan	MAKE LOVE, NOT WAR	NO NUKES	WHATEVER
Question	Where were you when JFK was shot?	Where's the beef?	Boxers or briefs?
Jewelry	Peace symbol necklace	POW bracelet	Nose ring
News	Walter Cronkite	CNN	CNN.com
War	Vietnam	Star Wars	Persian Gulf War
Hero	JFK	Jerry Brown	Jesse Ventura
Scandal	Profumo affair	Watergate	Monicagate
Poet	Bob Dylan	Bruce Springsteen	Kurt Cobain
Anti-	Anti-war	Anti-nuke	Anti–World Trade Organization

Source: Jonathan Pontell

While some marketers and historians are content to lump Baby Boomers into one large group, we see a clear line of demarcation that separates the leading edge from the trailing edge. Clearly, they do share some common traits, such as individualism and interest in health and wellness, but there are distinct differences in attitude and cohort values on both sides of this line. The year 1973 was the turning point, the year the idealism of the '60s began to unravel. Details about the Watergate break-in and the White House's involvement came to the surface during Senate hearings. And the Paris peace agreement with North Vietnam marked the official end of American involvement in the Vietnam War.

Trailing-Edge Boomer Defining Moments

+ Fall of Vietnam
+ Watergate
+ Nixon's resignation
+ Energy crisis
+ Stock market tumble

"I AM NOT A CROOK!"

Following the publication of the *Pentagon Papers* in the *New York Times* in June, 1971 — related classified Defense Department documents that showed a pattern of deception about the United States' role in Vietnam — Nixon grew more paranoid and obsessed with secrecy. This drove him to put together a team of "plumbers" to stop White House leaks, a practice that continued into the 1972 presidential campaign. A botched attempt to place wire taps at the Democratic National Committee's headquarters at the Watergate complex, and the ensuing cover-up, broke the lid off the pattern of wire-tapping, sabotage, and lies that led all the way to the White House.

When Senate hearings discovered that all of the president's conversations in the Oval Office had been recorded since 1971 at the president's own request, the fight was on to obtain the tapes. Nixon tried to block release of the tapes, but eventually was forced to turn over the lot. The tapes clearly implicated Nixon in the cover-up, and in 1974, he became the first president ever to resign from office. Later the same day, Gerald Ford was sworn in as president. Ford, the former House Minority Whip, had become vice president after Spiro Agnew resigned in a bribery scandal.

In his inauguration speech, Ford tried to close the door on Watergate and reassure Americans that he would restore integrity to the Oval Office. "Our long national nightmare is over," he said. Ford later pardoned Nixon from prosecution, an act that all but guaranteed he would never be elected to the presidency in his own right.

VIETNAM: SO-CALLED "PEACE WITH HONOR"

For more than a decade, Americans fought against the North Vietnamese. Public sentiment for the war had waned during Lyndon Johnson's presidency, as protestors spoke out against U.S. involvement. Nixon's secret bombing raids into Cambodia and the 1970 Kent State riots and shootings only prompted further disillusionment among the American public. By 1973, Nixon put aside hopes of ever winning the war and authorized Secretary of State Henry Kissinger to sign the Paris Peace Accord. While Nixon called the agreement an achievement of "peace with honor," most Americans saw it as defeat.

Famous Jonesers

Rosie O'Donnell

Bill Gates

Steve Jobs

Drew Carey

Quentin Tarantino

John F. Kennedy, Jr.

Whitney Houston

George Stephanopoulos

Jodie Foster

Michael Jordan

Madonna

Wayne Gretzky

Jerry Seinfeld

Oprah Winfrey

The 3 million Americans who served in Vietnam came home not as heroes, but as villains and "baby-killers." There were no ticker-tape parades or parties, like previous veterans had received, only small groups of soldiers quietly slipping through the lines of protestors, hoping to pick up the pieces of their lives.

The Trailing-Edge Boomers were too young to serve in Vietnam, but it heightened their consciousness about the cruel realities of war. It also sensitized them to be suspicious of authority figures and institutions in general.

With the fall of Saigon in 1975, Jonesers would forever have images of U.S. failure etched on their minds. Unlike the World War II and Postwar Cohorts, who came to expect success from American leadership, Generation Jones had just the opposite experience. To them, Vietnam was nothing more than proof of American arrogance and deception.

TURNING OUT THE LIGHTS

Beginning with the Yom Kippur War between Israel and its Arab neighbors in 1973, Arab members of the Organization of Petroleum Exporting Countries (OPEC) started an oil embargo against the United States and other allies of Israel. This shut off the supply of Middle East oil to the United States for five months, and drove up oil prices and the cost of gasoline, heating oil, and other petroleum-based products. Once the embargo was over, OPEC continued to flex its muscles, limiting oil production and export. Gas lines stretched for blocks, and then only a limited amount of gas could be purchased. Americans began to realize how dependent they were on foreign oil. They looked for ways to conserve energy — solar power, smaller fuel-efficient cars, turning thermostats down, and turning out the lights. This new focus on conservation was a foreign concept to Trailing-Edge Baby Boomers, who up until this time had been used to "having it their way." Now, with the cost of oil and products made from oil, such as plastic, at an all-time high, they had little choice but to get by with less.

The oil crisis, along with defense spending in Vietnam, the high cost of government social programs, rising unemployment, and several recessions only added fuel to the fire. Interest rates reached 20%, and high inflation plagued much of the '70s. After two decades of prosperity, Americans began to feel the pinch of recession. This sparked discontent, which became a part of the psyche of the Trailing-Edge Boomers. Having seen the prosperity that met the coming-of-age years of their older brothers and sisters, this cohort felt ripped off by the world that welcomed them into adulthood. This feeling of having missed out and of being disadvantaged remains with them to this day.

STOCK MARKET TUMBLE

The change in economic fortunes the Trailing-Edge Boomers experienced was more profound than is commonly realized today. Throughout their childhood and as they came of age, the older of the two Boomer Cohorts experienced good times; their expectations that these good times would continue were thus reinforced, and the cohort mind-set that was formed at that time can be seen today in a persistent resistance to begin saving for retirement. Things had been good, and they were going to *stay* good — somehow.

For the Trailing-Edge Boomer Cohort, the money mind-set was much different. The Oil Shock of 1973 sent the economy tumbling: The Standard & Poor's 500 lost 30% of its value between 1973–1975. At the same time, inflation began to resemble that of a banana republic, going from 5% to 13.5% to 18.8%. The *real* interest rate (the prime rate minus the interest rate) hit a record low of – 4%. Under these circumstances, debt as a means of maintaining a lifestyle made great economic sense, and a cohort with a "debt imprint" will never lose it. The Trailing-Edge Boomers aren't savers any more than the Leading-Edge Boomers are, but for different reasons. They assume that money will get even cheaper, that they can always get a loan, take out a second mortgage on the house, get another credit card, and never have to pay the piper.

ERA, AFFIRMATIVE ACTION, AND THREE MILE ISLAND

"The Times They Are A-Changin'," a song by Bob Dylan, was the unofficial anthem of the '60s, but it held true for the '70s as well. The women's movement picked up steam with Roe vs. Wade (the Supreme Court's decision to legalize abortion) in 1973. The Equal Rights Amendment, passed by Congress in 1972, was sent to the states for ratification (it later failed to gain the required two-thirds majority). Wives and mothers went to work in growing numbers, self-defense courses became popular, and feminism became a new rallying point for women. While sexual promiscuity and drug use were all part of the "Make-Love-Not-War" '60s, these things became ends in and of themselves in the '70s, as young people sought out new forms of self-fulfillment and self-expression. Hedonism became an American pastime.

Fads of the '70s and Early '80s

+ Pet Rocks
+ Streakers
+ CB radios
+ Shag carpeting
+ Mood rings
+ Platform shoes
+ Leisure suits
+ Wide ties
+ Wide-collar shirts
+ Annie Hall–look for women
+ Bell-bottoms
+ Hot tubs
+ Solar energy

African Americans also saw many of the civil rights dreams of the '60s come closer to reality. Affirmative action gave many blacks new opportunities and helped them break into the ranks of formerly all-white companies and institutions.

Environmental protests were a big part of the social landscape of the '70s, too. The nuclear meltdown at Three Mile Island, toxic waste at Love Canal, and other environmental disasters only added to the distrust many Americans already felt toward big business and government. It was further evidence of the crumbling of the old social structure, a dismantling that began in the '60s and continued throughout the '70s.

MUSIC "CH-CH-CH-CHANGES"

Popular music took off in every direction in the '70s and early '80s, from disco to hard rock to funk, to glamour rock, romantic ballads, and new wave. Performers as varied as KISS, Elton John, David Bowie, the Village People, Sly and the Family Stone, Queen, the Bee Gees, the Sex Pistols, and the Talking Heads gave audiences much more than a musical concert. Dressed in outrageous costumes (and in some cases, males dressed in high heels and make-up), they gave fans full-scale theatrical performances, complete with light shows, stunts, and dramatic climaxes. At the same time, there was also a move away from flashy stage shows and back to the roots of rock 'n' roll and rhythm and blues. Johnny Cougar (now known to younger audiences by his real name, John Mellencamp), the Police, Bruce Springsteen, and Dire Straits all hit it big with this approach, focusing more on lyrics and music and less on showmanship.

MOVIES AND TV: "YOU'RE GONNA MAKE IT AFTER ALL"

In the '70s, TV brought the major issues of the '60s (race relations, the sexual revolution, and the antiwar movement) into American living rooms with shows such as *All in the Family, Charlie's Angels, The Mary Tyler Moore Show, M*A*S*H,* and the miniseries *Roots. Saturday Night Live* pushed censors to the edge with raunchy humor and profanity. This was just the kind of irreverent, "in-your-face" antics that Trailing-Edge Boomers loved, the Leading-Edge Boomers liked . . . and that older cohorts hated.

Popular movies, including *Star Wars, Apocalypse Now, All the President's Men, Saturday Night Fever, Kramer vs. Kramer, Chinatown* and *Norma Rae,* reflected the move toward a high-tech society, new roles for women, and a growing distrust and disillusionment with the powers that be. They also reflected a yearning — or jonesin' — for innocence lost.

TRAILING-EDGE BOOMERS TODAY

Today, Trailing-Edge Boomers are 36–46, and they still carry with them much of the cynicism from their youth. They are juggling multiple demands, including parenting, step-parenting, and careers, while still trying to carve out time for their own fulfillment. The Snapshot feature shows a Multi-Dimensional Marketing™ overview of the Trailing-Edge Boomers, which we developed using the Lifestage Analytic Matrix™. These Boomers are interested first and foremost in convenience. They are behind the popularity of such new concepts as shuttle services for kids and personal chefs. While they are doing well financially, they tend to spend like there is no tomorrow, buying up electronic gadgets and feel-good products (such as Jacuzzis and aromatherapy products) at a fantastic rate. Their high propensity to consume is no doubt linked to their feelings of having missed out in their youth. Whatever the psychological underpinnings, this group is big on status objects, and they are very competitive. This makes them a marketer's dream! But they are price-conscious and savvy, too, having come of age at a time when people began to question everything.

The Joneser Sound

Bruce Springsteen

Boston

Styx

Bob Seger

Eagles

Seals and Crofts

David Bowie

Elton John

Queen

Jethro Tull

KISS

Village People

Bee Gees

SNAPSHOT OF THE TRAILING-EDGE BOOMER COHORT

Name of cohort:	Trailing-Edge Boomer or Generation Jones
Born between:	1955–65
Coming of age:	1973–83
Age in 2001:	36–46
Population:	49 million ✦ 22%

Key cohort values and concerns:

- ✦ Lonely individualism
- ✦ Cynicism and distrust of government
- ✦ Health and wellness
- ✦ Family commitments

Current and next lifestage:

- ✦ Homeownership
- ✦ Childrearing into teenage years
- ✦ Divorce and remarriage
- ✦ Career changes

Emotions and affinities:

- ✦ Informal
- ✦ Politically ambivalent
- ✦ Overtly materialistic
- ✦ Sexually liberated

Physiographic profile:

- ✦ First markers of aging
- ✦ Acute health conditions

Social activities and lifestyles:

- ✦ Physical fitness
- ✦ Possession experiences

Purchasing behavior:

- ✦ Feeling deprived
- ✦ Convenience
- ✦ Appeal to young kids
- ✦ Price and value

TAPPING THE TRAILING-EDGE BOOMER MARKET

At 49 million strong, Trailing-Edge Boomers make up the largest generational cohort segment of all — nearly one-fourth of all American adults. This group's large size, coupled with the fact that they crave the biggest and best of everything, both for themselves and their children, should put them at or near the top of your target audience wish list. Table 7.1 shows that they bring in more income than the average population ($53,579 versus $43,951 per year), but also spend more ($42,792 versus $36,995 per year). As a result, their net worth falls below the median ($51,000 versus $55,600). This cohort cuts across many markets, because of the multiple lifestages they are in right now. And because they want things to be easy and convenient, they are willing to pay big bucks for convenience products and service, such as pre-cooked meals, errand service, and nannies.

Popular Trailing-Edge Boomer Movies

+ American Graffiti (1973)
+ The Exorcist (1973)
+ Jaws (1975)
+ One Flew Over the Cuckoo's Nest (1975)
+ Saturday Night Fever (1977)
+ Star Wars (1977)
+ Animal House (1978)
+ Grease (1978)
+ The Blues Brothers (1980)
+ The Shining (1980)

TABLE 7.1: TRAILING-EDGE BABY BOOMER/ GENERATION JONES MARKET POTENTIAL

	Age 35–44	Total population
Median net worth (1995)	$51,000	$55,600
Median income (1999)	$53,579	$43,951
Avg. annual expenditures (1999)	$42,792	$36,995

Source: Consumer Expenditure Survey, 1999. Bureau of Labor Statistics

STEP 1: LOOK AT KEY COHORT VALUES AND CONCERNS

As we saw in the last chapter, the Leading-Edge Boomers were highly self-assured, and this manifested itself in two seemingly opposite ways. First, there was the rejection of authority and institutions, and the fervent embrace of causes (because they were sure they were right). Plus, there was the hedonistic embrace of pleasure and self-indulgence (because they were sure they deserved it). The Trailing-Edge Boomers, coming of age in a much harsher environment (and feeling neglected and under-privileged compared to their older siblings), were far less self-confident and focused more inwardly — because they felt they had to look out for themselves first. They, too, distrusted societal institutions, but rather than challenge and try to change them, they tried to figure out how they could personally benefit — "What's in it for me?" Not surprisingly, this attitude is reflected in their key cohort values and concerns.

LONELY INDIVIDUALISM: "DANCING WITH MYSELF"

Because so often during their coming-of-age years Trailing-Edge Boomers did not have a choice in what was happening around them (oil shocks, recession, and so on), many are now seeking greater control in more and more aspects of their lives. This lonely individualism is rein-forced by the belief that they have to take control if they are ever going to succeed. Rather than trust others, they would rather trust themselves.

In the workplace, this often leads to clashes. Jonesers, wanting to make sure everything gets done just so, often get the reputation for being control freaks or micro-managers. As more Trailing-Edge Boomers enter the ranks of middle management, this situation will provide greater opportunities for management and human resource consultants to help companies improve their work environment and boost employee morale.

For marketers, offering Jonesers greater choice and control in their lives will bring big returns. Unlike Generation-Xers, Jonesers typically love to negotiate on price, so they obviously are not prime targets for Saturn's no-haggling policy. But, they are prime targets for Internet websites, such as Priceline.com, eBay.com, and others that allow users to set their own price on everything from groceries to airline tickets.

CYNICISM AND DISTRUST OF GOVERNMENT

When coming of age, many Jonesers initially rejected the idea that marriage and family would satisfy their need for security. They learned to trust themselves — and money. Many Jonesers still carry this attitude with them today. As this generational cohort advances in age, we can expect an even greater emphasis on personal privacy craved ("jonesed") by this group. Internet security will increasingly become an issue in doing business with Trailing-Edge Baby Boomers. And marketers will have to seek new ways to reduce distrust in marketing pitches.

When it comes to politics, the civil rights movement and the Vietnam War created a sense of distrust, but the skepticism and extreme distrust of government didn't fully solidify until Watergate. After Nixon's resignation, it was assumed that whatever was old or established was automatically suspect. Modern-day politicians, including 2000 presidential contender John McCain and his "Straight Talk Express," have tried to appeal to this cohort by focusing on facts, not hype. In fact, all major candidates referred to Generation Jones by name, reflecting the importance of this group in the electorate. While the approach did not get McCain elected to the White House, it prompted Al Gore and George Bush to address key topics of interest to Jonesers and others. But there is a lot of history to overcome here, and it's unlikely that members of this cohort will ever have the trust in public officials that their parents did.

In trying to reach this group, political strategists and marketers of consumer products must provide Jonesers with plenty of facts and information. Sales pitches or campaign speeches based on emotion will have to have a substantive, rational appeal as well, or this cohort won't believe them.

HEALTH AND WELLNESS: "BORN TO RUN"

Health foods, physical fitness, and encounter groups were all the rage in the '70s and '80s when Trailing-Edge Boomers were coming of age. This emphasis on health and wellness still remains with this cohort today. While strapped for time like never before, this cohort still tries to find time to keep in shape and eat well. Even if they don't succeed, they know they should try harder. After all, it is something most members of this cohort value.

As Jonesers continue to age, health and wellness will become even more important during the next 25 years. Marketers can tap into this value and promote health foods, active living, and fitness programs for this cohort for many years to come. Food items need to be marketed with close attention to ingredients consistent with a healthful image. With promotions, spokespersons and models should be consistent with the Joneser image of wellness and fitness. This group has always embraced faddish ways to stay healthy — seaweed diets, avoidance of white wheat, abstinence from sugar, to name just a few — and this kind of approach will no doubt continue into the future.

FINDING TIME FOR THE KIDS

While the '80s and '90s were largely spent climbing the corporate ladder, family commitments are taking on a greater role with Jonesers in the new millennium. Today, more and more Jonesers are beginning to look for ways to balance work life with personal and family life. In 1999, for example, Microsoft's chief technology guru, Nathan Myhrvold — a Trailing-Edge Boomer — announced that he was taking a year-long sabbatical. What was he going to do with all of this free time? Pursue other scientific interests, travel to Europe with his kids, dig up dinosaurs, go fly-fishing, and goof off.[2] After having worked night and day for Microsoft for 13 years, Myhrvold realized there must be more to life than his high-paying job. His commitment to take time away from his career to re-dedicate himself to his children is a growing trend among Trailing-Edge Boomers.

This is true particularly among women. No longer referred to as "housewives," the "stay-at-home mom" is now making a comeback. Shunning old stereotypes that applied to their own mothers, these younger Boomer mothers see themselves as active, intelligent, and involved in their children's lives.

The female counterparts to the stay-at-home moms — those who work full time at outside jobs — are putting in longer hours than ever, leaving men with more responsibilities at home. Sociologists have found that men in their 40s spend nearly four hours more each week doing housework than men 20 years ago, and women do eight hours less each week. Despite these changes, women still do the bulk of the housework. But both men and women are making sacrifices to make sure they have time for family. Many working women are shunning the "Superwoman" designation for "Superdelegator," as more and more are calling for help from nannies, breast-feeding consultants, emergency baby-sitting services, agencies that focus on paying nanny taxes, birthday party planners, kiddie limo services, personal assistants, and household managers. Remember, Baby Boomers of all ages are apt to indulge themselves. We can look for more of these kinds of services in the future, but they will no doubt be geared toward caring for older children as this generational cohort ages.

SUV for Baby, Too

DaimlerChrysler's AG division recently licensed the Jeep name to a line of heavy-duty baby strollers, a move that combines the childrearing lifestage with Boomers' love affair with the SUV. The top model comes loaded with oversized phony chrome tires, fake lug nuts, gearshift, toy radio, and even a horn to drive Boomer parents nuts. This association between Boomer brand and parenting task clearly has the Trailing-Edge Boomer in the cross hairs.

Step 2: Analyze current and next lifestage

As Brad Edmondson, a former editor of *American Demographics,* points out, lifestage is one of the most important predictors of spending patterns.[3] For Trailing-Edge Boomers, who are busy with young families and careers, this means focusing on ways to do more in less time. Conven-ience is key in meeting the many demands associated with the hectic lifestages of today's Jonesers.

Home ownership: Living large

Many Trailing-Edge Boomers are looking for a reprieve from the stress of their daily lives. While vacation travel, dancing, and socializing appealed to them in younger years, they now often find the peace and contentment they crave in their own homes. As a result, houses are getting bigger and more extravagant. And with most consumers purchasing their most expensive homes in their early 40s, this puts Jonesers squarely in the limelight as a marketing demographic to watch.

This inner-directedness and emphasis on living large has pushed housing into the forefront as one of our society's ultimate status symbols. The family home is no longer just a retreat from the outside world, but an entertainment Mecca, shopping mall, workplace, and health club all rolled into one.

This all translates into very good news for contractors, real estate agents, and electronics, home furnishing, and fitness equipment manufacturers and retailers. For Jonesers, price is important, but status reigns supreme when it comes to building and furnishing the family home. This explains why Viking stoves (even for those who don't know how to cook) are now status symbols the way Gucci shoes and Burberry raincoats were for the Yuppies of the 1980s.

Joneser homes of the future could very well include such things as remote access to home information and a refrigerator that tracks contents inside and serves as a video and voice messaging center for the whole family. Other gadgets could include ovens that also act as refrigerators to keep food chilled until cooking starts and a dishwasher that senses when the machine needs repair and then contacts the service via Internet to fix the machine (a convenience-seeking Joneser's dream come true!). These new-age, high tech products are already in development, and they are likely to find Jonesers first in line at the check-out counter. They already are the prime market for at-home spas. In some affluent suburbs, 80% of upscale homes being built include elaborate home gyms. We can expect this trend to trickle down to more and more new homes as the Trailing-Edge Boomers come into their peak earning years over the next decade.

FROM INFANTS TO TEENAGERS

Many Trailing-Edge Boomers fall into the childrearing lifestage, but unlike their parents at this age, some have teenagers at home, while others are becoming parents for the first time. In fact, today's 40-year-old is much more likely to have a newborn than their parents were at the same age. The sexual revolution of the '60s and '70s made having children much more a matter of choice, not chance, leaving Jonesers more control over their lives. For those with children, they want the very best for their kids, and they tend to indulge them with the latest toys and technology.

Country Clubs Get Clubbed . . . by Jonesers with Different Ideas

As we enter the new millennium, only about 4,500 of that well-worn icon of the 1940s — the members-only country club — now remain.

In fact, the *Wall Street Journal* reports that about 500 dropped away during the last decade alone. Some are still thriving, but many are beset with major problems: fading facilities, a change in the tax code disallowing club dues as a business expense, a fall-off in tennis (once a big draw to joining such clubs), and competition from master-planned communities complete with golf courses. But an even bigger factor is that country clubs just don't jibe with Baby Boomers' values — particularly those of Trailing-Edge Boomers.

Many country clubs are living in the past. Some, for example, explicitly state that they are a "ladies' and gentlemen's club," not a "beepers, cell phones, and e-mail establishment." Now that just doesn't mesh with a Generation Jones lifestyle.

Going to some clubs is a lot like stepping back in time to the 1940s. Formal dress codes exist and are strictly enforced, and fly in the face of Boomer's penchant to be casual — all the time! The feminist movement was a Boomer phenomenon of the 1960s and 1970s, but country clubs all too often cordon off

---

To tap into this lifestage, General Motors has teamed up with Warner Brothers to introduce the Chevrolet Venture Warner Bros. Edition minivan. The vehicle, billed as the "ultimate family road trip machine," includes a stereo VCR with remote and an overhead flip-down video monitor so kids can watch their favorite Warner Bros. videos, or play video games while on the road. The package also includes 17 cup holders! Along with customized hardware, customers also receive "VentureTainment" — special access to free Warner Bros. videos, compact discs, discounts at Warner Bros. studio stores, and

parts of the facilities "For Men Only" and have restrictions on women golfers. Racial discrimination still runs rampant in many country clubs. And the thought of paying assessments for "communal responsibilities," such as facility renovations, are antithetical to Boomer individualism.

So what are country clubs doing to stem the tide? Once again, as is far too typical, superficial changes are being made instead of rethinking positioning. For example:

+ The Sequoia Country Club in Oakland, California, has turned to an aggressive recruiting campaign complete with a website.

+ The Country Club of Indianapolis, whose roster of members has included Eli Lilly and Benjamin Harrison, now allows jeans in the clubhouse up until 6 p.m. and holds a back-to-school bingo night.

These quick fixes clearly are no solution. What is needed is a total reassessment of what the country club concept can offer today's Baby Boomer market, from basic positioning all the way through to the tactical activities to achieve it. After all, the Trailing-Edge Baby Boomers will soon reach their peak incomes, and it won't be long before they are empty-nesters with all of the privileges that lifestage brings. It just may be time for the Boomers to enjoy a redefined club concept.

more. The standard Venture minivan with regular wheelbase starts at $20,650, but the extended wheelbase, Warner Bros. Edition can run as high as $28,995. That's quite a difference in price, but Jonesers see entertaining the kids as a top priority, and they are willing to pay the price to ensure their kids have every advantage.

But of course, all of this comes at a price. With Mom and Dad both working to provide the kids with the best money can buy, the kids are often left yearning for the one thing money can't buy — time together. That's where marketers are beginning to realize the real value of this lifestage. By offering Trailing-Edge Boomers the timesaving conveniences they crave, such as personal chefs, errand services, and online banking, they can help this cohort spend more time with their kids.

DIVORCE AND REMARRIAGE: "I GOT YOU, BABE"

Divorce and remarriage are about as common today as cell phones and SUVs. Nearly one out of seven 40-somethings is divorced—twice the rate of 1975. People in their 40s also have high rates for remarriage and blended families. As a result, step-parenting has become a big issue for this cohort. It is estimated that by 2007, blended families will outnumber traditional nuclear families.

Popular TV shows, such as *Once and Again* (starring Sela Ward and Billy Campbell), address the thorny issues of divorce, remarriage, and step-parenting that Trailing-Edge Boomers (and Leading-Edge Boomers, for that matter) are now facing. Blended families are becoming part of the norm, and kids are growing up with multiple sets of parents and siblings. This adds stress for both parents and kids. What do you call such a family? With multiple children taking on fathers' names, a blended family could easily include three or more last names. Then there's the question of "What do I call my step-parent? Dad . . . or Sam? Or, some new-age modification like 'Step-Sam'?" Religion, diet, family finances, and discipline all create new bones of contention that need addressing. The marketplace is ripe for a rash of self-help books and counseling services to help remove these difficulties. And as these issues become more recognized, marketers can construct promotional contexts reflecting these concerns that will promote immediate identification by blended families as a target market.

"I STILL HAVEN'T FOUND WHAT I'M LOOKING FOR"

Career changes are happening at an ever-faster pace as the downsizing of the '90s has left company loyalty at an all-time low. But that doesn't mean Trailing-Edge Boomers are above climbing the corporate ladder. In fact, like Generation X, they are very willing to climb one ladder until they see another ladder that looks more attractive, then they swing from one ladder to the next, pursuing their own inner-directed career path. Job-hopping and climbing the corporate beanstalk have helped Trailing-Edge Boomers increase their wealth over the years, with some striking it rich in the dot-com mania of the late '90s. But the long hours required to succeed in today's corporate environment, coupled with uncertainty about future career direction, have also added to this cohort's stress level.

And for some Jonesers, just as they have begun to accumulate valuable experience under their belts, many employers now see age and experience as liabilities, particularly when trying to implement new technologies or ideas. Youth, speed, and flexibility are today's hot job skills. But Jonesers shouldn't despair. Several studies have found that job performance rises with experience, so there is still plenty of demand in today's job market for experienced Jonesers.

Headhunters, job placement firms, and such websites as Monster.com are already tapping into this lifestage by offering online job postings. This gives Jonesers and others even more flexibility in seeking new career opportunities. Universities and community colleges can benefit by offering skill-building courses, such as computer programming and facilitated leadership classes, for mid-career employees. Long-distance learning, facilitated by the Internet, opens other opportunities. The University of Phoenix, for example, offers bachelor's and master's degrees in a wide variety of fields, with courses attended in large part online.

With most American workers having held an average of nine jobs by the time they reach their mid-30s, financial advisers are also experiencing an increased demand from clients who need help figuring out what to do with their 401(k)s from past employers.

Technology is making it easier to telecommute, and more and more Trailing-Edge Boomers are finding ways to work from home. This saves on commuting time and work-related expenses — such as clothing, dry-cleaning, and in some cases day care — and allows a whole new level of flexibility that appeals to this cohort. The recaptured time and money can then be spent with family.

To serve the growing work-at-home labor force, marketers need to offer telecommuters ways to get out of the house and reconnect with people. Fitness clubs could offer special packages to attract home-based workers, many of whom have the flexibility to work out during the day and make up the time later in the evening. Restaurants could host telecommuter roundtables — monthly or bi-monthly luncheons that would give home-based workers the opportunity to meet and network with new people.

STEP 3: EXAMINE EMOTIONS AND AFFINITIES

In keeping with the "insecure self-indulgence" that characterizes this cohort, Generation Jones is looking for ways to enjoy themselves that don't require too much effort or commitment. This is reflected in their social attitudes and affinities, which tend to be self-focused and quite materialistic (and even to the Leading-Edge Boomers, a bit shallow).

LAID-BACK STYLE

Like their older Boomer counterparts, Trailing-Edge Boomers also enjoy being casual. This includes anything from clothes to entertainment to an overall lifestyle and outlook on life. As with the Leading-Edge Boomers, this is quite a departure from the Postwar Cohort, who grew up with a strict set of rules about proper dress and behavior.

As a marketer, avoid staid, formal approaches in your advertising and marketing materials, and look to incorporate a subtle, laid-back style that taps into Trailing-Edge Boomers preference for casual living. L.L. Bean, Eddie Bauer, and Land's End are good examples of companies that have successfully used this affinity to their advantage.

POLITICS? WHAT'S IN IT FOR ME?

It's no wonder Trailing-Edge Boomers are ambivalent when it comes to politics. After all, they came of age during the end of the Vietnam War, Watergate, and Nixon's resignation — a time when trust in government and politicians was shaken to its core. These events contributed to a feeling that government, politicians, and institutions in general could not be trusted. This public trust never quite recovered, and, in fact, has continued to degrade in the years since.

While broader ideological issues, such as school prayer and flag burning, hold little interest for Trailing-Edge Boomers, issues that directly affect them or their families are hot topics. Examples include educational testing, school reform, gas prices, and healthcare reform.

WANTING THE LATEST AND GREATEST

Because they missed out on the prosperity enjoyed by older Boomers during their coming-of-age years, Trailing-Edge Boomers feel left out. Many have a deep sense of entitlement, and they are now trying to satisfy their unmet needs. As a result, they tend to be much more materialistic than other cohorts, especially when it comes to electronics and gadgetry. While very price sensitive, this cohort is often willing to forego a low price for the right image.

Appliance manufacturers, such as Whirlpool, Maytag, and General Electric, are trying to tap into this preference by offering sleek new designs that include high-end features. Five-burner stoves, space-age refrigerators, fast-cooking ovens, antibacterial dishwashers, and stain-fighting washing machines are just a few of the exclusive products now on the market. These luxury items appeal to Trailing-Edge Boomers' affinity to own the latest and greatest consumer products and technology available. And, lucky for manufacturers and retailers, these luxury models offer much higher profit margins than the basic stripped-down models preferred by older cohorts.

AFTER THE PILL AND BEFORE AIDS

While Trailing-Edge Boomers missed out on a lot during their coming-of-age years, sex was one area where they seemed to luck out. They came of age after the Pill and before AIDS — a blissful time when sex was experienced and enjoyed like a hot fudge sundae. The women's movement and sexual revolution contributed to a growing trend toward sexual freedom among this cohort in the '70s and '80s. Discos, nightclubs, and singles bars provided ample opportunities to meet partners, and one-night stands were often preferred to the commitment of a relationship.

While times have changed for Jonesers since those days, their affinity for sexual freedom remains. Nowadays, it translates into more liberal attitudes toward things such as living together, pre-marital sex, nudity, adult themes on TV, and more. The core audience of the immensely popular series *Sex in the City* on HBO is squarely centered on this cohort.

STEP 4: BUILD A PHYSIOGRAPHIC PROFILE

It's no secret that most people don't look forward to their 40th birthday the way they did their 20th. But physiographics aren't as strong of drivers of attitudes and behavior as they were for older cohorts, since fewer things have started to deteriorate. While cosmetic changes are becoming manifest, there is cause for optimism for the physical state of today's Jonesers as they begin to make their way into middle age.

A "TOUCH OF GRAY"

By the mid-30s, the earliest signs of aging begin to become apparent. Hair begins to gray at the temples, men continue to experience receding hairlines and hair loss, extra weight begins to collect around the mid-section, hearing declines become noticeable for the first time, and vision continues its downward spiral.

The good news is that people 35–44 years old today are much healthier than their parents were at the same age. Deaths from heart disease for this group have dropped by more than 50% in the last 30 years. Cancer deaths have dropped one third. This cohort is less likely to smoke and drink. And doctors say that if today's 35–44-year-olds exercise and eat right, they will be able to minimize aging effects and live happy, healthy lives for decades to come.

Cardiologists have shown that through exercise and a healthy diet, you can reverse age-related declines on a short-term basis even into your 80s. Although strength and endurance will continue to decline, a person can gain the muscle tone and cardiovascular capacity of someone 10–20 years younger. At least 30 minutes of exercise a day will also lower blood pressure, cholesterol, weight gain, and bone loss. Jonesers, who came of age during the fitness craze of the '70s and '80s, are particularly open to this message, and marketers of exercise equipment, fitness apparel and health clubs should use it to their advantage.

Like the Leading-Edge Boomers, this group also wants to look good, so marketers of hair dyes, wrinkle creams, beauty aids, and day spas are likely to find a captive audience with this cohort as well.

As noted in the last chapter, between 1992–1999, cosmetic-surgery procedures increased 153%, with women receiving 10 times more procedures than men. However, male cosmetic surgeries have increased from 55,000 in 1992 to 99,000 in 1999.[4] And 40% of these surgeries are to Baby Boomers. What is most intriguing is that these procedures are increasingly happening at earlier ages. Eyelifts and liposuction have become a cohort rite of passage not just for Leading-Edge Boomers, but for Trailing-Edge Boomers as well. We expect this trend to continue into the future.

ACUTE HEALTH CONDITIONS: "WE'VE ONLY JUST BEGUN"

While most Jonesers typically enjoy good health, high blood pressure and cholesterol levels, arthritis and other acute health conditions often become apparent in the late 30s and early 40s. In addition, annual screenings for breast cancer and prostate cancer also typically begin in one's 40s, and they sometimes turn up positive results.

While acute conditions are not the most prominent health concern of those in the Trailing-Edge Cohort, these individuals will be moving into the 45–55 age category over the next decade. We can expect to see a rising concern for a variety of physical ailments. Arthritis affects 40 million Americans and often begins in one's mid-40s. Heartburn is extremely common at this time and has created a great market for Zantac, Pepcid AC, and Prilosec. You now see advertising for these products that were not seen even 10 years ago. Pfizer has really hit it big with Viagra, just as the Trailing-Edge Boomers begin to cycle into penile dysfunction in large numbers. Because sexuality was such a part of their coming-of-age experience, this group is likely to provide a tremendous market for this drug well in the future.

STEP 5: UNDERSTAND SOCIAL ACTIVITIES AND LIFESTYLES

Trailing-Edge Boomers have reached perhaps the busiest time of their lives. Work and family commitments are pulling them in all directions, leaving them with precious little time for themselves. What free time they do have they spend on activities that reflect their collective vanity (like working out, done more for appearance than for fitness) or their materialism (like buying and displaying things that flaunt their status — a very different buying motive than the search for naturalness and authenticity that characterizes the Leading-Edge Boomers).

"LET'S GET PHYSICAL"

The fitness craze of the '70s and early '80s hit just as many Trailing-Edge Boomers reached their peak coming-of-age years. Jogging, yoga, aerobics, weight lifting, dancing, and other fitness activities were reflected in the popular culture of the day. Movies (*Flashdance, Rocky,* and *Fame*), music ("Let's Get Physical"), and fitness gurus such as Jane Fonda and Richard Simmons all helped fuel an inner focus on getting in shape and staying that way.

Jonesers today may not be as fanatical about staying in shape as they once were, but exercise is still a popular activity among this cohort, and this group tends to be very competitive. This makes them prime targets for fitness club memberships, exercise equipment, and athletic wear. Today, it is Tae-bo and rock-climbing at the club. Tomorrow, it will be some new form of getting or staying in shape. Even though it is well documented that exercise will not add years to your life, body strength, aerobic stamina, and flexibility all make getting around in older age easier and better. So expect all forms of fitness to be embraced by Trailing-Edge Boomers for many decades to come. But also look for new and better ways to treat the aches and pains that accompany this rigorous activity.

THE NEW STATUS POSSESSIONS GAME

As we saw earlier in the chapter, Trailing-Edge Boomers were financially deprived during their coming-of-age years. They were hit with excessive interest rates, high inflation, and an energy crisis. Remember that we value what we don't have when we are in late adolescence and early adulthood. So it's no wonder that they value money and what it can buy. We have seen evidence of this cohort's buying throughout this chapter. Services and products that provide convenience are central. But at the same time, many provide an important benefit in the message they convey about the owner. The Viking stove becomes a centerpiece of a fashionable kitchen, a place for entertaining as well as cooking. An in-home spa provides a stress-releasing experience with friends. A nanny opens up time to enjoy other things. And all of these status symbols convey to others an indisputable sense of economic success and social status.

The cruise industry today commands about 2–3% of the vacation market and has its eye on expanding that to 5%. Its target market is the Boomers. To capture their hearts and wallets, cruise lines are creating enormous floating resorts that offer ships two and three times the size of those built in the 1980s. They offer the ultimate in experiences — pizzerias open around the clock, cigar bars, and spas offering mini-facelifts and loofah treatments. The Royal Caribbean's *Voyager* even features a rock-climbing wall and an ice-skating rink.

You can help fulfill Trailing-Edge Boomers' quest for "possession experiences" like these by offering them novel activities and services that convey the achievement economic success and a high level of social status. Jonesers like nothing better than to talk about these kinds of experiences with friends and colleagues.

STEP 6: INVESTIGATE PURCHASING BEHAVIOR

Because of their large size, busy schedules, and their propensity to indulge themselves with status objects, this cohort represents a tremendous opportunity for marketers on a number of fronts. We think this cohort's tendency to "shop 'til you drop" — easily noticeable today — will persist as the Trailing-Edge Boomers move into old age. Whereas many of the Leading-Edge Boomers may become more ascetic in their later years, the Jonesers seem more likely to remain self-focused and self-indulgent right up to the end.

FEELING DEPRIVED: "IT'S MY TURN NOW"

This cohort has a real sense that it was born too late or too early. As a result, they feel as though they are "have nots" compared to older Boomers and younger Gen-Xers. Marketers can help alleviate these feelings by using messages such as "You deserve it"; "It's your turn now"; and "What you want, when you want it." Give Jonesers the feeling that they are important in your marketing messages. They feel left out and that they deserve more. The answer is in crafting subtle messages to uplift them.

In 1996 and 1997, Nissan aired an award-winning commercial, affectionately known as "toys." The advertisement featured an Indiana Jones–type action figure who falls out of the jaws of a dinosaur into the seat of a tiny sports car and speeds through a living room to a dollhouse to woo a doll that looks like Barbie dressed for tennis. She changes into a miniskirt and hastily jumps into his car as her apparent boyfriend, most likely Ken, watches in astonishment as they drive off and through the legs of an unknown Japanese man, all to the driving music of Van Halen's version of the Kinks' "You Really Got Me." The tagline hits right at the heart of the Joneser — "Life's a journey. Enjoy the ride." Conceptually, the commercial was on target, and even won a Clio for best Commercial of the Year. But Nissan sales did not improve, and the dealers hated the campaign (in part because the featured vehicle — the "Z" — was no longer being manufactured, so they couldn't even sell it) and the commercial was cancelled. This reminds us that no matter how good the marketing and communications, other factors can sometimes undermine a product's success.

Seven Tips for Selling to Generation Jones

- ✦ Persuade Jonesers that your product or service will take the edge off that Jonesin'.
- ✦ Use their music and other nostalgia in your advertising.
- ✦ Advertise on price.
- ✦ Play to Jonesers' feeling of entitlement.
- ✦ Make life easier for Jonesers, or at least make buying your product easier.
- ✦ Give Jonesers control, or the illusion of it.
- ✦ Tap into their sense that they need to seize the day.

Source: Tracy Staton, "Keeping Up With the Jonesers." American Way (15 November 2000): 146 .

TIME IS MONEY

Today's Trailing-Edge Boomers are facing an unprecedented time crunch. They work long hours, hurry home to care for young children and sometimes aging parents, and still try to find time for exercise. Because of their busy lifestyles, convenience is a key factor.

The need for convenience carries over to nearly every aspect of Jonesers' lives, and it provides a real marketing opportunity. Many grocery stores are now implementing new technology to improve and shorten the shopping experience. Kroger, for example, is a leader in installing self-automated U-Scan Express lanes. At these self-serve lanes, customers check out their own groceries, and pay a machine rather than a cashier. While customers have to do all of the work themselves, including bagging, these kind of devices give them more control over their time, which is of prime importance to Trailing-Edge Boomers. Next on the horizon is a device that will scan a whole cartload of groceries at once, similar to a metal detector, and then deduct the cost from a pre-paid grocery card. Already appearing are products such as the Mobil Speed Pass, which uses transponder technology to record and bill a gasoline purchase simply from the act of filling the tank, or a food purchase picked up in the drive-thru lane.

Even health insurance companies are tapping into this preference for convenience. Blue Cross and Blue Shield of South Carolina, for example, has customized its fulfillment program to better meet the needs of busy consumers. Instead of sending prospective clients huge packages of information that explain all of their programs and policies, they ask callers to answer a few quick questions, which allows them to tailor packets to fit callers' specific needs. In the end, this approach saves time, and has helped increase sales leads by 32%.[5] In addition to being a generational cohort value for the Jonesers, convenience naturally comes to the surface as one ages. As we get older, we feel we deserve a hassle-free lifestyle. The combination of the aging and cohort effects suggest that convenience is going to be a magnified "driver of behavior" for this cohort for decades to come.

SOMETHING FOR THE WHOLE FAMILY

We saw earlier how cruises are building in "possession experiences" to their voyages. But they are using more than experiences to lure the Jonesers. In the past, cruise lines focused on attracting middle-age to older couples or singles. But as we've pointed out in earlier chapters, the cruise industry is changing. These days, many cruise lines have switched gears and are marketing their "kid appeal" in an effort to attract Joneser families who want to indulge themselves and their kids while on vacation.

Disney Cruise Line is giving customers the option of combining a "magic voyage" to the Bahamas with "Walt Disney World fantasy and fun." Something for the whole family is the key marketing message here — and it works with Jonesers. Premier Cruise Line's Big Red Boat promises "the perfect summer vacation," with five different programs for kids aged 2–17, 25 youth counselors on every cruise, baby-sitting service until 2 am, a teen disco, a fun foods kids' menu, a video arcade, and more. And for Mom and Dad, there's "seven-star" hotel and dining service, a full casino, concerts, shows, and Godiva chocolates on the pillow each night. What more could a family ask for in a vacation? Many more marketers can take a cue from this industry. Supermarkets and other retailers can offer value by accommodating the desires of the entire family.

"LET'S MAKE A DEAL"

Jonesers love to haggle, and they love a bargain. As a result, they are particularly open to using the Internet to find the best deal. Some are even using websites to do their grocery shopping. Shoppers can also pre-pay their grocery bill over the Internet before picking up their groceries at the store. Or, if customers prefer, some grocery sites can deliver them to their door. Besides saving money, online shopping also saves valuable time — two things at the top of the list for most Trailing-Edge Boomers.

Advertisements, such as car ads, that emphasize low interest-rate promotions are particularly appealing to this cohort. And Expedia.com's TV ads that show an arrow pointing to a four-star hotel for $400, and another arrow pointing to a four-star hotel less than a block away for $225 also catch the attention of this group. Emphasize price and value in targeting Jonesers and your efforts are likely to get results.

FUTURE OUTLOOK: ON THEIR WAY UP

As Jonesers move into middle age, they will bring their free-spirited spending attitude with them, and will become an even more dominant force in our marketplace. Over the first decade of the new century, they will reach their peak income years, and empty-nest households are expected to increase 19% — twice the national average. And once the kids have gone, we expect these two-paycheck families to go on a spending spree. With time and money and the cohort value for "having," they should create a viable market segment.

Spending will increase on household items as nests are refeathered, and recreational second homes will continue to be in demand. The biggest leap in spending by this group will be healthcare, transportation and entertainment. Per capita spending on things such as food will increase, which will mean good news for gourmet food businesses, high quality fresh foods, and restaurants. Marketers will be well served to remember the value of convenience.

We believe that as the Leading-Edge Boomers reach retirement years, they will begin extracting funds from IRAs, 401(k)s and mutual funds. This will be somewhat offset by the Jonesers who will begin to funnel savings into their retirement. However, because the Trailing-Edge Boomers have not accumulated the wealth that their predecessors did, they will have less to add to these retirement funds. At the same time, we believe that the financial difficulties they wrestled with while coming of age will foster a greater anxiety about their financial security in later life. But will they do anything about it? We think not. The "spend-it-all-and-then-borrow-to-spend-some-more" philosophy that was imprinted during their coming-of-age years will persist. We're seeing it today in record lows in savings rates and record highs in personal bankruptcies. We believe that in their 50s, they will be no greater savers than the Leading-Edge Boomers are.

Trailing-Edge Boomers will continue to exhibit their individualism. They will redefine the products and services that they need and desire as they make their way through middle life. They will still be focused on their careers. Yet with more time and fewer financial responsibilities associated with childrearing, they will look to indulge themselves as their older Boomer counterparts have done. We expect continued emphasis on leisure time pursuits and on building "pleasure" into their jobs — more flextime, sabbaticals, exercise at the worksite, and the like. Self-indulgence will be central to their existence.

As they move into the grandparenting lifestage, the Jonesers will be "jonesin'" for their grandchildren more than the Leading-Edge Boomers can be expected to. But they will look to build into this role a sense of their own self-fulfillment and self-expression. Grandchildren will be integrated into their lifestyles, rather than focusing on the wants of the children.

The Jonesers will look for more and more security in their face-to-face and online transactions. They will expect meticulous attention to detail in marketing communications and in guarantees for product performance. They will also seek greater privacy. They are already besieged with invasions of it today as technology promotes one-to-one marketing. We expect a backlash of sorts where concerned groups rally together to call for more stringent rules on keeping their lives more private. Already the government is mandating strict privacy disclosure requirements, and the marketplace furor about Doubleclick's plan to merge Internet browsing behavior with demographic databases almost put them out of business. But while Jonesers are savvy consumers, they are still Boomers. Expect them to spend, and spend big, as long as marketers meet their requirements.

CONCLUSION: JONESERS DESERVE THE ATTENTION THEY "JONES" FOR

In both numbers and buying power, Trailing-Edge Boomers represent a tremendous opportunity for marketers of consumer products and services. This cohort has been neglected too long, and it's time they were given the attention they so badly crave. As you have seen in this chapter, they are as different from Leading-Edge Boomers as they are from Generation-Xers. Sure, they share some similarities, but they are a unique cohort unto themselves — a fact that is just now gaining awareness. But because their specialness is not so well known, it offers an open strategic window for the astute marketer willing to listen to the particular preferences and demands of this generational cohort. Multi-Dimensional Marketing can help you do precisely this. To get you started, we have put together a list of tips on how to begin to connect with this overlooked segment in Table 7.2. With these Jonesers soon coming into their high discretionary spending period, they certainly deserve the attention they "jones" for.

TABLE 7.2: HOW TO TAP THE TRAILING-EDGE BABY BOOMER MARKET

Cohort values	✦ Show their feeling of being robbed of their collective identity — they see themselves as "the next best thing" to their older Boomer predecessors.
	✦ Show less optimistic beliefs about their financial circumstances when compared to the older Boomer Cohort.
	✦ Reflect their distrust of government and other institutions.
	✦ Show their tension between the fading hopes of the '60s and the emerging cynicism of the '70s.
	✦ Depict them as spenders.
	✦ Characterize them as realistic idealists with concerns for practicality and results.
Lifestages	✦ Key on lifestages: Homeownership, childrearing into teenager years, divorce and remarriage, and career changes.
	✦ Show their desire to escape from the routine of childrearing.
	✦ Show Joneser mothers as multi-dimensional women who are pressed for time.

◆ Depict their need for success and meeting the challenges of their careers and lifestages.

◆ Show their focus on career and moving up the ladder of success.

Emotions and affinities	◆ Appeal to overt materialism; what's in it for me?
	◆ Provide a sense of novelty in their lives — a need to change and experience the unusual.
	◆ Show their appreciation for modern technology.
	◆ Reflect their liberal attitude toward sexual behavior.
Physiographics	◆ Combat their first markers of aging — hair graying, hair loss, and weight gain, with cosmetic products and/or cosmetic surgery procedures.
	◆ Accommodate for onset of acute health conditions such as high blood pressure and cholesterol levels, and arthritis.
Social activities and lifestyles	◆ Reflect their enjoyment of competitive rivalry and testing of one's skills through exercise and possession experiences.
Purchasing behavior	◆ Key on convenience — speed of delivery, ease of payment.
	◆ Use messages such as "You deserve it," "It's your turn now," and "What you need, when you want it."

ENDNOTES

1. Jonathan Pontell, "Why the name 'Generation Jones.'" GenerationJones.com.

2. "A Genius Breaks Away — Microsoft's chief technology guru takes a leave to dig up dinosaurs, go fishing and just plain goof off." *Newsweek* (14 June 1999): 55.

3. Brad Edmonson, "Do the Math." *American Demographics* (October 1999): 50.

4. Claudia Kalb, "Our Quest to Be Perfect." *Newsweek* (9 August 1999): 52–59.

5. Kendra L. Darko, "Shaking the Blues." *American Demographics* (October 1999): 47.

CHAPTER 8

THE GENERATION X COHORT

When the term "Generation X" first entered into our collective consciousness with the publication of Douglas Coupland's 1991 novel by the same name, the media went into a kind of frenzy for a few years. Here was a whole generation of self-interested "slackers," they proclaimed, working at McJobs, and lacking any real motivation to better themselves. This was a new generation distinctly different from the Baby Boomers — and that somehow made them suspect. They were hard to define, and so they became known as Generation X — where X meant generic, meaningless, different from the mainstream. Many in this cohort resisted the label. They didn't feel like a part of any larger cohesive group then, and many still don't today. But there are some clear commonalties that bind them together.

This generational cohort grew up at a time when mothers were entering the workforce in droves and divorce rates were skyrocketing. They were casualties in the upheaval of social change that began in the late '60s and continued on into the '70s. Then, as they begin to come of age in the mid-'80s and early '90s, the stock market crashed,

Reaganomics pushed the national debt to new heights, AIDS ruined sex, and suddenly the future lost its rosy allure. It seemed there was nothing left to look forward to.

Much has been made about the so-called "slacker" image of Generation X. But as media interest in this cohort has faded and the group has matured, they seemed to have outgrown the original stereotypes (if they were ever really true to begin with). This cohort clearly has received the most negative publicity of all. Some have blamed this on Boomer resentment. *New Republic* columnist and Boomer Michael Kinsley wrote:

> *X-ers are right to suspect that boomer complaints about them are based largely on resentment. No one was ever supposed to be younger than we are. Every generation feels that way; but probably none ever milked the Young Idea as successfully as the boomers did in our time.*
>
> *These kids today. They're soft. They don't know how good they have it. Not only did they never have to fight a war, like their grandparents, they never even had to dodge one.*[1]

Marketers also rushed into the fray, organizing Gen-X focus groups in a frantic attempt to get their hands around this amorphous cohort. Some of these efforts to tap into Generation X have fallen far short, while others have clearly hit the target. Online brokerage house Ameritrade struck gold, for instance, with its 1999 offbeat TV campaign that featured Stuart, a goofy, 20-something office boy who takes a break from photocopying his face for a party flyer to introduce his boss, Mr. P., to the world of online trading. When Mr. P. finally makes his stock selection and presses the send button, Stuart says, "Let's light this candle," and grinds his hips in a hilarious gyrating dance. The ad, which has been aired mostly on cable networks, hits home with Gen-Xers (and N-Gens, too, for that matter) because it uses humor to show them as brilliant, but misunderstood — a message many Gen-Xers identify with. It was an approach that worked with this cohort, and helped Ameritrade boost the number of its online customer accounts by about 40%.[2]

DEFINING MOMENTS: GLOOM AND DOOM

The oldest Baby Boomers grew up in secure, two-parent households. Generation X grew up with divorce and working mothers. The oldest Baby Boomers watched the first manned space walk. Generation X watched the *Challenger* explosion. The oldest Baby Boomers came of age during prosperous times. Generation X inherited a declining economy and a huge national debt. Boomers had free love. Generation X had AIDS. It all seemed so unfair to the 42 million Americans who were born from 1966–1976 and who came of age from 1984–1994. The promise and opportunity that had met previous generational cohorts as they entered adulthood had vanished by the time Generation X arrived on this threshold. Of course, the Baby Boomers also had Vietnam and the Kennedy Assassination, but Xers tended to focus on their own misery.

Gen-X Defining Moments

+ Reaganomics

+ AIDS crisis

+ *Challenger* explosion

+ Stock market crash of 1987

+ Fall of Berlin wall

+ Gulf War

REAGANOMICS: THE RICH GET RICHER

With double-digit inflation and high unemployment rates, the late '70s were a dismal time for the United States economy. When Ronald Reagan took office in 1981, he immediately set to work cutting taxes and social programs, while increasing spending on defense. "Reaganomics," as it was called, seemed to run counter to commonly held views about how to jumpstart a stalled economy. While Reaganomics did help to reduce interest rates and inflation, and resulted in millions of new jobs, it left a large percentage of Americans behind. The rich got richer and Wall Street went along for the ride, but the middle class and the poor stood still, or worse yet, fell behind. During the next 10 years, homelessness became a new social issue, and the number of children living in poverty increased to levels not seen since before Lyndon Johnson's Great Society. At the same time, by the early '90s, the national debt reached $4 trillion, leaving those just coming of age — Generation X — feeling like the race had already been lost before they ever got a chance to run. A feeling of bitterness began to emerge among the nation's youth. One protest group called Third Millennium, which was comprised of angry Gen-Xers, issued the following declaration in 1993: "Like Wile E. Coyote waiting for a twenty-ton anvil to fall on his head, our generation labors in the expanding shadow of a monstrous national debt." To make matters worse, Gen-Xers who graduated from college in the early '90s entered what was the worst job market since World War II.

AIDS CRISIS: FROM FREE LOVE TO SAFE SEX

The free love of the '60s and the Sexual Revolution of the '70s and early '80s disintegrated with the discovery and public awareness of acquired immune deficiency syndrome (AIDS) in the mid-'80s. Suddenly sex held even graver consequences than just the threat of pregnancy or venereal disease — death was now a part of the equation.

Although AIDS started as a disease that affected mostly homosexual men, it soon spread to the heterosexual population as well. Because AIDS awareness coincided with their formative coming-of-age years, the disease forever changed attitudes about sex among Generation X. So-called "safe sex" became a part of their lexicon, and free condom distribution made its way into many students' high school and college experiences. At a time when sexual experimentation and discovery were supposed to be the norm, fear, anxiety, and uncertainty seemed to over-shadow every sexual experience. Like other defining moments, AIDS has left a lasting impact on Gen-X attitudes and values.

CHALLENGER EXPLOSION: INNOCENCE LOST

By 1986, the launch of the space shuttle had become routine, even passé, for many Americans. For the previous 5 years, astronauts had successfully completed more than 20 missions. So the announcement that the space shuttle *Challenger* would include the first ordinary citizen, Christa McAuliffe, a social studies teacher from Concord, New Hampshire, helped to raise interest in the flight. While in space, McAuliffe, a mother of two, would appear in live broadcasts beamed to schools around the country via satellite. The flight started off as usual. But a little more than a minute into it, a booster rocket failed, igniting the rocket's external fuel tank. The *Challenger* exploded in a flash of light that instantly killed McAuliffe and the rest of the seven-member crew. Americans watched the explosion on TV in shock and horror. Because of the public interest in the flight, the viewing audience also included a large number of Gen-Xers who watched the flight on TVs in their classrooms. Like most Americans, they had taken the safety of manned space flight for granted. Now, they realized there were no guarantees.

STOCK MARKET CRASH OF 1987: BLACK MONDAY TAKES ITS TOLL

Junk bonds, mergers, leveraged buyouts, and hostile takeovers were the parlance of Wall Street in the early and mid-1980s. The Dow Jones Industrial Average more than tripled in five years. But bull markets don't last forever. The high-flying stock market that characterized much of the '80s came suddenly crashing to a halt on Black Monday — October 19, 1987 — when the market lost 22.6% of its value in a single day. It was the largest crash on record.

Greed also got the better of some traders in the '80s. By 1985, investigators for the Securities and Exchange Commission uncovered evidence of insider trading, fraud, stock manipulation, and other securities violations against Michael Milken and Ivan Boesky. The two became symbols of the greed that seemed to permeate the '80s.

FALL OF BERLIN WALL: THE NEW WORLD ORDER

Changes and reforms that swept the former Soviet Union beginning in the mid-'80s opened the floodgate to reform in the rest of Eastern Europe later in the decade. In 1989, the Berlin Wall, which was erected in 1961 to separate Communist, totalitarian East Berlin from free-market, democratic West Berlin, came tumbling down — figuratively, if not literally. Millions of East Germans poured over the wall and visited the West for the first time. Along with the destruction of the Berlin Wall came a call for reunification of the long-divided Germany.

The momentous opening of the Berlin Wall was a sign of hope for Generation X, which up to that point had experienced a string of mostly negative defining moments. Here was a glimmer of something brighter for the future, the beginning of a so-called New World Order.

GULF WAR: SMART BOMBS AND CNN

In January 1991, a U.S.-led coalition of 32 countries unleashed a massive air war against Iraq in retaliation for Iraq's invasion of Kuwait five months earlier. Millions of Americans watched Operation Desert Storm unfold on TV in the comfort of their own homes. CNN ran around-the-clock coverage, and the world was mesmerized. In fact, Iraqi President Saddam Hussein followed developments in the war the same way Americans did — watching CNN. In Hussein's case, the only difference was that he watched from his bunker underneath Baghdad. Suddenly terms such as surgical strikes, smart bombs, and Scud and Patriot missiles made their way into our vocabulary.

The war, which lasted less than two months, was unique for a number of reasons. For starters, it was very short. Secondly, it was very strategic and "surgical" in nature, not messy like Vietnam. Highly advanced missile systems were used to pinpoint strategic bombing targets, thus minimizing civilian bloodshed. Thirdly, because no draft was needed, it did not affect the American public as deeply as past wars had. Still, although many Gen-Xers served in Desert Storm, a larger number stayed home and watched the drama unfold on TV. For those at home, the war hardly affected them at all. It was just another violent confrontation between good and evil, just like the ones they saw in the movies, on TV, or in video games every day. And it was not on their soil like the attack on the twin towers on September 11, 2001.

POPULAR CULTURE: "SMELLS LIKE TEEN SPIRIT"

Popular culture from 1984–94 reflected Gen-Xer's growing disenfranchisement from a system they felt had failed them. They felt cheated, and this disillusionment was reflected in popular music, movies, books, TV shows, and fashions of the time.

Music was eclectic and all-encompassing, and it was not unusual for Gen-Xers to enjoy the hard rock sounds of Van Halen and Guns N' Roses, rap's L.L. Cool J and Ice T, and alternative artists such as Pearl Jam and Nirvana.

In the early '90s, "grunge" fashions emerged as a typically Gen-X look. It included such things as stained, ripped and/or faded jeans, earth-toned flannel shirts, and messy hair. It was just one more way for Xers to say, "Hey, we're different."

Most TV shows of the era focused on Boomers — *thirtysomething, Magnum, P.I.,* and *Moonlighting.* But a few shows, such as *The Simpsons* and *Beavis and Butt-Head,* reflected the edgier, free-agent mentality of Gen X. Other shows, including *Friends,* reflected Gen X's struggle with career, family, and relationships. And *The X-Files* tapped into Xers' distrust of authority. MTV was another popular form of entertainment, and that network's 1991 creation of *The Real World,* in which a group of diverse 20-somethings were chosen to live together in a house or apartment wired with microphones and cameras, marked the beginning of so-called reality TV. This appealed to Xers because it was unscripted and totally spontaneous . . . or so it seemed.

Popular Gen-X TV Shows

+ The Simpsons
+ Beverly Hills 90210
+ Melrose Place
+ Cops
+ The X-Files
+ Friends
+ Beavis and Butt-Head
+ Married with Children

Popular movies, including *Terminator, Rambo,* and *Die Hard,* showed a growing desensitization toward violence among young adults. On the big screen, killing was entertainment. Other movies, such as *The Breakfast Club, Sixteen Candles, Pretty in Pink, Ferris Bueller's Day Off,* and *Reality Bites,* spoke to the frustration, hopelessness, and disappointment Gen-Xers faced as they came of age. But all of these except *Reality Bites* focused on high school issues; attempts to create a true coming-of-age movie for Gen X, like *The Big Chill* was for the Boomers, fell completely flat. Movies such as *Reality Bites* and *Slacker* addressed important coming-of-age issues, but because Gen X resisted being categorized, these movies turned out to be box office disappointments.

Books were not particularly big sellers among Gen-Xers. The news media lamented the fact that young people were the least likely of all to read newspapers or magazines (see Figure 8.1). In an attempt to attract them, some newspapers devised special Gen-X sections that talked about everything from body piercing to the latest bands to how to find a job. It was an attempt to make what was going on in the rest of the world somehow relevant to this demographic. The efforts met with mixed success, because as a generalization, the Xers just weren't very interested in "The News." "Why should I give a s — about that stuff, dude? . . . I got my own problems!" With the rise of the Internet, if and when Xers did want to check out the news, they could do it online and have up-to-the-minute reports of world events. This has made the daily printed newspaper practically obsolete with younger readers.

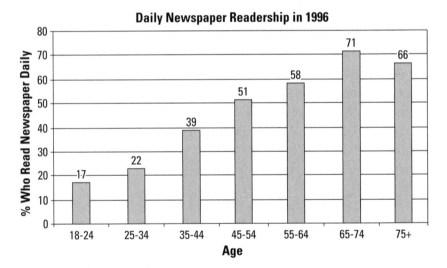

Figure 8.1.

GENERATION X TODAY: FREE AGENTS ON A MISSION

After the overblown slacker hype of the early '90s faded away, the Generation X Cohort has gone quietly about its business, eventually moving out of Mom and Dad's house, quitting their McJobs, and finding their way onto a real career path, many in high-paying, high-tech fields. This cohort is delaying marriage and children even longer than the Leading-Edge Boomers or Jonesers did. But when they finally do make commitments, they tend to keep them. They are taking marriage and family responsibilities much more seriously than many of their own parents did.

While they can be extremely hard workers, they still tend to be free agents, putting their own interests ahead of the team or company. They also tend to put the their personal lives ahead of work, which has run some of them into trouble at the office. They tend to clash with Leading-Edge and Trailing-Edge Boomers over values, and just about everything else.

Boomers feel Xers are whiners, who are unwilling to pay their dues and show the deference to authority Boomers feel they now deserve. Xers feel Boomers are self-righteous, materialistic control freaks who had their fun at other people's expense and spend way too much time politicking at the office. At the same time, though, Gen-Xers are proving that they are much more competitive than the old stereotypes allow. They made extreme sports, such as bungee jumping, snowboarding, sky surfing, and mountain biking, new (and lucrative) fads, and are now starting their own businesses in record numbers. Many of these businesses are of the dot.com variety, a trend that correlates with this cohort's coming-of-age affinity for high-risk activities.

As a whole, this group lacked the optimism and idealism of older generational cohorts during their coming-of-age years, and that is most what they crave today. Despite their tendency to separate from the rest of society, as they have gotten older, they have seen the value that comes with being a part of a community. And yet, they don't really see themselves as part of a generational community the way the Boomers did. In fact, many seem to resent the Xer label and see it as irrelevant, particularly now that they are full-blown adults with real jobs and families. The Snapshot feature shows a Multi-Dimensional Marketing™ overview of the Generation X Cohort, which we developed using the Lifestage Analytic Matrix™.

Gen-X Movies

✦ Back to the Future
✦ The Breakfast Club
✦ Die Hard
✦ Field of Dreams
✦ The Firm
✦ Forrest Gump
✦ Indiana Jones series
✦ Pulp Fiction
✦ Reality Bites
✦ Slacker
✦ Terminator
✦ Wayne's World

SNAPSHOT OF THE GENERATION X COHORT

Name of cohort:	Generation X
Born between:	1966–76
Coming of age:	1984–94
Age in 2001:	25–35
Population:	42 million ✦ 19%

Key cohort values and concerns:
- ✦ Free agency and independence
- ✦ Friendships important
- ✦ Acceptance of violence and sex
- ✦ Street-smart
- ✦ Pursuit of quality of life
- ✦ Cynical about future

Current and next lifestage:
- ✦ Graduate school
- ✦ Career search
- ✦ Cohabitation
- ✦ Marriage
- ✦ Homeownership
- ✦ First child

Emotions and affinities:
- ✦ Environmental concerns
- ✦ Social, sexual, and ethnic diversity
- ✦ Sexually cautious
- ✦ Global community

Physiographic profile:
- ✦ Invincible
- ✦ Earliest signs of aging

Social activities and lifestyles:
- ✦ Drinking with friends
- ✦ Technology-oriented
- ✦ Alternative religions

Purchasing behavior:
- ✦ Price conscious
- ✦ Internet buyers
- ✦ Credit card users

SNAPSHOT

TAPPING THE GENERATION-X MARKET

Gen X is considerably better off today than they were a few years ago. The economy has improved, and they have seen their economic situation improve as well. They have always been somewhat materialistic, at least when it comes to high-tech products, such as TVs and computers, and now they finally have the money to indulge themselves. About half are married and are part of dual-income households. They average more than $36,000 each year in expenditures — nearly as much as the total population average (see Table 8.1). But they are in the acquiring stage of life, where homeownership is a priority, and furniture, cars, baby equipment, and so on, are all necessities. This spells big bucks for marketers if you can figure out how to appeal to this hard-to-reach cohort.

TABLE 8.1: GENERATION-X MARKET POTENTIAL

	Age 25–34	Total population
Median net worth (1995)	$10,700 (under 35)	$55,600
Median income (1999)	$42,470	$43,951
Avg. annual expenditures (1999)	$36,158	$36,995

Source: Consumer Expenditure Survey, 1999. Bureau of Labor Statistics

STEP 1: LOOK AT KEY COHORT VALUES AND CONCERNS

Some have likened this cohort's pessimism about the future to that of the Depression Cohort. For both cohorts, their key values were formed during bad economic times and there seemed to be little room for improvement. While there are similarities between the two cohorts, Generation X shows a much greater sense of independence than the Depression Cohort and is willing to take much greater risks than the older cohort ever imagined.

FREE AGENCY AND INDEPENDENCE: A PIONEERING SPIRIT

A large percentage of this cohort grew up as latchkey children, due to divorce or both parents working full time, so they learned at an early age the importance of taking care of themselves and looking out for number one. This has carried over into their adult years as well. As this cohort has entered the job market and been forced to work on teams with older cohorts, their free-agency and independence has not been particularly welcomed. In fact, many Leading-Edge Boomers and Jonesers have seen this independence as a threat. They look at Xers and say, "What's wrong with you that you won't be part of the team?" But this is exactly why such characters as Ameritrade's Stuart are so popular among this cohort.

Gen-X Icons

Although not all are Xers, these people typify the Xer temperament — edgy, anti-establishment free-agents with a bit of an attitude.

Jim Carrey

Kurt Cobain

Tom Cruise

Michael Dell

Tonya Harding

Anita Hill

Michael Jordon

Madonna

Shaquille O'Neal

Queen Latifah

Bart Simpson

Quentin Tarantino

Thelma & Louise

Mike Tyson

Generation-Xers have always been more focused on individual achievement rather than loyalty to a team, and their pioneering spirit and rebelliousness has run them directly into conflict with Boomers. Because of Gen-Xer's free-agency, they have looked to build marketable skills in the workplace as soon as they could, and many have gone on to become self-employed entrepreneurs. In fact, Xers are starting companies at a faster rate than any other age group. A 1993 study by Marquette University and the University of Michigan found that people between the ages of 25–34 created 70% of all start-up businesses.[3]

The World Wide Web has become a Gen-X growth industry. Gen-Xers Jerry Yang and David Filo, founders of the web search engine Yahoo!, exemplify this entrepreneurial spirit, as does Laurie McCartney, founder of babystyle.com, a website that targets maternity fashions and baby clothes to expectant mothers. In fact, the majority of dot.com companies seems to be the brainchildren of Xers, reflecting this cohort's free-agency and pioneering spirit. The future will no doubt bring even more innovative and out-of-the-box Internet offerings, as well as Gen-X acceptance of new ways to buy and consume. To reach this cohort in the coming years, successful marketers will need to create an older, wiser Stuart, who has a real job and family responsibilities.

FRIENDSHIPS IMPORTANT: "SOMEBODY TO LEAN ON"

Because a large number came from divorced families, many Gen-Xers learned during their coming-of-age years that you couldn't necessarily count on family, but you could always count on friends. The TV sitcom *Friends* popularized this image: When all else fails, your friends will always be there to help. With this cohort, people and personal relationships almost always take precedence over most other interests, including corporate goals, job advancement, and civic obligations. The importance of friends in personal relationships contributed to Xers' marrying late, and may be a factor in their divorces — nights out with friends are still of very high importance, regardless of what a spouse may feel.

Gen-X Fads

+ Backward hats
+ Baggy clothes
+ Body piercing
+ Grunge look
+ MTV
+ Rap music
+ "Safe sex"
+ Stirrup pants
+ Tattoos
+ Valley girls

Gen X also was the first cohort to be born into an integrated society. As a result, they are more likely to have friends of different races than do older cohorts. In addition, they are much more racially diverse themselves. Only about 70% are white versus 77% of Baby Boomers.

Promotional campaigns for retailers, such as the Gap, Banana Republic and Old Navy, often depict young people of various cultural and ethnic backgrounds socializing together. This image appeals to Xers and reflects an acceptance of cultural diversity not seen in older cohorts. But image is not enough. These retailing forces are already beginning to experience trouble as Xers are straying from these once-popular retailers. To recapture market share, clothing makers need to reconnect with Xers desire for independence and more professional, yet up-to-date, styles, while still reflecting the key values of their coming of-age-years.

CYNICAL ABOUT FUTURE: "REALITY BITES"

Even though times have changed and the economy dramatically improved between the late '80s and early '90s and the early months of 2000, Gen-Xers still are cynical and pessimistic about the future. They can't help it.

It is one of those coming-of-age experiences they just can't shake. The 1994 movie *Reality Bites,* in which Winona Ryder plays a struggling Gen-Xer trying to make a living while staying true to her inner vision, is largely about a group of young adults who feel cheated by history. A series of negative defining moments, coupled with an ongoing stream of public scandals, including Iran-Contra, Clarence Thomas–Anita Hill, and Whitewater, just to name a few, have made Gen-Xers lose hope in public officials and government in general. One survey even found that 53% of Gen-Xers thought the soap opera *General Hospital* would outlast Medicare. And, if allowed, 59% of this group would prefer to opt out of Medicare and save on their own.[4] They also don't tend to trust the media, corporations, or anyone in a position of authority. While many are cynical about institutions, Xers tend to be very proactive about their own personal situations. In their book, *Rocking the Ages,* J. Walker Smith and Ann Clurman point out that 96% of surveyed Xers agreed with the following statement: "I am very sure that someday, I will get to where I want to be in life."[5]

Because they are cynical about the future, Gen-Xers are taking financial matters into their own hands at a much earlier age than did Leading-Edge Boomers or Jonesers. They tend to sign up for 401(k)s at a higher rate than older cohorts, and they are participating in IRAs, health savings accounts, and other tax-free investment accounts in droves. In all, they make up about 20% of all investors. Many feel they won't be able to count on pensions or Social Security, so they are planning for the worst possible scenario and setting up their own financial contingency plans for retirement. A marketing appeal based on the premise "Nobody's going to take care of you but *you* — better start preparing now!" would resonate with this cohort sentiment.

STREET-SMART: BAG THE HYPE

This cohort is very aware of being marketed to, and tends to be very street-smart when it comes to advertising. Oversold sales pitches full of hype fall flat with this group. They need to be spoken to in a way that says, "You're different. We respect that." Chrysler's Neon's "Hi" campaign, which showed the car with the simple message "Hi" written above it, was very effective with Xers mainly because it dropped all pretensions and talked directly to the customer in a non-threatening way. It also offered a car that was cute, fun-looking, fuel-efficient, and low-cost. In 1994, Xers bought 39% of all Neons, spending about $623 million.[6] This helped to make Neon one of the top five cars in the entry auto market. Saturn has had similar success using low-impact sales techniques, and focusing on a personalized approach and quality customer service. That's all Xers are really looking for.

While Boomers tend to respond to ads that make them look attractive or rich, or somehow enhance their image, Xers want no part of this ego-boost. "Cut the crap and give us the facts," they seem to be saying. But some advertisers, trying to be hip and tap the Gen-X crowd using grunge-themes have failed miserably. Subaru's grunge ad in which it said its cars were "like punk rock" fell flat with Xers.

You Can't Be Too Careful

"Generally speaking, would you say that most people can be trusted, or that you can't be too careful in dealing with people?"

Age	You can't be too careful	Most people can be trusted
Total	61%	34%
18–24	67%	27%
25–34	69%	27%
35–44	58%	37%
45–54	55%	40%
55–64	60%	36%
65+	59%	34%

While over-hyped and "in-your-face" ads don't work with this group, what does work with Gen-Xers are ads that include humor, music from their coming-of-age years, subtlety, irony, irreverence, and unexpected twists.

PURSUIT OF QUALITY OF LIFE: "HAVE SPOT, WILL TRAVEL"

In her book, *The Postponed Generation*, Susan Littwin says that most Generation-Xers — even those who grew up middle class — have a sense of entitlement that rivals that of children of the very rich. She writes, "They put great emphasis on the self, dislike answering to others, believe that things will somehow work out for the best, that their fantasies will come true. . . ."[7] In some ways, this sounds similar to the Baby Boomers — the difference being that with the Boomers, their expectations for the most part worked out just as they hoped. But for Generation X, just the opposite is true of their coming-of-age years. Now, they are part of a Boomer backlash that puts quality of life ahead of just about everything else. They have come to realize that enjoying life offers rewards not found on the corporate ladder.

In an attempt to tap this cohort, automakers — including Ford, General Motors, Volvo, and others — are redesigning their cars and their marketing strategies to fit in with Gen-X values. Ford, for example, introduced its new Focus with a variety of custom packages aimed squarely at Gen X and N-Gens. One is called "Have Spot, will travel." It offers a safety seat for pets, an air purifier, and a lint brush to clean dog hair off the seats. Other packages include the Sony Focus, which includes a 450-watt sound system, and Kona Focus, which comes with a customized mountain bike.

ACCEPTANCE OF VIOLENCE, SEX: "WHATEVER"

Generation X grew up surrounded by sex and violence on TV, so it is no wonder they are desensitized to it. It does not shock them like it once did older cohorts. They accept it as just another form of entertainment. In fact, about 75% of Xers describe themselves as heavy viewers of violence on TV.[8]

The music that Gen-Xers experienced during their coming-of-age years took a turn toward violence, and included much more graphically sexual themes. This was driven in part by the increasingly pervasive influence of inner city mores on popular culture, and continues to this day. This cohort saw the beginning of a new music rating system that prevented young teens from buying CDs that were considered too violent or sexually graphic. Groups as diverse as Public Enemy, Nine Inch Nails, and others all found their creative work slapped with the labels, which only made them more attractive to Gen X and younger audiences.

Products, but particularly promotions, can and do reflect this "at the edge" value. The music and movies just noted are product examples. The Calvin Klein ads of the '90s that displayed unusual sexual innuendos, such as a stack of naked bodies where you could not tell which arm fit with which leg and which torso, is one example. Benetton's death-row ad campaign, which featured the faces of death row inmates without mentioning their crimes or their victims, is another example. We can expect more advertisers to push the envelope of acceptability in coming years as they try to shock and engage Gen X and younger audiences.

STEP 2: ANALYZE CURRENT AND NEXT LIFESTAGE

In many ways, the lifestages in which Gen X now finds itself are not that much different than those of previous cohorts at the same age. The difference is that Gen X is waiting longer to get married, buy a house, and have children.

GRADUATE SCHOOL: THE REAL WORLD CAN WAIT

This cohort has achieved record high levels of education. In fact, in 1997, two-thirds of all students graduating from U.S. high schools went on to college. That represents an increase of about 20% since 1978. And this trend is expected to continue well into the future as N-Gens graduate from high school, and pursue higher education.

Having graduated from college at a time of high unemployment in the early '90s, many Gen-Xers decided to delay the real world and go to graduate school. Many are now finishing up advanced degrees and are finding the job market much more lucrative, if they are in engineering, computer science, or business, although less so for those in the liberal arts.

These grads are prime targets for apartment rentals, homes, household consumer goods, cars, and other necessities of life. High-end products are also big with this demographic. They have sacrificed for years, and now want to splurge and treat themselves to the good life. Messages that imply "You've earned this" will go over well for Gen-Xers leaving this lifestage.

For those just starting out in grad school, they have several more years of austerity ahead, therefore offering little opportunity for big-ticket sales. However, they still offer very real opportunities for marketers of typical college student purchases, such as casual clothes, fast food, and alcohol.

CAREER SEARCH: TIME TO BE ME

Unless they've opted to go to graduate school, most Generation-Xers are securely into their first career by now. What's unique about this group, though, is that their career search may never be over. In their minds, corporate loyalty is a relic of the past. To remain on top, Gen-Xers know they have to seize marketable job skills quickly, and then move on for better opportunities. They have no illusions about what the company is going to do for them long-term. After all, in their coming-of-age years, many saw their parents believe such promises, and then get downsized with a single chop of the corporate ax. While the Boomers and older cohorts may be ending their careers in cynical disillusionment about employer loyalty, the Xers are starting theirs that way.

This cohort wants more from a job than just a paycheck, and they are less interested in moving up the corporate ladder than in gaining new job skills that they can take with them elsewhere. They also change jobs not just for money, but for more time off to pursue their true interests, which, by the way, usually aren't work-related. With the low unemployment rates of recent years, the economy has worked to their advantage. Many now demand — and get — four weeks of vacation, the option to take time off without pay, flextime, the option to telecommute a few days a week, and the possibility to job share.

For employers looking to attract Gen-Xers, emphasize your company's fringe benefits, flexible working environment, generous vacation packages, and mentoring program. Company social functions or perks that require them to socialize with customers don't impress Xers. Rather than fly first class, many Gen-Xers would prefer to fly coach and pocket the difference.

COHABITATION: "THAT'S THE WAY LOVE GOES"

For most Gen-Xers, living together is a necessary lifestage before marriage. Of course, their parents don't like it one bit (even if they are Boomers), but they are learning to live with the idea. Having survived the aftermath of their parents' divorce, Xers know how devastating that lifestage can be and they want to avoid it at all costs. These days, almost half of all married people under 35 lived with their spouse before marriage. And, according to demographer Susan Mitchell, most people under 35 are likely to see cohabitation as a trial marriage — an opportunity to try the relationship on for size before making a lifelong commitment. "The low rate of marriage among young adults is partially offset by cohabitation," Mitchell writes in her book *Generation X: The Young Adult Market*. "Just because young adults are unmarried doesn't mean they are 'single.'"[9]

Having Children Out of Wedlock Is Growing Trend

While childbearing within marriage continues to be the norm, having a child as a single parent is a growing trend.

Since 1975, the percentage of children born out of wedlock has more than doubled. In 1992, 3 out of every 10 children were born to unwed or single parents compared to 1.4 in 1975.

Dewar's, maker of Scotch whisky, used this positioning to appeal to younger audiences. Its print ad shows a young 20-something female getting dressed for her professional job, while her boyfriend lies in bed with a pillow over his head. The copy appeals directly to Gen-Xers by acknowledging that they are successfully handling adulthood, so why not an adult drink, too? For Gen-Xers in the cohabitation lifestage, the lack of a lifetime commitment to a relationship also carries over to a lack of interest in establishing a permanent household. As a result, the marketing implications of this lifestage bode well for leases and rentals, including real estate, furniture, and household appliances.

MARRIAGE: "DO THE RIGHT THING"

Gen-Xers are delaying marriage longer than even the Boomers. Why? Because they are afraid — afraid of failing at marriage the way so many of their parents did. They are cautious about commitment and don't want to put their own kids through the pain of divorce. Today, about half of all Gen-Xers are married, but that number is expected to increase dramatically in the next few years as more and more Gen-Xers reach age 30. Since 1970, the average marriage age in the United States has increased from 23 to 27 for men, and from 21 to 25 for women.

Gen-Xers are looking to have fun in their early 20s, then settle down with the right mate and start a family in their 30s. Some marketers have described this cohort as nostalgic for the stereotypical family life of the 1950s: the one they've seen on cable network Nickelodeon's "Nick at Nite," where classic sitcom Moms and Dads are focused on hearth, home, and kids. While Gen-Xers idealize the childhood Boomers were supposed to have had, however, they want no part of the Boomer marriage and parenting models; they see them as self-serving.

Holiday Inn Taps into Boomerang Lifestage

On average, today's young adult leaves the family nest between the ages of 22–24 — much later than young people did 20–30 years ago. Even so, about half of all young adults will return home at least once. This boomerang phenomenon first became popular during the late '80s and early '90s — about the time when Gen-Xers were coming of age.

Most were either planners, who lived at home to save money before getting married, to save to pay off college debts, or to buy consumer items; or they were strugglers, who lived or returned home because they were unable to make it on their own (most often they suffered a failed relationship), but with no plans for moving out. Although most Xers have by now successfully flown the coop and have moved out of the boomerang lifestage, the recent downswing in the economy has somewhat prolonged its existence for this cohort.

Holiday Inn has tapped into this lifestage in its recent TV ad campaign. In one ad, a late 20s boomerang son walks into the living room and announces that he believes that his frequent-flyer miles were used by the family in the past and announces that he now thinks that he deserves brand-name merchandise for his donation to the family. He then walks over to the big-screen TV and asks his father to help him move it up to his room. His mother looks at him and says, "What does this look like, the Holiday Inn?" amid great laughter by his parents and grandmother. This add clearly targets young Xers still living at home and older Xers now living on their own, who remember all too well the added years they spent with Mom and Dad.

While Gen-Xers are delaying marriage longer than older cohorts, they seem to be more committed to making it work. As a result, we think the future will show a lower divorce rate for Gen-Xers than for older groups. After all, we tend to value most that which we lacked when coming of age. And for Xers, this was a happy, stable family environment.

To appeal to Xers in this lifestage, show young couples and young families enjoying spending time together. Blue Cross and Blue Shield's recent series of print ads uses this approach to connect with young parents. One ad, for example, shows a young, hipply dressed Xer father lying on the floor, sharing a laugh with his young son. The copy subtly implies that, unlike your own parents, you can choose to do what's right and in the best interest of your child.

HOMEOWNERSHIP: "LITTLE PINK HOUSES"

As they did with marriage and childrearing, Generation-Xers are also entering homeownership later than previous cohorts. Thanks to low interest rates and a soaring U.S. economy through the late '90s, Gen-Xers have finally begun to move into the homeowner lifestage. A growing number are even building brand-new houses. According to the Joint Center for Housing Studies at Harvard University, new household formations among Gen-Xers increased from 19.1 million in 1995 to 19.3 million in 1997.[10]

With homeownership, they've learned, come responsibilities and increased spending on mundane items, such as lawn equipment, household tools, and home repairs — all things previously handled by the landlord. This increase in spending on household equipment makes Gen X look particularly attractive to hardware stores, home superstores, and other home supply outlets. To attract this crowd, Home Depot, Lowe's and other home superstores have started to offer free home improvement mini-courses. This appeals not just to the Boomers and Jonesers, who also have an independent do-it-yourself streak, but to Xers as well. It gives them everything they want from a store — information, quality, a wide selection of products, and low prices.

For realtors and homebuilders looking to strike it rich in the Gen-X market, high-pressure sales tactics will not work with this cohort. A straightforward, genuine approach with a truckload of information is your best bet. That's why the Internet has become such a popular first stop for many Gen-Xers in their search for a home: They can avoid the sales pitch and get straight to the information they need to make a decision.

FIRST CHILD: AND BABY MAKES THREE

Many Xers are also delaying having children, wanting to first fulfill their own personal goals and make sure their marriage is going to stick before bringing kids into the picture. With the birth of the first child, responsibilities shift dramatically away from the self and on to the child. In this respect, Xers are no different than the millions of other people who have gone through this lifestage before them. However, they tend to be more committed to not screwing up with their kids. They know what it is like to be left aside, either through their own experience or that of their friends, and they don't want their own children to have to suffer the consequences.

The transition to parenthood is no longer marked by a retreat of mothers to the domestic sphere. Instead, it has become increasingly acceptable and even expected for women to continue to be breadwinners in addition to their new role as caretaker. As women continue to make important contributions to the family budget even after making the transition to parenthood, their role as breadwinner will continue to grow in importance.

For parents who do choose to stay home with the kids, the term "homemaker" has taken on less of a stigma than it did when Boomers were new parents. For this group, "stay-at-home moms" are increasingly likely to be "stay-at-home dads," and they are busy taking the kids to play groups as well as pursuing their own interests.

For Gen-X parents, online retailers who make it easy to buy baby items, children's clothes, and toys through the Internet are likely to win big with this group.

STEP 3: EXAMINE EMOTIONS AND AFFINITIES

Many of the social attitudes and affinities shared by Generation X are based on their coming-of-age experience during a time of uncertainty and lost hope about the future. At the same time, they grew up when the world was becoming a smaller place, so many of their attitudes reflect this globalization.

ENVIRONMENTAL CONCERNS: SAVE THE PLANET

This cohort is very concerned about the environment. Key events during their coming-of-age years, including the Exxon Valdez oil spill, the Chernobyl nuclear disaster, discovery of holes in the ozone layer, worries about global warming, and more emphasis on recycling, have helped raise awareness about the need to protect the environment among Gen-Xers.

Because of their heightened environmental sensibilities, this cohort will reward companies that appear to be making an effort to save the environment. As a result, to appeal to this group, marketers must be increasingly concerned with such things as recyclable packaging, the use of pollution-free ingredients, and reducing paper use to save trees.

Sweetheart Cup Co. and EarthShell Corp., for example, have teamed up to produce biodegradable food packaging for McDonald's and other restaurant and food service customers. Unlike most food packaging, which is made of plastic, this new packaging material is made from potato starch, calcium carbonate, and limestone. It is biodegradable, recyclable through composting, and it disintegrates in water once its coating is cracked. This environmentally friendly packaging is just one example of the kind of effort that is likely to be well received by Gen-Xers.

SOCIAL, SEXUAL, AND ETHNIC DIVERSITY: NOT AN ISSUE

Generation X is one of the most ethnically diverse cohorts of all. School segregation was a thing of the past by the time Gen-Xers entered the educational system. Most went to school with kids of all races and religions, and grew up thinking social and ethnic diversity was just a part of everyday living. As a result, Gen-Xers tend to be very accepting of people who are different from them with regard to sexual orientation as well. That gays have come out of the closet and now organize appearances in St. Patrick's Day and Halloween parades, as well as work in the next cubicle, is just the way the world is. Of course, there are exceptions. Some Caucasian Gen-Xers, as diversity widened, sought solace in splinter white supremacists groups, such as the skinheads and neo-Nazis. The pop singer Eminem — although mainly appealing to the N-Gen age group — embodies many of these sentiments in his lyrics, including homophobia. But in general, this is by far a small minority.

In advertising to Gen X, be sure to depict ethnic and religious diversity as much as possible. As mentioned earlier in this chapter, Calvin

Klein, the Gap, and Benetton have used this approach very successfully in recent years. Ikea, the inexpensive home furnishing chain, has run a series of television commercials featuring gay men shopping together, generating much publicity and presumably increased sales.

Sexually Cautious: "Let's Talk About Sex"

AIDS threw a monkey wrench into the sexual exploration of Xer's coming-of-age years. Sure, they were sexually active in their late teens and early 20s, but they worried more — not just about pregnancy and venereal diseases, but about the consequences of being infected with HIV and dying of AIDS. They were the first generation taught to have candid discussions with prospective sexual partners about their sexual pasts, which has a tendency to bank the fires of passion. But being the pragmatists that they are, Gen-Xers took the threat of AIDS seriously, and they still tend to be sexually cautious.

Global Community: "We Are the World"

While Xers don't really see themselves as part of a generational community, they do see themselves as part of a global community. The Internet, TV, movies, music, contact with other cultures through their own travel, and growing diversity within their peer group have all contributed to this feeling of being part of something larger.

As discussed later in Chapter 10, "Taking Generational Cohort Analysis Global," we have begun to see a convergence not just in fashions and musical tastes among younger cohorts, such as Gen X and N-Gens, but in lifestyles and values, too.

In targeting this group, appeal to their sense of living in a global community by showing people from different countries, cultures, and religions. Coca-Cola did this with the "I'd like to buy the world a Coke" commercial targeting first the Boomers in the '60s, and then reprising it for the Xers (as well as appealing nostalgically to the original target) with a sequel in the late '80s. Gen-Xers realize that they are just one part of the ethnic puzzle, and they are interested in learning about people in other parts of the world who may or may not share their same values.

Step 4: Build a Physiographic Profile

This cohort really doesn't know what it's in for when it comes to physiographics. As a result, marketers will have to wait a few more years until Xers reach middle age to cash in on this factor.

INVINCIBLE: NO FEAR

Gen-Xers are still young, so like most young people, they feel invincible. This leads some individuals to self-destructive behavior: binge drinking, psychoactive drugs, bungee jumping, tanning, and tattoos (which carry a substantial if largely unrecognized risk of transmitting Hepatitis C). Some are just now reaching their physical peak, while others are just past it. As a result, physiographics now plays little role in their lives. If anything, Xers are probably more likely to exercise and work out in order to help attract a mate. To tap into this feeling of invincibility, focus on messages that emphasize physical fitness and being in the prime of life.

EARLIEST SIGNS OF AGING: "BABY GOT BACK"

Despite their youth, the oldest Gen-Xers are just now beginning to notice the earliest signs of aging — receding hairlines is one example common among Gen-X men. This cohort is beginning to show interest in Rogaine and other hair loss remedies, but are not yet the heavy users that Boomers are.

Another consequence of getting older is that the junk food and snacks their bodies used to burn up with impunity now take longer to metabolize. As a result, many Gen-Xers are beginning to notice a few extra pounds around the middle. While some Gen-Xers are aware of why this is happening and have already made adjustments to their exercise routines and eating habits, most are not thinking seriously about the long-term health effects of eating Taco Bell, Pizza Hut, and McDonald's everyday for lunch. McDonald's offering salads for lunch and dinner is an attempt to anticipate an attitudinal change in this area, since it won't be long before the old kinds of eating habits catch up with the Xers.

STEP 5: UNDERSTAND ACTIVITIES AND LIFESTYLES

Gen-Xers tend to be very peer-oriented. As a result, social activities with friends tend to rank high on their list of priorities. They are also exploring new activities through the Internet — meeting new friends in chat rooms, and exploring new lifestyle options, such as job sharing and religion, via the web.

DRINKING WITH FRIENDS: HAIR OF THE DOG

For younger members of Generation X, drinking and going out to bars and nightclubs are often some of their favorite pastimes. This is pretty typical for most young adults of any cohort. But once the novelty of reaching 21 and being able to legally buy alcohol wears off, most people's alcohol consumption tends to back way off. Also, as responsibilities at work and home increase, it gets harder and harder to disguise a hangover and be effective.

While Gen-Xers like to party and have a good time with friends, most tend to take drunk driving seriously. This is largely due to stricter enforcement of drunk-driving laws, and educational efforts by organizations such as Mothers Against Drunk Driving and Anheuser-Busch. Anheuser-Busch's efforts have included national ad campaigns and more than a dozen community-based programs that discourage drunk driving and underage drinking, and promote the responsible use of alcohol by adults. The company's Budweiser Designated Driver Holiday Sweepstakes, for example, rewarded consumers for their efforts to select a designated driver. The interactive media promotion was held from Thanksgiving to New Year's Day, and used a variety of techniques, including an online sweepstakes entry form, outdoor billboards, print ads, and radio spots. Local Anheuser-Busch distributors have also reinforced efforts to promote responsible drinking by distributing literature to parents about underage drinking, training bartenders in responsible serving techniques, providing free cab rides home, and by paying for ads in local newspapers, on billboards, TV, and radio. These efforts have not gone unnoticed by Gen-Xers, many of whom came of age when awareness about responsible drinking was becoming more of a social obligation.

TECHNOLOGY-ORIENTED: FROM PAC-MAN TO THE WORLD WIDE WEB

This generational cohort grew up with video games, Nintendo, and the personal computer. Gen-Xers were some of the early adopters of the Internet and have no fear when it comes to technology. They are very willing to shop online and use the Internet as a tool to make their lives easier.

Gen-Xers like to stay on top of the latest technology, whether that be cable modems, the Internet, cell phones, electronic messaging, pagers, and so on. Because Xers are so technology-oriented, they respond well to web advertising. But keep in mind that they rely on friends' advice for many of their purchasing decisions, and they prefer cold, hard facts to overblown advertising hype.

Their technology focus has led many Gen-Xers to lucrative careers in information technology and the Internet. This has been their ticket up from slackerdom.

Online brokerage houses, sports providers, and other dot.coms are working hard to attract Gen-Xers. They are taking their message direct to this cohort through off-beat and humorous TV ads. Ameritrade's Stuart has been a huge success, and E*Trade is now getting into the game with a series of ads that poke fun at traditional brokers. One asks, "If your broker is so smart, how come he has to work?" A police officer is shown stopping a broker for speeding, confiscating his golf clubs, and sending him back to the office to work harder.

To grab a larger share of the Gen-X online sports market, Fox Sports Online has come out with a series of spoof situations that border on being politically incorrect. For example, in one ad, an elderly man struggles to get his medicine out of a cabinet, while his 20-something caregiver is absorbed with Fox Sports Online. When the man drops his pills, the caregiver rolls his eyes in irritation, but never once looks away from the computer screen. This is obviously not the kind of ad that would appeal to Postwars and older cohorts, but it seems to strike the funny bone of Gen-Xers, particularly male sports fans.

ALTERNATIVE FAITHS: "LOSING MY RELIGION"

As we have already pointed out, Gen-Xers don't tend to enjoy structured group activities. This holds true for organized religion as well. While many consider themselves spiritual and have a personal belief in God, they are reluctant to commit themselves to a single church or religion. Catholic theologian Tom Beaudoin, a Gen-Xer himself, has surmised that many Gen-Xers are finding spiritual themes outside of church in popular culture, such as popular music, music videos, and movies. For example, music group R.E.M. talks about "Losing My Religion," and rock singer Joan Osborne asks, in effect, if there is a God. Also, religious and spiritual websites are springing up all over the Web.

More than half of those aged 25–34 say they have no doubts that God exists, but only 21% attend religious services regularly. This poses serious problems for mainstream, organized religion, which relies on the tithes of regular churchgoers to remain afloat. Some churches are organizing less-ritualistic, more informal services in hopes of appealing to Gen-Xers and N-Gens. Others assume that Gen-Xers will return to the fold when they want their children baptized. While attending church regularly is not popular among Gen-Xers, alternative religions and spirituality are in.

STEP 6: INVESTIGATE PURCHASING BEHAVIOR

Gen-Xers are very willing to shop online and are more likely to use credit cards than cash. This group looks for ease, convenience, and value in deciding what to purchase — brand loyalty tends to be very low, and they do not buy for status. They are very cynical and street-smart about advertising, and will deride messages that hit a false note with a vengeance. As a group they are undermarketed to — yet they are just now entering high-need lifestages for big ticket items, and can be a lucrative target for the marketer that "cracks the code."

PRICE-CONSCIOUS: ONLINE AUCTIONS

Generation X is one of the most financially conservative and pragmatic cohorts since World War II. This stems from their coming-of-age years, when they found good jobs next to impossible to find, or saw friends, relatives, and parents downsized.

Many Gen-Xers grew up helping busy parents with the shopping, so they learned at an early age to clip coupons and look for the best value. They are still very price-conscious, and have little brand loyalty. They look for the best quality at the lowest price, but they aren't exactly frugal. Like Boomers, they want to indulge themselves, but they are not so taken in by image and the perceived status owning a certain high-end product will give them. This has caused concern among many high-end clothing and jewelry retailers, who expected to court Silicon Valley's new Gen-X dot.com millionaires the same way they did older cohorts. But this new breed of millionaire (so many of whom are gone in the dot.com crash of 2000–2001) often shuns image over substance — they prefer casual clothes and inexpensive watches to trendy togs and timepieces from Versace and Tiffany's.

To appeal to this group, emphasize value and getting a good deal. These messages will take you further with Gen X than a lot of phony, hyped-up sales pitches.

INTERNET BUYERS: MAKE IT EASY, THEY WILL COME

Because this cohort is so comfortable with technology, it was a logical next step for them to be some of the earliest consumers to buy online.

While going to the shopping mall appeals to younger cohorts, who see it as a social event, for Gen-Xers, who are increasingly busy with careers, family, and pursuing their own interests, Internet shopping is a useful way to do more with less time. Many Xers love to shop the Internet for the best deals, making sites such as Priceline.com, eBay.com, and other online auction sites popular outlets for Xer purchases. If you make it easy for them to buy online, they will come.

CREDIT CARD USERS: EASY MONEY

Credit cards, debit cards, and ATM cards are just another set of convenience tools for Generation X. They feel comfortable using plastic, mainly because credit card companies have aggressively recruited them since high school, and in some cases, even earlier. As a result, many Gen-Xers have multiple cards and carry a high level of debt. Unlike their grandparents or some of their parents, they are not accustomed to waiting to buy things they want or need. Credit cards are an easy way to get what you want now.

Some are having a hard time paying off debts, contributing to a rising rate of credit card delinquency and bankruptcy among people in their 20s and 30s. To make matters worse, many also still have a large number of student loans to pay off, and this also contributes to their high debt loads. In fact, Gen-Xers carry the highest debt at their age than any previous cohort.

While some Gen-Xers have acted irresponsibly with credit cards, others are even more fiscally responsible than their older Joneser brothers and sisters, and have already begun to save for retirement in a big way. After all, they have no illusions that Social Security will be there to support them in their retirement. This group is very financially literate and prefers to manage its own money rather than having a large company do it for them. Online investment firms, such as E*Trade, Ameritrade, and GenX Invest, appeal to the self-empowerment Gen-Xers crave. These firms make online trading fast, easy, and cheap, without any of the hefty fees, commissions, and investment advice of the old-school brokerage houses.

FUTURE OUTLOOK: SLACKERS NO MORE

Generation X is sandwiched between two larger cohorts — the Boomers (both Leading-Edge and Trailing-Edge) and the N Generation. Both these two groups dwarf the Xers in size, and see themselves as belonging to a large cohesive group that shares similar values. Xers, meanwhile, tend to fight being typecast and are often hard to predict. As a result, advertisers often sidestep Xers and focus their efforts on Boomers and N-Gens, who they see as offering a bigger bang for their buck. But Xers also offer very real opportunities for marketers.

As Xers have begun to move out of their coming of age years and into the adult lifestages of marriage, childrearing, and homeownership, they have more and more money to spend. They still rely on the buying patterns developed in early adulthood — and, like other generational cohorts, these will remain with them for life. They struggled early in their adult years, but have proven that the slacker image of their youth was nothing more than an overblown stereotype.

The future will see Gen-Xers continuing to dominate the infant and toddler market for a few more years as they continue to spend much more than the average household on such items as baby food, equipment, and toys. Other sectors likely to benefit include consumer electronics, furniture, travel, and casual clothing.

The current trend toward mass customization — being able to order clothes, salads, sandwiches, cars, shoes, and so forth exactly as you want them — is very appealing to this cohort. It taps directly into their affinity for individualism. As this group gets older, expect this "tailor-made approach" to continue to extend into such areas as retirement plans, benefit packages, healthcare, and an even wider range of consumer products.

Because Xers tend to have closer relationships with their parents than Boomers did (at least to the single parent that many of them grew up with), they are more likely to remain involved with them as adults. Similarly, because of this relationship, their parents may come to rely on them more in coming years as they get older and need help. Unlike Boomers, who often feel resentful about being pulled away from fast-track careers by their aging parents' needs, Xers are more likely to see eldercare as their chance to hold up their end of the bargain: It's a way for them to help re-create the stable family relationships so many of them yearned for when they were growing up.

As far as marriage goes, the future looks bright for Xers, many of whom have tried hard to avoid the pitfalls their own parents made. Xers are looking for more of a balance between work and family life than what Boomers have achieved, and chances look good that they will be able to do it. As marketing strategist Karen Ritchie writes in her book, *Marketing to Generation X:*

> *By delaying marriage until education is complete and careers have been established, they are increasing the economic stability of the future marriage. They are delaying the birth of their first child, which also helps to maximize resources. Both partners expect to work and to share in household chores, and that will make for less stressful partnerships.*
>
> *As a result, young married couples should enjoy greater financial security, more discretionary income, less conflict, and more stable marriages than Boomers. Generation X may, indeed, achieve its goal of marriage for life.*[11]

CONCLUSION: OPPORTUNITIES ABOUND

Generation X is more independent and technology-focused than any older cohort, but like other cohorts, they, too, require special care and handling when it comes to marketing. They are unique and they want to be treated as such, without any of the glitzy advertising ploys that worked so well for older cohorts.

This cohort is entering its busiest lifestages yet, with full-time work and family obligations topping the list. This poses a unique opportunity for marketers who are willing to take time to get to know this hard-to-classify cohort. Our advice is to provide Gen-Xers with goods and services that help to simplify their lives, thus giving them time to pursue their interests and to connect with family.

But this can be tricky. This group is very in-tune to hype, so proceed with caution. Use humor and offbeat approaches, and avoid Boomer status games at all cost. Xers will respond to genuine, artful, and funny ads that acknowledge their free-agency and pursuit of a higher quality of life. Also, use the Internet and other multimedia formats to tap into this group's penchant for high technology. See Table 8.2 for more how-to specifics.

Successful marketing to Gen X requires that you find a straight-forward way to convince young adults to buy your highly functional, totally practical, extremely affordable, and somewhat indulgent product while not offending them. Simple, right?

TABLE 8.2: HOW TO TAP THE GENERATION-X MARKET

Cohort values	◆ Depict their desire to be entrepreneurial in career pursuits and not confined to the career imprisonment of their parents.
	◆ Acknowledge free-agency by showing them as independent and doing their own thing.
	◆ Show you "understand" them by referencing the cynicism around sex and violence.
	◆ Reflect the importance of friends.
	◆ Avoid hype in ads; focus on "just the facts."
	◆ Help them obtain the security needs that came from seeing parents downsized.
	◆ Characterize their dogged pursuit of quality of personal life.
Lifestages	◆ Show them in early-adult lifestages — grad school, career search, cohabitation, marriage, homeownership, and birth of first child.
	◆ Show their lack of satisfaction with work.
Emotions and affinities	◆ Reflect their focus and fulfillment from family, not their job.
	◆ Show their environmental concerns.
	◆ Show them as part of a "world family," not just their native country.
	◆ Show their acceptance of cultural diversity — racial and sexual.

Physiographics	✦ Reflect their high energy and strong bodies at the top of their physical form.
	✦ Depict their feeling of invincibility and "no fear."
	✦ Offer them a healthier-eating alternative, but in a less regimented fashion than for older cohorts.
Social activities and lifestyles	✦ Show technology as a way of life.
	✦ Avoid references to organized religion and group orientation.
Purchasing behavior	✦ Position on price and value.
	✦ Use Internet to make shopping easy, and to provide detailed information about your product or service.

ENDNOTES

1. Michael Kinsley, *Generations Apart: Xers vs. Boomers vs. the Elderly,* edited by Richard D. Thau and Jay S. Heflin. Prometeus Books: Amherst, N.Y., 1997.

2. Rebecca Buckman, "Rock On! 'Stuart' Rules as Web Trader." *The Wall Street Journal* (7 December 1999): sec. C, p. 17.

3. Warren Cohen and John Simmon, "A new spin on the economy." *U.S. News & World Report* (8 May 1995): 54–55.

4. Margot Hornblower, "Great Expectations: slackers? Hardly. The so-called Generation X turns out to be full of go-getters who are just doing it — but their way." *Time* (9 June 1997): 58.

5. J. Walker Smith and Ann Clurman, *Rocking the Ages: The Yankelovich Report on Generational Marketing.* Harper Business: New York, 1997.

6. Warren Cohen and John Simons, "A new spin on the economy." *U.S. News & World Report* (8 May 1995): 54–55.

7. Susan Littwin, *The Postponed Generation: Why America's Grown-Up Kids Are Growing Up Later.* Morrow: New York, 1986.

8. Margot Hornblower, "Great Expectations: slackers? Hardly. The so-called Generation X turns out to be full of go-getters who are just doing it — but their way." *Time* (9 June 1997): 58.

9. Susan Mitchell, *Generation X: The Young Adult Market.* 2nd ed. New Strategist Publications: Ithaca, N.Y., 1999.

10. Boyce Thompson, "X marks the spot." *Builder* (November 1998): 19.

11. Karen Ritchie, *Marketing to Generation X.* The Free Press: New York, N.Y., 1995.

CHAPTER 9

THE N GENERATION COHORT

Most studio buyers who saw *The Blair Witch Project* at the Sundance Film Festival in early 1999 were not impressed. In fact, some walked out in the middle of it, annoyed by the film's low-budget cinematography, which included jumpy, hand-held camera shots, out-of-focus and grainy footage, and scratchy audio. The movie chronicles the experience of three film students who disappear in the Maryland woods while shooting a documentary about the legend of a local witch.

When the film — which was shot for an initial cost of about $30,000 — became the summer box office smash of 1999, Hollywood execs just scratched their heads in disbelief. Here was a low quality movie that broke all of the rules. In fact, it looked a lot like a bad home movie. It bypassed the typical Hollywood distribution and marketing channels and went straight to its target audience — teens and young adults.

Directors Daniel Myrick and Eduardo Sanchez purposely sought the low-budget documentary effect. They felt that the poor quality somehow made it more authentic and more immediate. Artisan Entertainment eventually picked up the film for $1 million at the Sundance festival, and then put another $15 million into marketing it to teen and young adults. A key element of the marketing plan was the Blair Witch website, which was packed full of bogus historical research about the Blair Witch legend, fake newspaper articles, a fabricated diary of one of the students, and even a fake interview with one student's mother.

Myrick and Sanchez had initially marketed the film via the Internet to people interested in the occult and a core audience of independent film aficionados. Artisan built on this base, making the movie seem like an extension of the website, rather than the other way around. To attract younger audiences, Artisan also focused its marketing efforts on building "anti-hype hype" — they posted missing persons flyers on college campuses (so-called "wild postings") just before school let out, leaked "news" about the film to websites and MTV, ran trailers that included nothing but a blurry shot, a scream and a stick figure, and worked with the Sci-Fi channel to develop a "mockumentary" about the Blair Witch legend. All of these efforts were beneath the radar of typical Hollywood big media pushes, which made the movie all the more attractive to young audiences.

N-Gen Movies

+ American Pie
+ The Blair Witch Project
+ I Know What You Did Last Summer
+ The Matrix
+ Scream
+ She's All That
+ There's Something About Mary
+ Titanic

The effort paid off big as teens and young adults flocked to the box office to see the movie. Many initially believed the story to be real. The film earned $48 million in its first week of wide release — making it one of the most profitable films ever.[1] The movie taught Hollywood the incredible subtlety and power of the Internet as a marketing tool.

Blair Witch proved, without question, that today's teens and young adults are a whole new breed of consumer, one easily turned off by hype, and who seek at least the appearance of reality and authenticity, if not the actual thing itself. The point was proved even more emphatically by *Blair Witch II,* a typical Hollywood attempt to wring money from a derivative sequel. *Witch II* was everything *Witch I* was not: slick, transparently promoted, and hype, not anti-hype. It was not gritty and independent — and it bombed, despite (or perhaps because of) being technically far superior to the original.

INTRODUCING . . . THE INTERNET GENERATION

We call the youngest American cohort the N Generation, N-Gen, or Internet Generation, because the Internet is a defining event for them, and because they will be the "engine" of growth over the next two decades. This cohort is clearly still emerging and is in its formative stage. The oldest *adult* members of this cohort are currently 24 and the youngest adults 18. From a purely demographic standpoint (looking at the N-Gen, as demographers do, as the offspring of the Boomers), the case can be made that N-Gens extend downward to at least age 7 as of this writing. If so, it will be a very large cohort indeed, with more than 79 million members. However, it's unclear at this time how big the N-Gen Cohort will prove to be — stay tuned for the sequel to this book, which will analyze whether the 18-year-olds 5 years from now are still N-Gens, or are part of another new cohort yet to be defined. That said, in the absence of some unforeseen cataclysm, we see no reason why the N-Gen Cohort will end anytime soon.

The World Trade Center and Pentagon tragedy of September 11, 2001, is clearly a defining moment for this cohort and, as noted in the addendum to the Prologue, will instill and magnify certain core values, such as patriotism and perhaps physical fear. But unless the horrific events of that day escalate, our guess is that it will not result in a new cohort formation, but rather the coalescing of the current N-Gen Cohort into an even more cohesive group.

Although technically not adults, who are legally defined as having reached age 18, we have also included 17-year-olds in our analysis, since they are just now coming of age. Adult N-Gens who have come of age represent a small percentage of the adult population now, but their numbers will swell as more and more turn 18. They are the children of the Baby Boomers, and so have been nicknamed the Echo Boom, the Baby Boomlet, Generation Y, and the Millennials, among others.

For the most part, the N Generation have been growing up in two-income households and early on are developing a level of self-sufficiency that surpasses even Gen X. They are more diverse than the rest of the population (about one-third are minorities, compared to one-fourth of the general population), and are more likely to come from single parent households (about one-fourth versus one-eighth in 1970). They have grown up with computers, CD-ROMs, the Internet, and other forms of interactive learning, and they have come to expect this kind of instantaneous response from the marketplace.

As the children of the Baby Boomers, they are part of a child-safety push that includes car seats, bicycle helmets, and training on "good touch–bad touch." They eat Happy Meals and ride in minivans. As a result of all of this attentiveness to their every need, they have a strong sense of entitlement. Like Generation X, Jonesers, and Leading-Edge Baby Boomers, they are very independent and like to pursue their own interests. Unlike these other cohorts at the same age, however, they are much more technologically savvy and aware that marketers are courting them. Thus, they are more skeptical of those very marketing efforts.

DEFINING MOMENTS: TIME WILL TELL

So far, there have been few truly galvanizing defining moments to unite this cohort. But there's no question that the Internet and the roaring economy of the '90s have definitely made a permanent positive mark. The tragic events of September 11, 2001, Clinton's impeachment, and numerous school shootings have also left a mark, although in a negative way. One thing that binds N-Gens together is their rejection of their Boomer parent's anti-institutional mind-set. This rejection of some parental values is a recurring theme — we have noted it, for example, in the cycles of attitudes towards sexual permissiveness. In this case, the older Boomers were an unusually strong and cohesive cohort, with an absolute conviction that they were right and that *institutions* — be they government, church, or school — were wrong. The reaction to this attitude on the part of their N-Gen offspring is also strong and cohesive, but in the other direction — the institutions, if not exactly "right," are to be honored and ultimately obeyed. Idealistic and team-players, similar to the World War II Cohort in their respect for institutional values, the N-Gen is as much different from Gen X as the Boomers were from the Postwars.

THE INTERNET: GROWING UP WIRED

This is the first generational cohort to grow up with the Internet. As a result, they look to the web first for just about everything — from doing their homework, listening to the latest music, accessing the latest movie reviews, and keeping in touch with friends, to researching consumer products and meeting new friends. Unlike older cohorts, they tend to take the interactivity that the Internet offers for granted. They have an expectation that information will be provided instantaneously, whether that be from the government, their school, or consumer product companies. If information isn't readily available, they are unlikely to dig too deep. They consider having the latest technology, such as high-speed computers, cable modems, cell phones, and pagers, not as luxuries, but as necessities. A recent study of kids aged 12–17 by the Pew Internet & American Life Project showed that nearly 75 percent of youths surveyed use instant messaging — a technology that allows them to electronically communicate in real time with multiple friends.[2] This kind of multi-tasking lets them be two places (or more) at once, simultaneously carrying on several different conversations.

This is truly a wired cohort. Because they have never known life without computers, remote controls, compact discs, and cellular phones, new technologies have allowed them to avoid personal face-to-face interactions in a way not previously possible. And over the next decade, evolving technologies such as person-to-person, easy and cheap videotelephony and video mail will offer much more powerful new vehicles for communicating with the N-Gen Cohort. "Voice-activated," "wireless" and "digital" will be watchwords for marketers. And this cohort will increasingly accept "virtual connectivity", as they turn to technology rather than flesh-and-blood interactions.

N-Gen Defining Moments to Date

✦ The Internet

✦ Good economic times

✦ School shootings

✦ Clinton's impeachment

✦ Terrorist attack on World Trade Center and Pentagon

"WHO WANTS TO BE A MILLIONAIRE?"

Following a recession in the early '90s, the economy took off in the middle of the decade and climbed to new heights. The stock market soared, unemployment dropped to new lows, and most people had a sense that they were better off than in previous years. This feeling of euphoria was not wasted on N-Gens, who have come to expect the economy and the stock market to continue their upward spiral indefinitely. With Baby Boomers as parents, many N-Gens have grown up in dual-income families and have greater disposable income available to them. And many more work part-time jobs to be able to afford the latest fashions, movies, and music CDs.

It's no accident that the hit TV show *Who Wants to be a Millionaire?* garnered such appeal in the new millennium. In this day and age, everybody wants to be a millionaire, and many N-Gens see this as an achievable goal. Despite the sharp stock market correction of 2000 and 2001, N-Gens remain very optimistic about the future and see themselves achieving a high level of success. This is probably the biggest attitudinal difference between them and Gen-Xers.

A NEW MEANING FOR "DUCK AND COVER"

School violence dramatically increased in the '90s, heightening fears about personal safety among teens and young adults. Some people blame absentee parenting for the increase in violence, while others blame the loss of community, the glorification of violence in the media, or other social factors. The April 20, 1999, massacre at Columbine High School in Littleton, Colorado, in which 14 students and 1 teacher were killed and 23 others were wounded, capped a decade in which students brought weapons to school in growing numbers. It was an alarming new trend that prompted schools to install metal detectors, hire security guards, and develop readiness plans to deal with violence. It gave new meaning to the "duck-and-cover" drills of the '50s, and it shows just how much things have changed in a half century. It also shows why many N-Gens

Popular N-Gen TV Shows

+ *Boy Meets World*
+ *Buffy the Vampire Slayer*
+ *Dawson's Creek*
+ *Felicity*
+ *Real World/Road Rules*
+ *Sabrina, the Teenage Witch*

are fearful about their own safety. They are not the carefree teens their parents were.

CLINTON'S IMPEACHMENT

When allegations that the president of the United States had had sexual relations with White House intern Monica Lewinsky — a woman just a few years older than his own daughter — turned out to be true, Americans were stunned. For many, an even greater sin was Bill Clinton's lying about his escapades in a brazen, boldfaced way. It seemed unbelievable that a man in such a position of power and authority would stoop to such a level. The extensive investigation and eventual impeachment divided the country and showed a relaxing moral attitude among many Americans.

For some N-Gens, many of whom sympathized with the humiliation that must have been felt by Clinton's daughter, Chelsea Clinton, the event caused them to lose faith in politicians and engendered two opposite reactions. For one group, it engendered a cynical attitude toward government, which they withdraw from. For another, it has led to a desire to really reform the system; to make it better for us all in the future. It remains to be seen which group will prove dominant in the years to come.

THE TERRORIST ATTACKS OF SEPTEMBER 11, 2001

As we have referenced, the horrible tragedy of the terrorist attacks on the World Trade Center and the Pentagon constitutes a profoundly negative defining moment for the N-Gen Cohort. The events of that day are likely to intensify the fears of physical harm that were first planted by the Columbine shootings and instill the core value of physical safety to a greater extent than seen since the World War II Cohort was coming of age. It will also magnify the value of patriotism, something already felt by the N-Gens, but now in a more top-of-mind, activist way.

Assuming that September 11 is not the trigger point for the Crisis discussed in the Epilogue, September 11th's events will serve to reinforce and make stronger the core value tendencies the N-Gen Cohort already exhibits: teamwork, acceptance of institutions, anti-hype, and ambition. From a values standpoint, it will make them even more like the World War II Cohort than they already are.

"LIVING LA VIDA LOCA"

Popular culture in the late '90s and early twenty-first century has taken on a distinctly N-Gen flavor. Movie and TV executives, record producers, and fashion designers now realize that this emerging cohort represents a huge population surge over Generation X. They also have a lot of free time on their hands, and — more importantly — a lot of money to spend.

REALITY TV AND INDIES

TV shows, such as *Dawson's Creek, Felicity,* and *Making the Band,* now target teen and young adult audiences. Advertisers now fully grasp the value of this particular cohort group. Unlike Gen-Xers when they were the same age, N-Gens have more money to spend; plus, there are a whole lot more of them.

N-Gen Icons

Christina Aguilera

Backstreet Boys

Matt Damon

Claire Danes

Leonardo DiCaprio

Eminem

Sarah Michelle Gellar

Melissa Joan Hart

Monica Lewinsky

Ricky Martin

Brad Pitt

Freddie Prinze, Jr.

Britney Spears

Spice Girls

Tiger Woods

Because of the size of the cohort, the N-Gens can drive media representations the way the Boomers did. When the Boomers were truly babies, the emphasis was on babies (remember the birth of "Leetle Ricky" Ricardo, the highest-rated episode of the nation's highest-rated series?). When they were in grade school, they had *Leave it to Beaver.* When the Boomers were teens, television featured — teens! David and Ricky Nelson. *The Monkees. Gilligan's Island.* The N-Gen childhood was spent with Disney cartoons, such as *The Little Mermaid.* Then they graduated to movies such as *Home Alone* and *Jurassic Park.* Now that they are in their coming-of-age years, their tastes have evolved to reflect a more eclectic style. They made a $1 billion box office smash out of *Titanic,* and multimillion-dollar successes out of *Scream* and *The Blair Witch Project* (all with coming-of age protagonists). Independent films — or indies — are the latest rage with this group, and they can often be downloaded for free off the Internet. These movies reflect art untouched (or so it seems) by corporate movie studios and a new way around typical distribution channels. N-Gens love them. The N-Gen hits on MTV — *Real World* and *Road Rules,* which were also popular with Gen X — are the precursors of the more mainstream "reality TV" shows, such as *Survivor.*

MUSIC AND MAGALOGS

Reflecting greater multiculturalism, Latin singers, such as Ricky Martin and Enrique Iglesias, are topping the record charts. There has also been a revival of the concept of "boy bands" ('NSync, 98°, and the Backstreet Boys) and "girl bands" (The Spice Girls and Destiny's Child), which target young adults and teens. Paralleling television, these types of youth-only groups haven't been popular since the Baby Boomers were teens. But the paradoxical concepts they represent align perfectly with the conflicting N-Gen psyche. They simultaneously embrace:

- ✦ Sex and virginity (as do Britney Spears, Christina Aguilera, and Jessica Simpson)

- ✦ Hipness and morality

- ✦ Youth and religion

As such, they are in many ways the opposite of the druggie, alcoholic, sex-crazed bands of the '70s, '80s and early '90s, such as the Rolling Stones, the Doors, Van Halen, and Nirvana. The message, although complex and confused, is far less nihilistic and anarchic than that of Kurt Cobain.

Magalogs or catazines — which combine catalog sales content with magazine articles and reader submissions — are a another hot item, as companies, such as Abercrombie & Fitch and Delia, develop unique content and fashions geared specifically for N-Gens. Things like baby doll T-shirts, glitter makeup, and skater shorts are all the rage with younger N-Gens. Most adults would not be caught dead in these fashions, which is precisely why N-Gens flock to them. And watch for more and more technology-based marketing, such as online advertising, but more targeted to the recipient (one-on-one marketing).

N-GEN TODAY: WELCOME TO ADULTHOOD

The N Generation is just now coming into adulthood. Because this group is so young and has not yet formed the values that will guide them in later life, there are few conclusions that can be drawn about their long-range buying habits at this time. Generation X proved that trying to characterize a young cohort just entering its coming-of-age years can often lead to misunderstandings and mistargeted marketing approaches. As a result, in this chapter, we have focused on the short-term for N-Gens.

N-Gen Fads & Fashions

- ✦ Body piercing and tattoos
- ✦ Chat rooms
- ✦ Dark nail polish (black, green, and blue)
- ✦ E-zines
- ✦ '50s, '60s and '70s fashion revival (capri pants, bell-bottoms, and platform shoes)
- ✦ Glitter makeup
- ✦ High-tech video games
- ✦ Instant messaging
- ✦ Magalogs (catalog and magazine hybrids, such as Abercrombie & Fitch and Delia)
- ✦ Raves
- ✦ Tommy Hilfiger

They are distinctly different from older cohorts (more optimistic than Gen X and more technology driven than Jonesers and Leading-Edge Boomers), and they expect marketers to recognize this uniqueness. Like the Xers, they have been exposed to commercials since they were born, and because of their large numbers, they have grown up the target of very sophisticated marketing campaigns. As a result, they are very skeptical of being sold to. They refuse to be sucked in by broad-based approaches designed for mass audiences. They expect greater options to be available to them, and they want to be treated as individuals. This can pose a serious challenge for marketers, but not an insurmountable one, as you will see.

Although N-Gens haven't solidified their key cohort values yet, we have put together a tentative Multi-Dimensional Marketing™ snapshot (see Snapshot feature) of this cohort based on the Lifestage Analytic

Matrix™ (see Chapter 2, "What Makes Us Tick: Using the Lifestage Analytic Matrix™") and current popular trends among this group. This provides a framework from which to tap into the current 17–24-year-olds in this cohort group.

In reading through this chapter, please keep in mind that this cohort is a work in progress, and only time will tell what values and affinities they will carry with them for the long term.

TAPPING THE N-GEN MARKET

Although this generational cohort is just now beginning to enter adulthood, as time goes on, they will likely become a much larger force in the marketplace. Many high school and college-age N-Gens work at part-time jobs after school or full time in the summer, and they spend much of the money they bring in on entertainment, from movies to MP3 players to lattes at coffeehouses. It's no wonder we have seen such a large number of teen- and young adult–oriented movies, TV shows, music, and fashions in recent years. This group wants the best money can buy, and if deciding whether to buy two cheaper pairs of off-brand jeans or one pair of Hilfigers, they will choose the higher status — and usually more expensive — brand name every time. Table 9.1 gives a preliminary overview of N-Gens' market potential. Not all Census numbers correlate with our age breakdown for this cohort, but the table gives you an idea of the opportunities this group offers.

TABLE 9.1: N-GENERATION MARKET POTENTIAL

	N-Gens	Total Population
Median net Worth (1995)	$10,700 (under 35)	$55,600
Median income (1999)	$18,276 (under 25)	$43,951
Avg. annual expenditures (1999)	$21,704 (under 25)	$36,995

Source: Consumer Expenditure Survey, 1999. Bureau of Labor Statistics

INITIAL SNAPSHOT OF THE N GENERATION COHORT

Name of cohort:	N Generation
Born between:	1977–1984 (17–23 only)
Coming of age:	1995–present
Age in 2001:	17–24
Population:	26 Million ✦ 12% (17–23 only)

Key cohort values and concerns:
- ✦ Hopeful about future
- ✦ Respect for institutions
- ✦ Team players
- ✦ Heightened fears
- ✦ Change is good
- ✦ Tolerance and diversity

Current and next lifestage:
- ✦ High school graduation
- ✦ College
- ✦ First job
- ✦ Dating
- ✦ Early marriage

Emotions and affinities:
- ✦ Brand conscious
- ✦ Retro and eclectic styles
- ✦ Street-smart
- ✦ Socially and environmentally aware

Physiographic profile:
- ✦ Physical peak

Social activities and lifestyles:
- ✦ Internet
- ✦ Electronic media
- ✦ Shopping
- ✦ Skateboarding and snowboarding

Purchasing behavior:
- ✦ Internet shopping
- ✦ Entertainment at center of interests

STEP 1: LOOK AT KEY COHORT VALUES AND CONCERNS

So far, the core value structure of N-Gens seems to be quite different from that of Gen-Xers. They are more idealistic and social cause–oriented, without the cynical, "What's in it for me?" free agent mind-set of many Xers. They are attitudinally stronger, with more deeply held, more conventional values, and with far more structured life goals. Perhaps in a reaction to the strongly held, anti-institution mind-set of their Boomer parents, the N-Gens tend to respect and honor institutions — to "play by the rules." And they are team players, not freelancers or "free agents." As noted above, they are far more optimistic about the future and their role in it than were the Xers, and even the Jonesers. In addition, we have begun to see that many of these same values are holding true for youth in other developed countries around the world as well. We think this is due to the pervasiveness of the Internet and the globalization of telecommunications and media. (We will explore this phenomenon further in Chapter 10, "Taking Generational Cohort Analysis Global.")

HOPEFUL ABOUT THE FUTURE

The soaring stock market of the late '90s (the S&P 500 Index increased an average of 28.6% per year for the five year period from 1995–99!) contributed to this cohort's feeling of optimism about the future. So did the fact that they are, for the most part, the children of the Leading-Edge Boomer Cohort — parents who were themselves more protective, attentive, optimistic, and outgoing than the Postwar parents of the Xers. This puts N-Gens in stark contrast to Gen X, who at this point in their lives largely saw the future as pretty bleak. N-Gens tend to have high expectations about what they will achieve, both personally and financially. For the oldest of the N-Gens, especially those working in high-tech industries, the dramatic fall in the NASDAQ from March 2000 to March 2001 is a reminder that their optimistic world view is subject to hiccups. It did not impact most of the N-Gens, however. There are signs that the downturn was in fact a hiccup, and that the recovery will be rapid. In any case, we will monitor this closely to see if future economic trends represent a "defining moment" that can form a new cohort.

The N-Gen learned about money at an early age and see the stock market and entrepreneurship as easy ways to get rich quick. N-Gens are hopeful about the future, and they are eager to strike out on their own. A 1999 Nickelodeon/Yankelovich Youth Monitor survey reported that 64% of surveyed teens aged 12–17 want to own their own companies, and 59% said they expect to be wealthier than their parents.[3] And because they have grown up during one of the most prosperous times in U.S. history, many N-Gens have come to expect 20% annual returns on investments, even though at this point most are not investing their own hard-earned money.

Some investment firms, such as Fidelity Investments, the country's largest mutual fund company, are keeping a close eye on N-Gens. They are trying to encourage N-Gen loyalty now by marketing to their parents, and by putting billions of dollars into electronic commerce.

At the same time, because money has come so freely and financial responsibility never made a priority, many N-Gens have not learned sound money management skills. Credit cards are now readily available to teens as young as 16. As a result, some N-Gens are now finding themselves deeply in debt.

RESPECT FOR INSTITUTIONS

By citing respect for institutions as a value, we do not mean that N-Gens are as committed in that regard as were the World War II and Depression Cohorts. The respect is not absolute, as it was for many members of the older cohorts, for whom the family, the church, the school and the government were central to their core being. However, within the N-Gen Cohort, respect has *increased* relative to the ingrained rejection of institutions that was begun by the Leading-Edge Boomers (who sought to substitute their own higher, personal ethos) and culminated in the Xers, a small portion of whom today seem to be engaged in virtual nihilism.

Unfortunately, the visibility of those that embrace this nihilistic mentality (a kind of "thug code" — in other words, getting what you want at all costs) has been vastly increased by broad (and admiring) exposure in the media through sports, entertainment and — by extension — advertising. Why this has happened is unclear, but it has resulted (at least in the context we are best qualified to comment on) in advertising that no longer resonates with most of the N-Gens because it is too edgy, too inner-city for most N-Gens to relate to. The thug code proactively "disses" the institutions of civil society. While some (mostly the downscale part) of the N-Gen Cohort go along with this, many more do not.

N-Gens don't have the absolute and unquestioning obedience to institutional authority that characterized many of the World War II Cohort, but they want to get good grades, they believe in organized religion, and they want a stable and supportive family structure. They can even believe that positive societal change can result from the political process, although they also believe that major change in the process itself must occur first.

TEAM PLAYERS

N-Gens, as opposed to Gen X, are team players. As we noted in the last chapter, the Gen X Cohort can be characterized by a kind of "What's in it for me?" mentality, a sense of "I gotta look out for myself, 'cause no one else is going to!" This is the epitome of the free-agent mind-set. It's rampant in sports, from baseball (where it's not uncommon for a player to be on four teams in five years) to basketball (where the team often seems to be letting Michael Jordan, or Shaq, or Allan Iverson carry the load). It's also rampant in business, where loyalty to a company, as well as a team, is a flagrant violation of the thug code.

N-Gens are different. Perhaps because their intra-peer communication technology is so much better (cell phones, 3-way telephone calls, Internet chat rooms and instant messages), they relate much better to others in a cooperative, collaborative sense. They are not yet the quintessential team players the Depression and World War II Cohorts were (the Princeton class of 1934's beer jackets proudly featured the National Recovery Act logo and slogan, "We did our part"), but they believe the power of teamwork can achieve more than they can as individuals. If the Xers are symbolized by their youthful toys, the "Teenage Mutant Ninja Turtles" — individualists who fought their battles alone — N-Gens align with the "Mighty Morphin' Power Rangers," who conquer evil through the power of teamwork.

HEIGHTENED FEARS

Increasing school violence throughout the '90s and into the new millennium has had a lasting effect on N-Gens. A quick look at Table 9.2 shows a disturbing trend: Having grown up with the threat of violence in a place once considered safe (schools), many N-Gens have heightened fears about their own safety compared to older cohorts. Metal detectors, security guards, bans on backpacks, and drug- and bomb-sniffing dogs have all been part of their school experience. This is of limited utility from a marketing standpoint — although they may have heightened fears compared to other cohorts in their youth. At the moment the N-Gens are still youths — and as with all youths, they tend to think that they, personally, are immortal. The fear is more of an abstraction, something they will play back when asked, but it doesn't drive their personal behavior very often. As with other contradictory tendencies, N-Gens are complex in this area as well, as is evidenced by splinter groups espousing neonazism or the "Goth" cults.

CHANGE IS GOOD

Because this cohort grew up with the Internet, they have come to expect that change is just a natural part of life. They expect to see websites updated frequently with the very latest content. There is no shortage of distractions. Music, video games, the Internet, radio, and more than 100 TV channels are easily accessible to most teens and young adults. If one medium doesn't meet their needs, they are likely to find another one that does. With advertising, they expect to be entertained and to see new material on a frequent basis. They have little patience with the same old thing.

To keep your message fresh, use an integrated approach to marketing. Don't put all of your money into network TV ads. Branch out into cable, the Web, cinema ads, sponsorship of music and sporting events, and depending on your product, you may even want to consider wild postings on the Internet and college campuses. Play into the "change-is-good" theme by acknowledging N-Gens' eagerness to be on the forefront of new trends.

TABLE 9.2: RECENT SCHOOL MASSACRES

Date	Location	Number Dead	Age of Shooter(s)
Feb. 2, 1996	Moses Lake, Washington	3	14
Feb. 19, 1997	Bethel, Alaska	2	16
Oct. 1, 1997	Pearl, Mississippi	2	16
Dec. 1, 1997	West Paducah, Kentucky	3	14
March 24, 1998	Jonesboro, Arkansas	5	11, 13
April 24, 1998	Edinboro, Pennsylvania	1	14
May 19, 1998	Fayetteville, Tennessee	1	18
May 21, 1998	Springfield, Oregon	2	15
April 20, 1999	Littleton, Colorado	14	17, 18
Feb. 29, 2000	Mount Morris Township, Michigan	1	6
May 26, 2000	Lake Worth, Florida	1	13
March 5, 2001	Santee, California	2	15

TOLERANCE AND DIVERSITY

The N Generation is the most diverse cohort of all. One-third are from minority groups, compared to one-fourth of the total population. Because they have grown up with people of various races and religions, they don't tend to equate being different as a negative. Even the definition of family is different for this group. It now includes homosexual couples, single parents, and siblings from different racial backgrounds.

Compared to older cohorts, N-Gens tend to hang around a much more diverse group of friends. This diversity includes not just friends of other races, but of other socio-economic groups as well. In marketing to this group, reflect greater diversity in your ads. Benetton has been particularly effective in mirroring diversity in its advertising, using photographs of inter-racial partners and gays in billboards and magazines. Even Ralph Lauren's "wasp-ish" lines of clothing have embraced racial and ethnic diversity. It is one good way to reach the hearts and minds of this cohort.

STEP 2: ANALYZE CURRENT AND NEXT LIFESTAGE

Because the leading edge of this cohort is just now coming to the end of its coming-of-age years, many new lifestages are now opening up. As time goes on, this cohort will no doubt make its own mark on the various lifestages, just as other cohorts before them have done.

HIGH SCHOOL GRADUATION

High school graduation is a rite of passage that the earliest wave of N-Gens have already passed through, but there are many more still in school. This may well be the very first lifestage recognized by those coming of age, and it can be a serious step in the life of this generational cohort. Marketers have a great opportunity to memorialize this moment with innovative products that reflect N-Gens' individuality. New "prom" clothing lines or creative limousine services are all possibilities. Advertising and other promotional executions can also reflect the importance of this day. There also seems to be a resurgence of "retro" importance attached to this right of passage. Formalwear, corsages, and the ever-present limo seem *de rigueur.* This is a manifestation of the N-Gen embrace of traditional institutions. Coming-of-age Boomers would not have been caught dead in a limo. The N-Gens are rebelling against their parents' rebellion.

Broadening this lifestage to include high school in general probably offers many more marketing opportunities. Teenagers of other generational cohorts have always been interested in high school themes, as evidenced by the popularity of *American Graffiti, Risky Business, Ferris Bueller's Day Off, Fast Times at Ridgemont High, 90210,* and now *Dawson's Creek.* This will no doubt be a fertile field to plow well into the future.

LEAVING THE NEST

For many N-Gens, college has always been a part of their parents' and their own high expectations. This cohort has the potential to be the most highly educated cohort of all.

Education started at an earlier age for N-Gens than for any other cohort. A large number were in preschool by the time they were 3. After graduating from high school, 65% are expected to go on to college, compared to just over half in 1986. Because of increasing college costs and tighter rules on student grants and loans, however, this cohort is expected to have one of the highest student debt ratios of all time. As a result, getting a good-paying job right out of college will be a top priority. This is doubly true because N-Gens have been raised with generally privileged lifestyles — few of them have had to go without up to this point. Unlike many of the Xers however, they don't necessarily have the expectation of "easy money" — they are willing to work very hard to get it. As a result, they don't show the apathy toward being financially successful that we observed just a few short years ago with some segments of the Gen-Xers.

The percentage of students who expect to get an advanced degree is also on the rise. But despite this interest in getting degrees, some educators have said that N-Gens are more interested in obtaining the "credentials" — the diploma — than in learning. This cohort sees higher education as a means to a good job, rather than as an end in and of itself. As a result, some of them can be a bit disengaged from the learning process.

The leaving-the-nest lifestage (empty-nesting from the parent's point-of-view) offers some opportunities for marketers. The nest-leavers have not accumulated a lot of material possessions, so they have buying motivation. Unfortunately, most are students or in entry-level jobs, so they don't have a lot of disposable income. They are particularly receptive to offers and discounts that recognize their starting out status — student or recent-grad discounts, reduced membership fees for those under 21 or 23 or 25, extending family memberships even to those no longer living at home, liberalized credit terms for those with short work histories, and so forth. As with everybody, the marketer who shows he *understands* their lifestage and empathizes with them generates a lot of goodwill, even if the monetary reward offered may not be that large. In the long run, this approach will pay off.

FIRST JOB: LIFE'S A BEACH

Job fairs on the beach were just one tactic desperate companies used to attract N-Gens during the labor shortage of the late '90s and early 2000. Panama City, Florida, hosted just such a job fair during Spring Break

2000, and more than 50 corporate recruiters showed up looking for new hires. These days, two-week vacations and a good benefits package aren't enough to attract most Gen-Xers and N-Gens. Unlike older cohorts who expected to put their time in and work their way up the ranks, these younger cohorts don't want work to consume them the way it has their parents. N-Gens, in particular, are not into corporate ladder-climbing, and they see office cubicles as a new form of prison. While they do want to make good money to buy the finer things in life, many are more interested in jobs that have social impact — such as teaching — rather than in business or finance. Others have seen Generation X make fortunes in the dot.com world and they see themselves striking it rich, too, despite the recent downturn in the technology sector. Unlike Gen X, though, N-Gens are much more likely to see working in a team environment as a positive thing.

CHAT ROOMS ARE THE NEW SINGLES BARS

Because sexual intercourse can lead to so many pitfalls (AIDS, sexually transmitted diseases, and pregnancy), many N-Gens are playing it safe when it comes to love. The Internet has become a popular screening tool.

Chat rooms have become the singles bar of the new millennium. They provide a safer forum in which to meet and get to know new people. If things go well with the initial chat, couples "go to voice," then follow up with an F2F — a face-to-face meeting. Of course, there are pitfalls to dating in cyberspace. Misrepresentation — sending fake information or photos — can be a big problem, and chatters must still proceed with caution.

Because of the risks associated with intimacy, many N-Gens are waiting until they are into their 20s before having sex . . . or at least they say they are. Of course, for many who report this, the definition of "sex" is very precise: It refers only to vaginal intercourse. As did former President Bill Clinton, N-Gens believe oral sex is not sex. It is "fooling around," "making out," "petting" (all curiously archaic terms), or "hooking up"(more current) — but definitely not sex. A far larger group than in the past is also choosing to remain virgins until marriage, bucking a 30-year liberal trend started by their own parents, and a trend most notable among the Xer Cohort — "The youngest to copulate and the oldest to marry!"

From an N-Gen Perspective

The people who started college in the fall of 1998 were born in 1980. Here is a perspective on their experience:

+ They have no meaningful recollection of the Reagan Era and did not know he had ever been shot.

+ They have only known one Germany, although they remember the fall of the Berlin Wall from childhood.

+ They have no idea that Americans were held hostage in Iran.

+ Their lifetime has always included AIDS.

+ Roller skating has always meant "in-line" skating.

+ They likely never played Pac-Man, and have never heard of Pong.

+ The compact disc was introduced when they were 1-year-olds.

+ They have always had an answering machine, remote control, and cable TV.

+ The *Tonight Show* has always been hosted by Jay Leno.

+ Popcorn has always been cooked in a microwave.

+ Kansas, Chicago, Boston, America, and Alabama are places, not musical groups.

A NEW TWIST ON TRADITIONAL VALUES

This cohort has voiced conservative opinions about everything from marriage to sex to government to religion, and this comes as quite a change to attitudes held by many Xers, Jonesers, and Leading-Edge Boomers. "Neo-traditionalism" — or a return to old-fashioned values, such as no sex before marriage — is the new trend among this cohort.

This group has not had a lot of stability in their lives, and now they are looking for it in traditional institutions such as marriage and family. Remember, we often value what we don't have while coming of age.

N-Gens are increasingly saving sex until marriage, getting married younger, having children earlier, having more children, and having one parent stay home with the kids. Since 1994, the number of 18–24 year olds who said having sex before marriage is always wrong has been on the increase, with 1998 figures topping 20%.[4] In some ways, these attitudes are reminiscent of the '50s, but with a new twist. Instead of Mom staying home with the kids, this cohort feels that it could be either Mom *or* Dad — just as long as one parent is there. The economic boom of the '90s led many to believe that they could one day expect to live at a comfortable lifestyle and still afford to have one parent stay home. They, along with Generation X, are finding new ways to make this work, either through quitting work completely, working part-time, telecommuting, job sharing, or taking sabbaticals from work.

Although N-Gens tend to be somewhat conservative, in trying to appeal to this cohort, avoid old-fashioned approaches that might appeal to their grandparents. While some attitudes may be similar, they are definitely not the same. Instead, reflect N-Gens' neo-traditionalism in your communications by depicting more modern themes — show the husband staying home with the kids, or the wife in workout clothes, for example.

STEP 3: EXAMINE EMOTIONS AND AFFINITIES

Partly due to lifestage, N-Gens are currently very focused on developing their own identities and making their mark in the world. They are experimenting with a wide range of social attitudes and affinities, trying to discover their own authentic self.

BRAND CONSCIOUSNESS: NICHE IS IT

Overall, N-Gens are very brand conscious and brand loyal. Because the economy has been so good for so long, they have gotten used to the finer things in life. They have a penchant for luxurious, branded items, and they are willing and able to pay for the highest quality goods.

Concerned with the status certain brand names convey, N-Gens are more likely to pay more for an individual item than Gen-Xers, who tend to be more caught up in getting the most value for their money. This tendency also illustrates the eclectic, self-contradictory nature of the

N-Gens. While they are anti-hype and find the smaller, offbeat brands appealing, they also are strongly drawn to the big names in certain categories, such as Tommy Hilfiger, Calvin Klein, and Abercrombie & Fitch. According to a 1998 article in *Restaurant Business* magazine, N-Gens are more likely to pay $5 for a high-end cup of coffee or $9 for a special appetizer than Gen-Xers. And, says one advertising executive, "In the past kids were more likely to save up and go bigger. Not these kids. They don't want to delay things . . . they want to move ahead — now."[5]

Brands that Boomers, Jonesers, and Xers liked, such as Levi's and Reebok, are taboo with this group. Instead, they prefer labels geared specifically to them, niche brands such as Greed Girl, Juicy, Tag Rag, L.E.I., 26 Red Sugar, and Steve Madden. This group is much more fragmented than other cohorts, and niche brands have sprung up practically overnight to meet their seemingly insatiable buying habits.

For the most part, big brands are out with this cohort. Old-style image campaigns that worked with Boomers are not going to work with N-Gens. This cohort prefers to discover its own brands. Larger companies can accommodate this preference by coming out with new line extensions geared to N-Gens, while smaller brands can play up the fact that they are small and are at the forefront of the latest trends.

Companies such as Nike, Levi's, Cover Girl, and Maybelline have had to rethink how they market to this cohort. Nike is trying to improve its corporate image after allegations surfaced that it used inhumane labor practices overseas. Levi's is now working to integrate more entertainment venues into its advertising, and it's coming out with new ads, new styles, a more interactive website, and it's paying closer attention to teen focus groups. Cover Girl has introduced a new "Rhythm & Blues Back to School Collection." The makeup line offers hip new shades, such as Jammin', Green Groove, and Disco Ball. Maybelline has signed *Buffy the Vampire Slayer* star Sarah Michelle Gellar to pitch its Express Makeup 3-in-1 line, which squarely targets teenage girls and young adults.

RETRO AND ECLECTIC STYLES

Capri pants, bell-bottoms, platform shoes, tight fitting shirts with zippers, and cat-eye glasses. These are just a few of the retro fashions popular with N-Gens. They are creating their own unique look by putting together eclectic fashions first discovered by older cohorts. We at Lifestage have found that fads often skip a generational cohort and then reappear. The Boomer bell-bottoms, for example, missed Generation X but found interest in the N-Gens. Clogs are now making a comeback from the 1960s. And so it goes. If you are looking for a repeat performer, we suggest searching the fads and fashions of two cohorts ago, making some adjustments to reflect modern tastes, and repositioning it to the new generation — the "Grandfather Law" at work!

Another marketing mandate is that no manufacturer or retailer can afford to become locked into a particular look or style. This eclecticism must carry through to product offerings — there is no such thing as the "timeless look," as such currently struggling companies such as the Gap and Banana Republic are discovering.

SOCIALLY AND ENVIRONMENTAL AWARENESS

N-Gens are more socially conscious and environmentally aware than Gen X. Companies believed to be socially and environmentally irresponsible turn this cohort off. Take Nike, for example. When news broke that the athletic shoe and apparel maker was accused of relying on sweatshop labor to produce its goods, the company lost favor with N-Gens. A boycott ensued, which punished Nike for its image as a bad corporate citizen.

With N-Gens, a negative company profile on social or environmental issues can lead to lost sales. Keep this in mind when marketing to this group. Promote efforts to reduce waste, help the needy, or somehow make the world a better place to live. Even though this kind of message may have little to do with the product you are selling, it will help to build a positive image about your company among N-Gens, and this can help to increase sales.

UNDERGROUND AND HONEST

This cohort has grown up in an age of instantaneous communication and advertising saturation. Concepts such as Baby Gap, advertiser-supported Channel One in schools, magazines such as *Sports Illustrated for Kids* and cable networks such as Nickelodeon were all a part of their childhood experience. They have become the most marketed-to cohort since the Boomers.

As a result, like Gen X, this cohort is very aware of and turned off by "hype." They prefer honesty and the *appearance* of authenticity — if not the real thing itself — in all advertising. The movie *The Blair Witch*

Project was a great example of this. As we mentioned earlier in this chapter, the movie didn't follow the conventional approach used by most Hollywood movies, yet it clearly took the country by storm. Gen-Xers and N-Gens both loved this film, and it squarely beat out more heavily hyped, big-budget movies released around the same time.

Another example of this "underground" marketing has just been launched as we write in the Spring of 2001. Steven Spielberg's movie *A.I.* — Artificial Intelligence — has a Web-based publicity campaign built around a highly involving game. Website movie credits include an obscure reference to a "sentient machine therapist" named Jeanine Salla, Professor at Bangalore University. Checking this reference leads to game participation, which results in faxes, e-mails, and phone calls to the players referencing the "anti-robot militia" and their opponents. These and other Web links are clues to solving the game. Other clues require a level of attention bordering on the obsessive. For instance, one clue emerges only after game players zoom in on a tiny screen in a web photo, process it through Microsoft Paint program (Microsoft participated in the game's development), and discover a message invisible to the naked eye. Other puzzles involve literary references, chemistry and computer-programming skills. It's too soon to know how successful this promotional event will be in hyping ticket sales for *A.I.,* but it's a new spin on the Blair Witch formula, and a unique way of getting an N-Gen target audience really *involved* with the movie.

Lee's Co. Dungarees line of clothing has found sponsorship of the X-Games — an extreme sports competition — to be a good way to reach N-Gens. The company has moved away from network TV ads and now focuses on sports sponsorships, print, cable, and cinema ads to tap into N-Gen audiences. When Lee introduced a line of oversized cargo pants that targeted young skateboarders, instead of spending big bucks on TV ads, the jeans maker put its money into marketing on the Internet, outdoor posters, and in skateboarding magazines, which turned out to be a smart move.

In marketing to N-Gens, use a more grassroots approach to convince this group that they are the first to discover you. Some companies are going so far as to use "street teams" of young people that go out to nightclubs, malls, and other hot spots to talk with N-Gens about fashion, finance, buying habits, and so on. It is an effort to spot trends that can be used in cutting-edge marketing campaigns.

Volkswagen's quirky and offbeat TV commercials appeal directly to N-Gens' and Gen-Xers' penchant for unpretentious advertising. One ad showed two guys picking up an old chair that had been discarded by the side of the road, and then stopping to dump it out when it became obvious that it smelled bad. Another VW ad showed a young couple driving through what appears to be New Orleans. All of the people they pass on the sidewalk are moving in sync with the music on their radio. These ads are far from the typical image-building approach taken by most car makers, but they are a hit with younger audiences because they don't try to sell them on status and hype. It should also be noted that trying too hard to be anti-hype doesn't work either. Sprite tried a campaign that said "Image is nothing, thirst is everything." This was such an obvious gimmick that the cynical, street-smart N-Gens saw through this ploy and instantly rejected it.

STEP 4: BUILD A PHYSIOGRAPHIC PROFILE

At this young age, N-Gens are not at all concerned with physiographics. They tend to take more risks, eat a lot of junk food and fast food, and are not much concerned with eating a healthy diet or exercising for health reasons. But they are extremely appearance-conscious — everyone and everything is evaluated on the basis of looks, and to the extent that one's diet can promote slimness or exacerbate acne, it is a key consideration.

"I'M THE KING OF THE WORLD"

This cohort is at its physical peak. As a result, N-Gens often see themselves as invincible. Those who are working full-time often don't see the need to pay for health insurance. But accidents do happen, and insurers would be wise to court this group for one simple reason: The healthier the people you insure, the higher your profit margins will be. By courting N-Gens now, insurance companies can build long-term relationships with this emerging demographic.

According to a 1999 *American Demographics* article by Alison Steinwellner, this cohort likely will be less tolerant of health plans that limit their choices. "They want the flexibility to choose alternative medical care, for example, including acupuncture and herbal supplements, things that are often not covered by health plans but are very popular among young adults." They are more likely to want a plan that offers them "cafeteria-style" benefits, such as birth control pills, vision and dental benefits, and an option to use alternative herbal remedies.[6]

Girl Power

While team sports are not as popular among N-Gens as they once were with Boomers, a new sports phenomenon has taken hold with this younger group — the "female jock." Professional female sports stars, such as Olympic soccer player Brandi Chastain and professional basketball player Lisa Leslie, have become idols for many young N-Gens, popularizing the image of the girl athlete. Sporting goods manufacturers have been slow to serve this market segment, but some, including Nike and surfwear maker Roxy, are beginning to get the picture.

Step 5: Understand Social Activities and Lifestyles

N-Gens have a very active social life, and technology is playing an even larger role in helping to facilitate these activities. The Internet has sometimes been criticized for promoting impersonality and a lack of social skills, but this is starting to change with the advent of always-on, high-speed broadband connections (which almost all N-Gen college students have access to). Instant messaging is here now, and with the coming video conferencing capabilities, the Internet will greatly expand its role as an interactive social force.

Internet: A new social force

For N-Gens, the Internet has become more than just an easy way to find information. Many N-Gens go online from home several times a day, every day. For them, the Internet has become a way of life, a social force that has expanded the realm of possibility. It is helping to expand definitions of family, community, and friendship, and is breaking down time, cultural, and ethnic barriers like never before. It is also, along with cable TV and other electronic media, helping to break down regional differences and promote a national teen culture.

For marketers, the immediacy of information available on the Internet is affecting the speed at which trends spread both within the United States and globally. In the past, new trends typically emerged in the East and West Coasts, then spread to the Midwest, and then overseas.

Now, with the wide spread use of the Internet, trends can start anywhere, and they spread in a matter of weeks, not months.

The popularity of the Internet has contributed to an increasingly fragmented N-Gen market. For Boomers, network TV was the medium of choice and, for the most part, everyone watched the same limited content. But for the N-Gen, network TV has taken a back seat to the Internet, a medium in which content is very much a personal matter. TV tends to lump everyone together, while the Internet allows everyone to be an individual. This is precisely why it is so popular with N-Gens. As a result, a well-designed, informative, interactive and updated website is crucial for reaching this cohort. The word interactive is critical — a static website may attract an experienced Web-surfer *once,* but unless it is involving, providing an interactive experience, they will never return.

Chat rooms, mentioned earlier, have become virtual singles bars to meet new people and to connect with old friends online. Instant messaging, or IM, is another popular tool among N-Gens. It is similar to e-mail, but is quicker and more secure than an e-mail chat room. Users can typically include up to 10 people in their IM session. America Online has mined this technology by introducing "Buddy Lists" to its users. This feature is popular with N-Gens because it gives them another quick and easy way to communicate with friends. To keep up with the fast speed of communications, IM and chat rooms have spawned their own shorthand language (see the sidebar "Know What I Mean?" later in this chapter).

While the Internet has its advantages, it also has its downside. The impersonality of cyberspace can lead to isolation, diminished social skills, and a feeling of being cut off from society. While this has been a problem for some N-Gens, others have used the Net to connect even more firmly with their friends. We believe that opt-in e-mail lists (where Web users volunteer their addresses so they can receive messages) will explode with the N-Gen Cohort and provide another surge in permission marketing. As the G-3 wireless technology becomes available, "handies," which are like cell phones but provide wireless instantaneous messaging, will begin sweeping the United States as the N-Gen Cohort looks for even more outlets to satisfy their instant communication desires. This is already a craze among youth in Japan, much of Scandanavia, and Germany.

The MP3 technology pioneered by Napster, the formerly-free Internet music-swapping service, is a phenomenon that is not going to go away, either — even if Napster as a company is litigated into oblivion.

First, music is critically important. A cohort that has grown up multi-tasking sees music in the background as essential to daily living as food or water. Napster made music instantly available, affordable, and with unlimited access and options. It also had the anti-hype element — simply because is has (to date) not been under the control of the big music companies. It's hip and cool and oh so alluring in a thumb-your-nose at the establishment kind of way. If not Napster, then a new technology will evolve, or perhaps a licensing arrangement with the music houses will permit Napster to remain in business, with users paying a fee. But in any case, music-swapping in some form will endure.

Know What I Mean?

Users of electronic instant messaging and chat rooms have developed their own shorthand language and jokes to keep communications moving along. Here are just a few examples:

+ **AFAIK:** As far as I know
+ **BRB:** Be right back
+ **BTW:** By the way
+ **GD&R:** Grin, duck and run (after snide remark)
+ **LOL:** Laughing out loud
+ **OTOH:** On the other hand
+ **POS:** Parent over shoulder (change the topic quickly)
+ **ROTFL:** Rolling on the floor laughing
+ **SWALK:** Sealed with a loving kiss

COMPUTER IS NEW HOT ROD

Realizing that many of its customers love electronic media and computer games, clothing-maker Tommy Hilfiger sponsored a Nintendo competition and installed Nintendo terminals in many of its stores. This played on the N-Gens' love of technology, while providing a comfortable place to meet and socialize.

In an effort to appeal to N-Gens, computer makers are trying to design products that look less office-like and more colorful and stylish. Macintosh led the way with the trendy iMac computer in colors such as blueberry and tangerine. Some have said the computer is this cohort's hot rod. N-Gens want the fastest, sleekest computers they can possibly afford.

This movement toward the trendy also extends into other electronic products. One of Panasonic's most popular CD players is red with silver-metal trim. And Zenith Electronics has plans to introduce Kid's TVs in blue, green and purple. Other new products aimed squarely at N-Gens include a combination camera and MP3 music player for use with PCs, cellular phone and MP3 music players, and for younger N-Gens, backpacks with built-in speakers for use with MP3 music players.

N-Gens' affinity for technology is spilling over into a wide range of areas. McDonald's, for example, is testing out self-serve kiosks at a few of its restaurants. Customers place their orders by touching pictures on a screen, pay with cash, then wait at a table for their food to be delivered. Although the new system has only been used on a limited basis, the ATM-like machines are a hit with younger customers. "It's pretty cool," said one 14-year-old girl. "It's something different. And sometimes when I don't feel like talking, I can use it."[7] As noted earlier, McDonald's is also testing Speed Pass, using a transponder to transmit billing information remotely as you use the drive-thru.

MALLS, CATAZINES, AND MORE

The shopping mall has become the center of social activity for many younger N-Gens as they seek independence from their parents' watchful eye. Teenage Research Unlimited, a market-research firm in Northbrook, Illinois, estimates that 75% of teens aged 12–17 spend an average of four hours a week at the mall to hang out with friends and to shop.[8]

But shopping malls aren't the only option. "Magalogs" and "catazines" are the latest rage with N-Gens, particularly females. They are magazine-catalog hybrids that offer targeted content in between sales space. MoXiegirl (MXG), Delia, Droog, Alloy, and Abercrombie & Fitch are just a few examples of this booming new medium. Most magalogs also have websites, and MXG has even branched out into TV. To receive the monthly or quarterly magalogs, readers typically pay subscription fees of up to $10 per year. MXG has a circulation of 500,000 and estimates readership at about 2.9 million.

Alloy uses an integrated print and online approach to target N-Gens. The company's print catalog goes out to about 20 million young adults, and helps point readers to the company's website. There, customers can fill out a questionnaire to receive the company's bi-weekly electronic magazine. This is permission marketing at its finest. This approach has enabled Alloy to collect demographic data from about 480,000 readers. This information is then used in negotiations with website sponsors.[9]

SKATEBOARDING AND SNOWBOARDING

Team sports are losing popularity with this group for two reasons:

1. N-Gens seek to show their individualism with sports such as skateboarding and snowboarding.

2. Big salaries and the corporatization of professional sports have turned this group off.

According to the Sporting Goods Manufacturers Association, more than 93% of snowboarders and skateboarders are male. And a large percentage of this group are teens between the ages of 12–17. Niche sports magazines, such as Times Mirror's *Transworld Skateboarding,* have sprung up in recent years to serve this demographic, and they have enjoyed booming success. In fact, Times Mirror publishes seven special-interest titles that target young snowboarding, skateboarding, BMX-biking, and surfing enthusiasts.

Skateboarders and snowboarders have created their own subculture that includes their own style of clothing, shoes (Vans), lingo, magazines, and websites. Marketers serving this demographic have proven that niche marketing works with N-Gens, mainly because it acknowledges their need to be unique.

STEP 6: INVESTIGATE PURCHASING BEHAVIOR

As we have shown, this generational cohort is very much into building a unique image for themselves. Their purchasing behavior reflects this value and gives us clues as to where to focus future marketing efforts.

DRIVING ONLINE SALES

Because of their affinity for the Internet, N-Gens are becoming an important catalyst in boosting online sales. NFO Worldwide Inc., a Connecticut research firm, estimates that by 2002, kids ages 5–18 will each spend $1,259 a year on the Internet.[10] Most of this will be through their parents' credit cards.

Retailers are taking note, and coming out with enhanced websites designed to attract N-Gen shoppers. Since they are comfortable with the technology, they are more likely to look to the Internet for purchases. Having a quick-loading, easy-to-use website with e-commerce capabilities is critical to attract and retain this cohort. But keep in mind that the shopping mall is an important social outlet for many teens.

ENTERTAINMENT AT CENTER OF INTERESTS

For most N-Gens, entertainment is at the top of their list of priorities. And this is largely true for any cohort in their prime coming-of-age years. But compared to older cohorts at the same age, N-Gens have more available cash, due to part-time jobs, and more affluent parents. And nearly all of the money they bring in is spent on entertainment.

Movies, music, TV, video games, sports, and nightclubs are all popular ways for N-Gens to spend time and money. In trying to reach this group, go where they are, not where you think they should be. Consider entertainment-related advertising, such as music concerts and sports sponsorships. The X-Games, cybergrrl, clickchick, and spark.com are popular venues that attract crowds of N-Gens. Hotornot.com is a good example of peer-generated content: N-Gens upload their pictures for others to evaluate!

FUTURE OUTLOOK: NEW AND CHALLENGING INTERESTS AND DESIRES

Our N-Gen Cohort is currently a subset of the demographically defined Echo Boomers. We define it by the advancement of the Internet and the positive change in the economic circumstances that began to be felt in 1995. These driving forces have formed this cohort's new value set. But the future will perhaps create new defining moments that will further subdivide this population group.

Like other cohorts, the N-Gens are not a homogeneous group, although perhaps to an even greater extent. Much of the segment distinctions arise from differing socio-economic conditions of their parents. Those N-Gens with generally affluent and educated Boomer parents are the idealistic, overachieving team players that characterize the cohort as a whole. Those who come from disadvantaged situations seem more similar to the youngest Xers — antagonistic to society, more out for themselves, and free-agents. These are the stoners and the gang-bangers, pessimistic, violence- and drug-prone, and very out-of-sync with their numerous and far more sunny and cooperative peers. Setting the "dark ones" aside, the larger group will be different from the Xers by exhibiting:

- ✦ Less sexual intercourse, although there are equal or increasing amounts of "making out."

- ✦ More group activities, as opposed to strictly individual behavior.

- ✦ Generally more wholesome activities and an outlook reflecting more of the traditional family values of the Depression and World War II Cohorts.

In his bestselling book *The Roaring 2000s,* Harry Dent points to the correlation between demographics and the stock market. His data suggest a strong market for this first decade of the new millennium but a drastic downturn as the oldest Baby Boomers, who are now in their peak earning years, move into retirement and take money out of the financial market to support their leisure years.[11] If this comes to pass, Echo Boomers (today aged 13 and younger) will face a new defining moment — one that will likely create strong security and safety values. But that is perhaps 10 years away, and the sky's the limit on what might happen in the meantime.

That said, a growing number of young adults entering the job market in the next few years could drive down wages and increase competition for jobs. They could also help fill the current void in highly educated technology workers. We expect that the N-Gen Cohort will continue to extend their college years beyond the typical four and will continue to feather their parents' nests to gain economic stability and asset accumulation as they resist adulthood as long as possible. The soaring stock market of the last half of the '90s has provided their parents with the wherewithal to allow their children to push off acceptance of adulthood responsibilities — and the downturn since March 2000 hasn't yet impacted this (and perhaps never will). At the same time, Boomer parents at some point will resist this ongoing drain of cash and choose to serve their own indulgent desires. We believe this will cause intergenerational conflict.

You can expect interracial marriages to increase in number and the "salad bowl" cultural blending to pervade more and more aspects of life. Advertising and other promotional vehicles and messages must mirror this strong value. Environmentalism and ecology are simply a way of life. Products and packaging must be in sync with this demand. As permission marketing and technological advancements go hand in hand, sound marketing must eliminate the sizzle and provide the substance to these "cut-to-the-chase" N-Gens.

Marketing to the N-Gen must utilize the Internet to an even greater extent, as broadband, always-on Internet access becomes taken for granted. Marketing communications will be even more fragmented than they are now as full-motion video becomes available over the Internet, and the more traditional, intrusive model of advertising will become obsolete. N-Gen will *expect* commercials to be entertaining — they have too many ways of avoiding them otherwise. The next few years will be a time of "permission marketing" beyond even the wildest dreams of Seth Godin, the concept's originator.

All this amounts to an interesting period ahead. It should be a time when the emotional mind-set of N-Gens provides a new and challenging set of marketplace interests and desires.

CONCLUSION: REINVENTING MIDDLE-CLASS LIFE IN AMERICA

N-Gens are just now beginning to come of age, and they will no doubt have a growing impact on society and the marketplace in the coming years. They are the largest generational cohort since the Baby Boomers, and marketers have been courting them practically since birth. As they come of age and form lasting values, N-Gens are likely to add their own twist to the various lifestages they pass through. The real test is whether marketers will be able to keep one step ahead of this savvy cohort.

Expectations have always been high when it comes to this group. Since childhood, they have been pushed and scheduled and challenged. And now their parents have high hopes that they will one day find a cure for cancer, or find a way to make space travel possible for the average American. On a simpler scale, though, this cohort seems to have the best chance yet of finding a balance between the competing forces of work and family life that has so eluded other cohorts.

TABLE 9.3: HOW TO TAP THE N GENERATION

Cohort values	✦ Appeal to their desire to be team players, not independent free agents
	✦ Recognize that they tend to respect the institutions of society, not reject them; they want to "play by the rules."
	✦ Play on their generally upbeat, positive view of the future.
	✦ Acknowledge their sense of belonging to a global community.
	✦ Don't make fun of people in ads — this turns N-Gens off.
	✦ Use multi-cultural and inter-racial themes in advertising.
	✦ Strive for a broad ethnic mix in casting for ads.
Lifestage	✦ Reflect teen and young-adult lifestages — high school graduation, college, first job, dating, and early marriage.
Emotions and affinities	✦ Use sophistication, a sense of humor, and honesty in devising marketing messages.
	✦ Entertain them with spoofs and ads that make them laugh.
	✦ Focus on messages that emphasize the environment and make the world a better place to live for everyone.
	✦ Use integrated marketing that doesn't have the feel of advertising.
	✦ Don't fall back on advertising hype; be authentic.
	✦ Word-of-mouth advertising, in which one person recommends your product to a friend, can be highly effective. So can "viral marketing," where one group of users recruits others (as in Instant Messaging).
	✦ Design products and messages to appeal to the N-Gens' love for "retro" styling
Physiographics	✦ Portray them as being at their physical peak.
Social activities and lifestyles	✦ Use the Internet and other new technologies such as magalogs and catazines, as a medium.
	✦ Recognize the importance of niche markets.

TABLE 9.3: (CONT.)

Purchasing behavior	✦ Use popular music and icons.
	✦ Use radio, cable TV, the Internet, and street marketing (wild postings, give-aways, samples and special events) to reach them.
	✦ N-Gens love information, so use your website to provide them with comparative breakdowns about how your product stacks up with the competition.
	✦ Use event marketing — hosting the event, or just advertising at it — to gain awareness and generate goodwill.

ENDNOTES

1. John Leland, "The Blair Witch Cult." *Newsweek* (16 August 1999): 44.

2. Karen Thomas, "Instant messaging: It's a teen thing." *USAToday.com,* June 21, 2001.

3. Mara DerHovanesian, "Coming On Strong." *The Wall Street Journal, Interactive Edition,* 29 November 1999.

4. Helene Stapinski, "Y Not Love?" *American Demographics* (February 1999): 63.

5. Marjorie Coeyman, "Do You Know Y?" *Restaurant Business* (15 March 1998): 4.

6. Alison Steinwellner, "The Young & The Uninsured." *American Demographics* (February 1999): 73.

7. Associated Press. "McDonald's tests self-serve machines." *Midland Daily News* (12 August 1999): sec. B, p. 4.

8. Mara DerHovanesian, "Coming On Strong." *The Wall Street Journal, Interactive Edition,* 29 November 1999.

9. Cristina Merrill, "Keeping Up With Teens." *American Demographics* (October 1999): 27.

10. Mara DerHovanesian, "Coming On Strong." *The Wall Street Journal, Interactive Edition,* 29 November 1999.

11. Harry S. Dent, *The Roaring 2000s.* Simon and Schuster: New York, 1998.

CHAPTER 10

TAKING GENERATIONAL COHORT ANALYSIS GLOBAL

W e've seen that generational cohorts can be used to segment various age groups in the United States. This begs the question, "Do other countries have well-defined cohorts like the United States?"

The short answer is that other *developed* countries have cohorts. In those where the defining events that form a particular cohort are the same as in the United States, the cohorts are similar in length and tend to share many (although not all) of the United States cohorts' values. In countries where the defining moments are different, the cohorts are different as well — different dates, different lengths, and different values.

For example, the United States and the United Kingdom share many striking similarities in terms of defining moments and cohort values. The Great Depression, World War II, and the Cold War were all important events that shaped the coming-of-age years of youth in both countries. This is not unexpected, given the extremely close cultural and historical ties between the two nations. The result is a cohort structure in the United Kingdom that closely resembles that of the United States. The dates are similar, and many, but not all, of the cohort values are similar as well.

In Brazil, however, where we determined the cohort structure for one of our multinational clients, we were surprised to find that there was no World War II Cohort at all! World War II did not really impact Brazil in any meaningful way — therefore it was not a "defining event" as it was in most of the developed countries around the world.

In contrast, in Russia (another country in which we did extensive primary and secondary research), not only was there a World War II Cohort, but the coming of age of the cohort spanned at least 12 years, from the beginning of the war in 1941 until the death of Stalin in 1953. In Russia, World War II was such an overwhelmingly important defining event (23 million killed) that its influence lingered more than a decade — well after other countries had moved on.

This has led us to conclude that countries with different cultures and histories can have very different cohort structures, but that those with similar cultures and histories often share similar cohort classifications. But what is necessary for a country to have cohorts that are national in scope?

CONDITIONS NECESSARY FOR COHORT FORMATION

It is our belief that not all countries have a number of well-defined and widespread cohorts. We have looked at various countries around the world to determine whether any noticeable cohort structure exists, and if so, what it is. In each case, our methodology first entailed extensive secondary research: sifting through books, academic and business research, business publications, newspaper stories, photographs, advertisements, music, and even museum artifacts. Next we conducted interviews with historians, sociologists, social demographers, social psychologists, social workers, educators, and economists — experts in their field who might shed light on the nature of defining moments and the resultant cohort values. The investigation of these sources was exhaustive. Finally, to help validate the findings, primary field research was conducted with actual members of the cohorts to verify the value assumptions for each age group. These individuals were asked about their defining moments and consequent social values, attitudes, and preferences. What we have learned is that for cohorts on a national scale to form, three key requirements must be met. These include:

+ Mass communication capabilities.

+ A high degree of literacy.

+ Social consequences.

MASS COMMUNICATIONS CAPABILITIES

For the impact of a defining moment to be felt by a society, people have to know about it. And to state the obvious, there must actually *be* a defining moment — an event of great historical or social significance — to form a cohort. In today's fast-paced society, there is no shortage of such events. However, it can be imagined that in centuries past, when change happened very slowly, cohorts might have been very long — because there could be many decades, or even hundreds of years, between defining moments. Today, most developed countries are technologically advanced, and have highly advanced communication capabilities. In the United States, local, national, or world events are broadcast to almost every home within minutes of occurring, allowing each individual to be apprised of historical events. And this happens throughout many countries of the world — Saddam Hussein, for instance, received much of his intelligence information about the Gulf War in 1991 from watching CNN in his bunker. However, this fast and continuous flow of information does not occur in many *developing* countries.

When events are communicated by word-of-mouth, they appear to have less of an impact than if communicated by the mass media. We can only imagine how information is transferred in undeveloped areas of Africa, Tibet, Mongolia, or Borneo. In such situations, the impact of events on large proportions of the population would be severely diminished as time and interpretation take their toll. The cohorts that exist under these conditions are probably quite localized, to villages or groups that experienced the event first-hand, and thus they are of limited utility for the mass marketer.

A high degree of literacy

Education affects all aspects of a country's culture, from economic development to consumer behavior. And literacy has a profound effect on the existence and formation of cohorts. In countries where the literacy rate is low, many people may not understand the implications, importance, or impact of a defining event. Thus, it is unlikely that this event will influence their values.

Social consequences

Defining moments need to have societal consequences for them to be cohort forming. For example, the death of Princess Diana, even though it emotionally affected many people, is unlikely to be a cohort-defining event in most countries because it didn't cause a broad change in values. In fact, it is not even a defining moment in England. In sharp contrast, the death of President John F. Kennedy was a defining moment because it stole from the American public the optimism that the Camelot White House provided. And for an event to form a global cohort, the impact must have *global* consequences. As we saw above, even World War II was not global enough in scope to produce a *worldwide* World War II Cohort.

These three conditions — mass communications, high literacy, and social consequences — are certainly found in all developed countries of the world and in some emerging countries, such as Eastern European nations, Lebanon, and China. But most developing countries today do not provide fertile ground for cohort analysis and cohort segmentation marketing. However, technology is changing so rapidly that this assessment should be revisited on a regular basis for reasons shown below.

Cohorts and Defining Moments Around the World

Within a given country, defining moments come from both national and international events. Some cohort defining moments are unique to a nation, such as economic or political change, or even the spread of technology within a society. Other defining moments come from events that occur outside the country. Random samplings of people from various countries show certain twentieth-century events (see Table 10.1) as examples of defining moments that had an extremely broad reach, while those listed in Table 10.2 had more of a country-specific or regional impact. Whether defining moments are regional or more global in scope, they all contribute to the development of shared values. These values can, in turn, be plugged into the Lifestage Analytic Matrix™ (see Chapter 2, "What Makes Us Tick: Using the Lifestage Analytic Matrix™,") and used to develop Multi-Dimensional Marketing™ snapshots of particular cohorts anywhere they exist.

TABLE 10.1: EXAMPLES OF
WIDESPREAD DEFINING MOMENTS*

Date	Time period event occurred
1914–18	World War I
1920s and 30s	Great Depression
1940–45	World War II
1946–53	Cold War and threat of nuclear war
1940s and 50s	Advent of television
1970s	Energy Crisis
1989	Fall of Berlin Wall
1990s	Development of the Internet
1991	Dissolution of Soviet Union
1991	Gulf War
2001	Terrorist attacks in U.S.

Note: These events are not ranked in order of importance, but by date.

World War II was mentioned as key for almost all countries (with some exceptions), but its interpretation is different in different countries, as Jacqueline Scott and Lilian Zac found in their 1993 study of collective memories in Britain and the United States:

. . . Although both Britain and America regard World War II as the most important event of the last half-century, the meaning attached to the war is different in the two countries. In the United States, the war was associated, especially by younger respondents, with the prosperity that followed the war, an association that does not figure in British responses at all. More interestingly, mentions of patriotism and the common spirit of the wartime years is also absent from British recollections.[1]

TABLE 10.2: EXAMPLES OF COUNTRY-SPECIFIC OR REGIONAL DEFINING MOMENTS

Event	Date	Country Affected
John Profumo scandal	1963	United Kingdom
Nelson Mandela's imprisonment and release	1964 and 1990	South Africa
Cultural Revolution	1966–76	China
Six Days War	1967	Jordan, Israel, and Egypt
Khmer Rouge rule	1975–79	Cambodia and Southeast Asia
Assassination of Anwar Sadat	1981	Egypt
Falklands War	1982	United Kingdom and Argentina
Assassination of Olof Palme	1986	Sweden
Tiananmen Square massacre	1989	China
Manuel Noriega's arrest and extradition to United States	1989	Panama
Japanese economic "bubble" bursts	1991	Japan
Irish legalization of divorce	1995	Ireland

This shows that while many countries may experience the same defining moments, socioeconomic, cultural, geographical, and religious and political differences can profoundly change the impact these events have from country to country. In Britain, the war was actually fought on their soil. The sound of air raid sirens was often heard, and fear of bombings became a part of daily life. Meanwhile in America, except for the 450,000 who actually fought the battles, the war was more of a distant story. This may account for the differences in patriotism and spirit.

Cohort Points to Ponder

✦ Were the Japanese as intensely patriotic as Americans who fought in World War II?

✦ Did the Germans who rebuilt their country after the World War II embrace the "Can Do!" attitude of Americans who helped rebuild the United States during the Great Depression?

✦ Did the Six Days War in 1967, in which the Israeli military completely destroyed Egyptian air forces and swept through the Sinai to the Suez Canal routing the Egyptian army, create a sense of heightened nationalism or just the opposite with Egyptian citizens?

✦ Are individuals who came of age in Chile during the Pinochot dictatorship of the 1970s likely to value freedom because they were denied freedom of speech and were highly censored during their young adulthood?

✦ With its devastating campaign of genocide, did the Khmer Rouge's rule from 1975–79 in Cambodia create values of insecurity and political distrust in Cambodians coming of age during that time?

✦ Did the end of apartheid in 1990 create a strong sense of optimism for the future in those South Africans coming of age during this time?

To show you how the Lifestage Analytic Matrix and Multi-Dimensional Marketing can be used in other countries, we present three examples from our work in Russia, Germany, and Brazil — three countries that have a clear cohort structure. While there are some similarities, *each country's cohort structure is quite different from that found in the United States.* To avoid redundancy, we will start with Russia and show an in-depth analysis of that country's cohorts, then go on to Germany, where we will more directly apply the Lifestage Analytic Matrix. In Brazil, we will use the matrix to show specific marketing implications and offer tips on how to reach the various cohorts. This will give you an overview of how Multi-Dimensional Marketing and the Lifestage Analytic Matrix can be used outside the United States.

RUSSIA: 12-YEAR WORLD WAR II COHORT

During the last century, Russia has gone through tremendous social and political change — a situation that has had a very real impact on the country's cohort structure. In Russia, we have identified six different cohort groups (see Table 10.3), discussed in the sections below.

THE COLLECTIVIZATION COHORT

The Collectivization Cohort came of age from 1929–40, and thus roughly corresponds to the Depression Cohort in the United States in terms of time period. Cohort members are aged 78–89 in 2001. This cohort experienced Stalin's massive campaign to force Russian peasants into collective and state-run farms operated by communist party representatives. Several million peasants (*Kulaks*) who had the misfortune of accumulating more property than their neighbors were killed during this time. The plummeting agricultural production that resulted from collectivization (combined with terrible growing conditions) precipitated the famine that is forever etched in this cohort's memory. As if this weren't bad enough, to maintain absolute control and to divert blame away from failed central state policies, Stalin held minor officials responsible for the famine. Millions more people were arrested by the secret police and either shot in the dead of night or placed in "corrective labor colonies." Few returned.

Despite the horrid outcomes of these events, this cohort as a whole regards the period somewhat benignly. As bad as it was, for many former serfs (who had, in truth, been slaves as we would define the term), collectivization was an economic improvement. And because the later purges were not publicized (indeed, not revealed at all, until recently) people tended not to know about them unless a family member was taken. Without group awareness, an event cannot be broadly cohort-defining. The state was seen as the liberator of the masses, and a protector and savior from the predatory West. Thus, this cohort values dedication to the communist party, nationalism, and belief in the state. They also tend to be suspicious of the West.

THE GREAT PATRIOTIC WAR (OR WORLD WAR II) COHORT

The Great Patriotic War Cohort spanned 12 years, from the beginning of World War II in 1941 to Stalin's death in 1953. Cohort members were 65–77 in 2001. World War II was a unifying event that brought Russians together like no other official government campaign could. It gave the people oppressed by hardships a sense of purpose and pride in a job well done. Young soldiers were taught not to fear death and not to lose their heads under fire. The Cold War and the death of Stalin are two other important defining moments of this era.

The World War II Cohort enjoyed greater freedom and personal initiative than its predecessor, the Collectivization Cohort. Through the schools, the Soviet propaganda machine produced youth who were fiercely ideological. Over and over again, they were taught that only the Soviet state would protect them against the evil and decadent aggressors — not only Germany, but England and France as well. For a time, the United States enjoyed a somewhat more positive status due to the war material provided by the Lend-Lease Program. However, this ended with the bombing of Hiroshima, as Stalinist propaganda charged that "Russia is next!" Even today, this cohort is intensely patriotic and nationalistic; they resent the "freedom" of today's Russian youth (which seems to them undisciplined and self-indulgent), feel unappreciated, and many are against the reforms of perestroika.

THE THAW COHORT

The Thaw Cohort includes what would be (in terms of the same coming-of-age period) the Postwar and the Leading-Edge Boomer Cohorts in the United States. Their coming-of-age years span from 1954–69, and they are aged 49–64 in 2001. It's hard for us to imagine how these two cohorts in the United States could be grouped together, but clearly the Russian cohort's defining moments take a sharp departure from those in the United States during the same time period. After Stalin died in 1953, the country began to change its course. Nikita Khrushchev denounced past abuses and freed the survivors of the gulag. As a result, this cohort absorbed the spirit of liberal reforms that swept the country during this time. Western products and fashions also began to be allowed during this time, and this helped to give Russians a taste of the value of capitalism. Sputnik, the International Youth Festival, Yuri Gagarin's orbit of the Earth, and the "Prague Spring" are all defining events for this group. Even today, this cohort values greater social and economic freedom, idealism, and individuality, and they tend to be supportive of perestroika.

THE STAGNATION COHORT

The Stagnation Cohort came of age from 1970–85, a time when the Soviet economy deteriorated, hopes of liberalization faded away, and the Soviet regime began to lose its legitimacy under the leadership of Leonid Brezhnev. This cohort is aged 33–48 in 2001, and roughly corresponds to the Trailing-Edge Boomers (Jonesers) and Generation X Cohorts in the United States. No one particular event stands out as a defining experience for this group. Rather, a series of tactical and strategic retreats sapped this cohort's collective energy. Defining moments included bad economic times, an increase in emigration to the West, and Mikhail Gorbachev's rise to power.

Key cohort values include the erosion of faith in communism, an inner-directedness, pessimism about the future, a tendency to be cynical and withdrawn, and a preference for living outside of Russia. Despite this negativity, this cohort also retains a perverse nostalgia for the stagnation years. Those times might not have been so good — but at least there was stability! This is something that is sorely lacking in Russia today.

THE PERESTROIKA COHORT

The Perestroika Cohort came of age from 1986–91 and are aged 27–32 in 2001. This group roughly corresponds with the Generation X Cohort in the United States. This era of liberalization began with Mikhail Gorbachev's 1986 campaign for *glasnost* (openness) and *perestroika* (political and economic restructuring). Other defining moments included the Chernobyl nuclear disaster, the first parliamentary elections, the fall of the Berlin Wall, Boris Yeltsin's election as president, the dissolution of the Soviet Union, and the 1991 communist coup attempt. Unlike Generation X in the United States, the Perestroika Cohort has played an active role in the momentous social and political changes sweeping the country. They attended political rallies, advocated parliamentary reforms, and more. Members of this cohort value political activism, are opposed to centralized authority, prefer to live outside of Russia, and tend to be somewhat materialistic.

THE POST-SOVIET COHORT

The Post-Soviet Cohort began coming of age in 1992, and they are largely still a work in progress. This cohort roughly corresponds to the N Generation Cohort in the United States. The Post-Soviet Cohort witnessed the dissolution of the Soviet Union, followed by hyperinflation, privatization and economic reforms, the devaluation of the ruble (which wiped out people's life savings), the confrontation between Boris Yeltsin and the Russian parliament, the Chechnya War, the bitter 1996 presidential campaign, the increasingly erratic behavior of Boris Yeltsin, and the 1998 stock market crash.

One thing that sets this group apart is the lack of parental supervision. Their parents were too preoccupied with what was going on around them to pay much attention to their children, and teachers did not know how to teach history and social science during a time when the official dogmas suddenly lost their meaning. Many have called this cohort "an abandoned generation" because they have gotten lost in the shuffle. As a result, gang and drug activity have been on the increase among Russian youth in recent years. Key cohort values include self-sufficiency, cynicism, street smarts, materialism, amoralism, and a strong interest in living outside of Russia. It will be interesting to see in a few years if the devolution of Russian society into one run by organized and white-collar criminals will result in an even more cynical value structure in this cohort and/or the one that follows it.

TABLE 10.3: RUSSIAN COHORTS

Cohort	Born	Coming of age	Age in 2001	Defining moments	Key cohort values
Collectivization	1912–23	1929–40	78–89	✦ Collectivization of agriculture	✦ Dedication to party ✦ Nationalistic ✦ Believe in and rely on state ✦ Suspicious of West
Great Patriotic War (WWII)	1924–36	1941–53	65–77	✦ World War II ✦ Cold War ✦ Death of Stalin	✦ Intensely patriotic ✦ Nationalistic ✦ Resent youth ✦ Feel unappreciated ✦ Against perestroika
The Thaw	1937–52	1954–69	49–64	✦ Sputnik ✦ International Youth Festival ✦ Gagarin first man to orbit Earth ✦ "Prague Spring"	✦ Greater social and economic freedom ✦ Idealism ✦ Individuality ✦ Support perestroika
Stagnation	1953–68	1970–85	33–48	✦ Bad economic times ✦ Emigration to the West ✦ Gorbachev's rise to power ✦ Cynical and withdrawn	✦ Erosion of faith in communism ✦ Inner-directedness ✦ Pessimistic about future ✦ 30% prefer to live outside Russia

Cohort	Born	Coming of age	Age in 2001	Defining moments	Key cohort values
Perestroika	1969–74	1986–91	27–32	◆ Perestroika and glasnost ◆ Chernobyl ◆ Parliamentary elections ◆ Fall of Berlin Wall ◆ Soviet Union dissolved ◆ 1991 communist coup attempt	◆ Political activists ◆ Against central authority ◆ 50% prefer to live outside Russia ◆ Materialistic ◆ Yeltsin elected president
Post-Soviet	1975–?	1992–?	26 and under	◆ Privatization and economic reforms ◆ Chechnya War ◆ Stock market collapse ◆ Amoral	◆ Self-sufficient ◆ Cynical, street-smart ◆ Materialistic ◆ Actively want to leave Russia

TABLE 10.4: WEST GERMAN COHORTS

Cohort	Born	Coming of age	Age in 2001	Defining moments	Key cohort values
Post–World War I	1901–18	1918–35	83–100	◆ End of World War I ◆ Hitler's rise to power	◆ Discipline ◆ Collectivity ◆ Order ◆ Honor ◆ National Pride
Opportunists and Followers	1919–28	1936–45	73–82	◆ World War II	◆ Discipline ◆ Leadership and subordination ◆ Social equality ◆ Do one's duty ◆ Do your best
Post–World War II	1929–48	1946–65	53–72	◆ End of World War II ◆ Rebuilding after the war	◆ Hard Work ◆ Hierarchy ◆ Importance of family ◆ Diligence ◆ Contentedness ◆ Austerity ◆ Punctuality ◆ Good manners
Wild Sixties	1949–68	1966–85	33–52	◆ End of Conservative Era ◆ Coal crisis ◆ Vietnam War ◆ Social protests ◆ Oil shocks ◆ High unemployment	◆ Individualism ◆ Personal and social expression ◆ Pacifism ◆ Social justice and tolerance

TABLE 10.4: (CONTINUED)

Cohort	Born	Coming of age	Age in 2001	Defining moments	Key cohort values
Generation X	1969–78	1986–95	23–32	◆ Protests against government ◆ Government scandals and corruption ◆ High unemployment	◆ Individualism ◆ Indifference ◆ Tolerance ◆ Convenience
Internet Junkies	1979 or after	1996–Present	22 and under	◆ Internet ◆ Information Age	◆ Mobility ◆ Flexibility ◆ Openness ◆ Having fun ◆ Convenience

Germany: 9-year World War II cohort

Germany, too, has experienced tremendous social and political change during the twentieth century, but particularly in the last 50 years with its division and reunification. East Germany came into existence after World War II. Until the reunification, it, too, experienced its own separate defining moments. But here, we simply focus on Western German cohorts during that period. Some examples include (see Table 10.4 for more details):

- ✦ **Post–World War I Cohort** — Came of age during World War I and Hitler's rise to power

- ✦ **Opportunists and Followers Cohort** — Came of age during World War II

- ✦ **Post–World War II Cohort** — Came of age in the postwar era and experienced the rebuilding of Germany

- ✦ **Wild Sixties Cohort** — Came of age during the turbulent end of a conservative era, social protests, the Vietnam War, and other social turmoil

- ✦ **Generation X Cohort** — Came of age during a time of protests against the government, government scandals, and high unemployment

- ✦ **Internet Junkies Cohort** — Came of age during the dawn of the Internet and the Information Age

While many of these German cohorts seem to correspond to cohorts in the United States, a closer look reveals significant differences. For example, Germany's Opportunists and Followers Cohort started as early as 1936 and did not end until 1945. This was much longer than the five years the World War II era lasted in the U.S. This cohort's National-Socialistic education, their involvement in the war, and its disillusioning end played a major role in their lives. Most spent their youth as members of the Hitler Jugend (HJ) or Bund Deutscher

Maedel (BDM) — government-sponsored youth training programs designed to teach Nazi principles to young Germans. Within these organizations, youth experienced a strict hierarchy. For the young men, this was later reinforced by their service in the military. Members of the Hitler youth organizations were encouraged to take on positions of leadership and responsibility, which resulted in high self-esteem for the cohort. Later, however, the collapse of the Third Reich led to deep disillusionment and guilt. Despite these losses, they still held onto the values they learned before and during the war, which included such things as the willingness to do one's duty, the willingness to give everything one has for a cause, pride in personal achievement, and the willingness to work hard. Some of these values are clearly shared with the World War II Cohort in the United States, but missing is the strong sense of patriotism and romance that is still valued by the American World War II Cohort today.

West Germany's Post–World War II Cohort stands in stark contrast to that of the United States, even though they both shared the same defining moment of the end of the war. While Americans were living the good life after the war, German Post–World War IIs were rebuilding their country literally from the ground up. They were faced with a collapsed infrastructure, millions of dead and missing, food shortages, and a decimated economy.

As a result of this hardship, they came to value hard work, hierarchy, the importance of family, and a rebirth of conservative values, such as diligence, contentedness, austerity, punctuality and good manners. Using the Lifestage Analytic Matrix, we developed an overview of this cohort in the Snapshot feature. While American Postwars like to indulge themselves now and then and are part of a new trend toward adventure travel and active lifestyles, German Post–WWIIs are still haunted by the hard times that plagued their coming-of-age years. They are still saving and looking for the stability that they lacked as young adults.

SNAPSHOT OF GERMANY'S POST–WWII COHORT

Name of cohort:	Post–WWII
Born between:	1929–48
Coming of age:	1946–65
Age in 2001:	53–72

Key cohort values and concerns:

- ◆ Hard work
- ◆ Hierarchy
- ◆ Importance of family
- ◆ Diligence
- ◆ Contentedness
- ◆ Austerity
- ◆ Punctuality
- ◆ Good manners

Current and next lifestage:

- ◆ Retirement
- ◆ Grandparenting

Emotions and affinities:

- ◆ Nostalgia
- ◆ Tradition
- ◆ Respect for authority

Physiographic profile:

- ◆ Vision and hearing problems
- ◆ Hypertension
- ◆ Arthritis
- ◆ Gray hair and hair loss

Social activities and lifestyles:

- ◆ Reliance on self for determining lifestyle
- ◆ Classical music

Purchasing behavior:

- ◆ Very price sensitive
- ◆ Still saving
- ◆ Convenience services becoming more important

From Sports Clubs to Sports Boutiques: A Sign of the Times

Just like in the United States, different German cohorts often put their own spin on the very same activities. Take sports, for example.

After World War II, sports clubs for group sports, such as soccer, became a popular pastime among Germans. In addition to offering exercise, these clubs also provided a social and recreational outlet that helped Germans forget about the war and its devastating aftermath.

But in recent years, while exercise is still a priority, sports clubs have lost favor in Germany. Fitness studios are now the latest rage. Mountain biking, jogging, squash, tennis, and badminton are also popular. With the popularity of these non-team activities, you can clearly see the move away from the camaraderie of group-oriented sports to more individualistic pursuits.

This correlates with the shift in Germany's youth from older, more collectivist cohorts, to younger, more individualistic ones.

The German Wild Sixties Cohort very closely mirrors that of the Leading-Edge Baby Boomers in the United States. In fact, there was a small Baby Boom in Germany as reconstruction reached the point where people felt secure enough to start having children — around 1954. In many ways they resemble the Leading-Edge Boomers in the United States and use 1968 as kind of a denominator of their generation — they even call themselves the "Achtundsechzigers" — "the 1968ers."

The Vietnam War and student protests were two important defining moments for both The Wild Sixties and the Leading-Edge Boomer Cohorts. The social change that took place during these two cohorts' coming-of-age years resulted in a completely new value system. There was a rebellion against conservatism and tradition. Social justice and tolerance were popular ideals, and intellectual and sexual freedom reached new heights. As a result, the values that both of these cohorts adopted included individualism, personal and social expression, pacifism, social justice and tolerance. The Snapshot feature shows an overview of Germany's Wild Sixties Cohort, which again, we developed using the Lifestage Analytic Matrix. Compare this to the snapshot of Leading-Edge Boomers in Chapter 6 and you will see many similarities. In fact, it's difficult to tell these two cohorts apart.

Finally, according to a Roper Starch global values survey conducted in 1999, 50% of the Internet Junkies Cohort are primarily "Funseekers," while 25% are "Intimates." This is somewhat at odds with the preceding cohorts, who have a much greater tendency to be intimates. According to Roper Starch, intimates are people who place higher-than-average value on stable personal relationships, protecting the family, friendship, romance, sex, and intimacy. Their attitude can be summed up in the message, "I want to simply enjoy life with those I am close to."

In contrast, "Funseekers" are partygoers who place higher-than-average value on having fun, adventure, pleasure, excitement, a varied life, romance, music, and looking good. The key message for them is: "I want fun, friends, and fantasy. Entertain me!"

This is a major attitudinal shift in Germany, and it may be the point at which there is a significant generational divide. Certainly this new funseeking German is at serious odds with the stereotype of the strict, methodical and ordered German.

BRAZIL: WORLD WAR II PLAYED MINOR ROLE

Like Russia and Germany, Brazil was found to have six distinct cohorts (see Table 10.5, later in this chapter). Interestingly enough, while World War II shaped the majority of young people coming of age in the early 1940s in North America, Europe, and Asia, in Brazil, it had little impact. As a result, the country has no World War II Cohort. Instead, it has the Vargas-Era Cohort, whose members came of age from 1930–45. This cohort was named after Getulio Vargas, a charismatic leader who ruled the country with an iron fist through two coup d'état attempts and two constitutions.

SNAPSHOT OF GERMANY'S WILD SIXTIES COHORT

Name of cohort:	Wild Sixties
Born between:	1949–68
Coming of age:	1966–85
Age in 2001:	33–52

Key cohort values and concerns:
- Individualism
- Personal and social expression
- Pacifism
- Social justice and tolerance

Current and next lifestage:
- Children in high school and college
- Empty-nesters
- Second careers for some
- Divorce and remarriage for some
- Some grandparenting

Emotions and affinities:
- Sexually experimental
- Good relationship with their children
- Nostalgia
- Still challenging authority, but less provocative

Physiographic profile:
- Vision and weight problems
- Hypertension
- Gray hair and hair loss
- Menopause
- Arthritis

Social activities and lifestyles:
- Spiritualism and transcendentalism
- Active life
- Nostalgia (Rolling Stones concerts, the Beatles, and so on)

Purchasing behavior:
- Debt is okay
- Convenience very important
- Services increasingly important

The middle class resented the economic pressure of this era, the terror with which they lived, the persecution of political opponents, and the repression of all kinds of dissent that was inherited from the Great Depression of the late 1920s. In fact, the middle class resented the economic pressure more than the authoritarian regime. On the other hand, the masses surrendered entirely to Vargas' skills as a strategist. Protective labor laws and other benefits counterbalanced extreme poverty and massive unemployment. Their access to formal education was limited. The scarcity of industrialized products led them to put more emphasis on "being" rather than "having." Lack of imported goods hindered dreams of consumption. Due to massive, biased government propaganda and the exaltation of national values, members of this cohort developed a strong cult of nationalism as well as a perception of the state as the solution for all national problems. In general, people of this cohort are nationalistic, look to the state for solutions, accept authority, and feel that having experiences is better than having material possessions.

Another interesting Brazilian cohort is the Iron Years Cohort. Its members came of age from 1968–79. Defining moments included a widespread social crisis that resulted from the political reigns being taken over by a dictatorship, and the implementation of Institutional Act No. 5, which abolished the democratic congress. While the Leading-Edge Baby Boomers in the United States were enjoying ever-greater freedoms and liberalism, the Iron Years Cohort in Brazil lived through a repressive and violent regime of military dictatorship that often led to hostility or alienation. Civil Rights were significantly reduced, censorship was instituted, and political opposition was not tolerated. Peaceful protest was everywhere — in the form of lyrics of popular music and in the people's emphatic and steadfast silence.

In order to counterbalance its own authoritarianism, the military regime was lenient toward violations of traditional ethical and moral values. The dictatorship used sports, festivals, porno-farce movies, and soap operas to camouflage its savagery, resulting in a system of programmed alienation of the population. Taking advantage of others was praised as a virtue on TV. The harmony of interpersonal relationships was definitely broken, as wariness, suspicion, and cynicism became, for the most part, substitutes for genuine, candid, and honest relations among people. While these social problems were running rampant, the dictatorship provided economic prosperity. There was increased economic growth, an increase in imports and exports, rapid industrialization and urbanization, huge investments in large infrastructure projects, and an expansion of the educational system. But these economic improvements were viewed as taking place at the expense of social justice. As a result, the sense of economic accomplishment was reduced to a myth.

Key cohort values that this era produced were a sense of belligerence about government institutions, alienation, repressed silence as a means of survival, pride in what was Brazil's myth of success, and the importance of education, which was seen as a way out of the social crisis.

Once a clear cohort structure is understood, the Lifestage Analytic Matrix can be used to develop a country-specific model for developing marketing strategies and tactics. Professor Paulo Cesar Motta, an executive consultant at Lifestage Matrix Marketing and a professor at Catholic University in Rio de Janeiro, worked with us to develop marketing implications for Brazil's six cohort groups based on the values we found (see Table 10.6).

Because each cohort group has unique values and experiences, marketers need to treat them with care in designing products, planning marketing executions, and developing promotional pitches. Consider the Iron Years Cohort: Because of the distrust that came with alienation, products targeting this group should be filled with guarantees, and promotions should stress the quality of the product's features. Tag lines could associate the product with the cohort's sense of lost freedom. "The Bank of Brazil will provide you freedom from worry about the safety of your hard-earned money!" "Grab for freedom . . . Brahma Beer is your accomplice in the Great Escape!" Also playing off the concern for freedom, products that hint of finding new ways to use them reflect an opportunity for freethinking, something this cohort was denied during its oppressed coming-of-age years. And because cohort members saw the economic surge accompanied by social injustice and the hope for better times ahead, marketers might use spokespersons and product demonstrators that appear ahead of their time to play off the optimism that this cohort still has about the future.

TABLE 10.5: BRAZILIAN COHORTS

Cohort	Born	Coming of age	Age in 2001	Defining moments	Key cohort values
Vargas-Era	1913–28	1930–45	73–88	◆ Vargas's coup d'état	◆ Nationalism ◆ State as a solution ◆ Having experiences is better than having material possessions ◆ Acceptance of authority
Postwar	1929–37	1946–54	64–72	◆ Vargas' deposition and Dutra's election to president	◆ Moral tradition ◆ Value of having
Optimism	1938–50	1955–67	51–63	◆ Vargas' suicide and President Kubitschek's election	◆ Country of the future ◆ Youth culture and looking abroad
The Iron Years	1951–62	1968–79	39–50	◆ Dictatorship instituted ◆ Social Crisis ◆ Institutional Act No. 5 (abolished democratic congress)	◆ Belligerence ◆ Alienation ◆ Repressed silence ◆ Myth of grandiosity ◆ Value of education
The Lost Decade	1963–74	1980–91	27–38	◆ Amnesty for activists ◆ End of Economic Growth	◆ Fear ◆ Frustration ◆ Materialism ◆ Individualism ◆ Hopelessness
Be On Your Own	1975 and after	1992–Present	25 and under	◆ Government crisis ◆ President Collor's impeachment ◆ Change in currency to the *real*	◆ Self-sufficiency ◆ Consumerism ◆ Recovery of ethical and moral values

Table 10.6: How to Tap the Brazilian Market

Cohort	Marketing implications
Vargas-Era	✦ Provide detailed information about the products. ✦ Adopt entertaining marketing communications backed by Brazilian culture and conditions.
Postwar	✦ Provide products that may benefit the whole family. ✦ Emphasize simplicity. ✦ Show the virtues of those who prefer the products and use spokespersons that appear to be honest.
Optimism	✦ Show people actually using the products. ✦ Avoid putting pressure on buyers. ✦ Occasionally remind potential buyers of the country's economic progress, its industries, and national pride.
The Iron Years	✦ Offer guarantees of all kinds. ✦ Develop promotions based on the idea of freedom. ✦ Use endorsers that appear to be ahead of their times, and that are shown as users of the products.
The Lost Decade	✦ Emphasize fashionable products and fashionable users. ✦ Favor products that can benefit their users' individuality. ✦ State that everybody in the crowd already has the products. ✦ Employ spokespersons of high visibility that transmit an image of honesty.
Be On Your Own	✦ Stress variety, as tailor-made products will appeal to this group. ✦ Resort to one-to-one marketing with a personal reply whenever possible. ✦ Use global themes in promotions. ✦ Avoid erotic appeals. ✦ Associate promotions with honesty values. ✦ Favor mechanisms that allow bargaining (e.g., variable price structure).

YOUNGER COHORTS CONVERGING

Lifestage Matrix Marketing's research shows that, for the most part, global cohorts really don't exist for older age groups. While there are similarities between countries that share the same history, such as the

United States and the United Kingdom, most cohorts develop independently within a country's borders. But with younger age groups, such as Gen X and N-Gen, we find increasing similarities in values, attitudes, and preferences around the world. Young people in so many countries now travel extensively and influence their peers back home with their new experiences. With the globalization of U.S. television programming and movies, youths around the world tune into MTV, Jerry Springer, and Oprah with a click of the remote control. And with the popularity of Internet chat rooms, youth can just as easily meet and exchange ideas with a friend in The Netherlands as they can with someone from their own school. It's no wonder that younger age groups are finding convergence in values, including independence, self-expression, an openness to new ideas and cultures, flexibility, mobility, and most importantly, having fun and enjoying life. Consider these facts:

+ Young adults are delaying acceptance of responsibility. Going to college is increasingly becoming the norm in developed and developing countries. In the United States, the average length of time to obtain a college degree is now 5 years, up from 4.5 in 1982. In Sweden, students get paid by the government to be students for up to 6 years. Therefore, with little incentive to graduate, students are spending more time in higher education.

+ In both the United States and Brazil, living with one's parents in one's 20s is quite common. In the United States, two out of three people aged 18–25 live with their parents or another relative. In Brazil, average upper- and middle-class 20-year-olds live at home with their parents.

+ First marriages are occurring later in life. In the United States, the average age at first marriage in 1970 was 23.2 for men and 20.8 for women. In 1997, that stood at 26.8 for men and 25.0 for women. In Japan, in 1979 men married on average at age 28.7, while women were 25.9 on average. Today, the average in Japan is 29.9 for men and 27.5 for women. And young Swedes today actually show a disdain for marriage. They find cohabitation a more desirable alternative. In fact, Sweden has a legal "marriage-like" status called *sambo* (defined as a couple living together in a semi-long-term relationship, but unmarried). Of the 90,000 Swedish couples that move in together each year, eight out of nine do so sambo.

+ Transition to parenthood occurs later and with fewer children. In the United States, the average age of mothers at first birth increased by 1.5 years between 1975–96, from 22.3–23.8. Women aged 15–24 are bearing 1.5 children. In Sweden, the age when women have their first child has increased considerably over the past two decades. In 1980, 37% of 25-year-old Swedish women had had their first baby. By the 1990s, this number dropped to below 25%. The average number of children in a Swedish family is between 1.5–1.6, very similar to the United States. In 1995, Brazilian women gave birth to 2.3 children, down from 6.0 in 1960. And in Japan, the birth rate is now 1.39, well below the 2.08 replacement rate. In fact, the incidence of more Japanese families with an only child has led to overindulgence of this offspring.

+ Divorce rates for young people are skyrocketing around the globe. It is no longer a social negative to be divorced. Having children out of wedlock also has lost its stigma. In most developed countries, mothers are shunning the traditional role of withdrawing from the workforce and remaining at home with the children. More and more modern young women are committing themselves to a career. In short, there is a resounding convergence of values around delaying responsibility, valuing education as a license to a better career, awarding lower status given to familial duties over career, putting concern for self over concern for others, and gaining greater self-esteem and freedom for women.

+ Throughout Europe, North America, and Asia, teens and young adults are getting pierced, tattooed — and in some extreme cases, even branded — to show their unique style and to assert independence. In the United States, an estimated 7 million adults have tattoos, and that number is growing as more and more young people see tattoos and piercing as the ultimate form of self-expression. Lips, noses, eyebrows, tongues, genitals — you name it — are all prime targets for piercing, as a growing number of teens and young adults experiment with new forms of body art.

Body Art Undercover

Some United States companies, such as Marriott Corp. and electronics superstore Best Buy, have implemented rules requiring employees to cover all body art while on the job.

But with the current shortage of workers, at least in the United States, Gen-Xers and N-Gens know they have the upper hand. "I'm not going to change myself for anyone," these teens and young adults say. "If employers won't accept me the way I am, I don't want to work for them."

These value shifts in the young might well be attributable in good part to expansion of world travel, advances in communication technology, the emergence of global media, and declining trade barriers. These are all factors contributing to the acceleration of a global village. These trends suggest that consumers socialized in this global market should experience more similar environments than their predecessors. Japan and Germany offer two good cases in point.

JAPANESE YOUTH: "WE JUST WANT TO HAVE FUN"

Challenging long-held beliefs about the value of hard work and discipline, some Japanese youth are choosing to throw future plans out the window in favor of just having fun. Young girls in their teens prowl the trendy locales of Shibuya, Tokyo's night district. Dressed in avant-garde fashions, with bleach-blond hair and paste-white makeup, they wander the narrow streets, respond to advances of admirers of all ages, and dance at nightclubs until the wee hours of the morning. Often returning home as the sun comes up, they sleep the day away, only to return to the wild side again that evening. They favor "sex friends" over serious boyfriends and prefer the excitement of nightlife to the discipline and drudgery of school. After all, this hedonistic image is just what they see in American films, movies, and TV shows.

In Japan today, plenty of youngsters still work hard, but an increasing number are joining the ranks of an emerging youth sub-culture. In 1999, there were 10 million junior and senior high school–aged teens. Of them, 120,000 dropped out of school, a 20% surge over 1997. And in terms of sexual promiscuity, a 1999 survey found that 50% of high school senior girls had had sexual intercourse by senior year, an increase of 10% over 1993.[2] And this new value system obviously does not exclude teen boys either. Wearing baseball jackets and billed-caps turned backwards American-style, they exhibit the same casual, "I-want-no-part-of-responsibility" way of life.

This is in sharp contrast to the Japanese youth of 20 years ago. Then, teenagers were leading an increasingly regimented and "managed" lifestyle. Japanese parents pushed their children to excel in school and aimed at sending their sons and daughters to top universities. A degree from one of these schools meant better marriage prospects for women, and a ticket to secure lifetime employment at a prestigious firm for men. The company took care of you, promoted from within, and gave priority to seniority. The image of the "salary man" has dominated Japanese culture since World War II. Self-sacrifice for the company was the top priority, outranking family obligations and self-interest. As a result, so-called "overwork death" was not uncommon among Japanese men.

But recently, Japanese 20-somethings have dramatically changed their preferences and values, moving away from corporate loyalty and toward greater individualism and enjoyment of their lives. Why? A protracted recession that began in 1991 has led many Japanese companies to turn their backs on the old social contract, which included life-long employment, seniority-based advancement, and internal promotion. Workers have been increasingly subject to demotions and firings. The concept of "downsizing" was totally foreign to the Japanese, whose hierarchical job system was completely based on the paternalism of the company they worked for.

These "defining moments" explain, at least in part, the shift in cohort values shared by Japanese youth who have just come of age, and even the values of teens and young adults still in this stage. If their parents worked so hard, sacrificed for them, and then were confronted with losing their jobs in mid-career, why should they embrace those "old-school" ideals? In fact, they appear to embrace just the opposite. Even for Japanese youth and young adults who aren't a part of any sub-culture, values have shifted sharply as a result of these coming-of-age experiences. Plus, greater exposure to Western lifestyles through movies, TV, music, and the Internet has given Japanese youth a taste of the good life.

Corporate Casual Makes Its Way to Japan

Dark suits, white shirts and neckties used to be standard uniform for Japanese "salarymen." But these days, corporate casual is beginning to make its way to Japan.

Nearly a decade of recession has younger, more Western-oriented managers looking for ways to loosen up the workplace and help reduce employee stress. A more relaxed dress code is one way to do that. And that suits younger workers just fine.

With the move toward a more casual workplace, discount chains and warehouse clothing outlets are popping up all over Japan, as more and more Japanese make the switch from high-priced status labels to "cheap-chic" casual.

But old habits die hard. Many salarymen, particularly older ones, still keep a black jacket and white shirt at the office — just in case they have an important business meeting or a funeral to attend.

GERMAN YOUTH: "IN TOUCH AND IN DEMAND"

In Germany, like Japan, chronic unemployment and a stagnant economy have put limits on growth and led to disillusionment among the country's youth. Divorce and dysfunctional families have become a part of their everyday experience, and these trends are reflected in popular TV shows and movies. Many lack goals and are either unemployed or unhappy in their current jobs. So, like many American Gen-Xers and N-Gens, they have turned to their friends for support and focus their efforts on enjoying life to the fullest. After all, trying to follow their parents' path only leads to anxiety.

Some enjoy vacationing on the Spanish island of Ibiza, where drugs, casual sex, and dancing until dawn at anything-goes nightclubs are all part of the allure. The island has become a kind of party mecca for Europe's fun-seeking youth.

Technology is another area that binds these young people together. The Internet provides instant access to information, and provides seemingly unlimited possibilities. Having grown up with computers, this group is not intimidated by the Internet, but rather sees it as a convenient tool they can't live without. Pagers and cell phones have become the new status symbol among Germany's youth. This mirrors a similar trend in the rest of the developed world. Wireless technology allows youth to remain constantly "in-touch" with friends, and is a symbol of being popular and in demand.

Global Youth — In Some Ways the Same, in Many Ways Different

While there is a growing homogenization among the tastes of young people around the world, there is also a growing trend toward celebrating regional differences. For example, rather than relying on the United States, many countries are now producing their own popular music stars, which are a huge hit with local audiences.

Because of this simultaneous convergence of values and divergence of regional tastes, marketers can't just assume that what works in the United States will work abroad. They need to cater to local tastes.

CONCLUSION: COHORT VALUES CAN HELP TAP GLOBAL MARKETS

Before reading this chapter, you probably would have agreed that applying generational cohort analysis to other cultures makes sense — and our work has shown that definitely to be the case. Of course, we have only scratched the surface, but we have found some foreign cohorts share similarities with those in the United States, and many more are completely different.

Developed countries tend to mirror the international defining moments that have changed our values in the United States — for example, the Great Depression, World War II, the energy crisis of the '70s, and the dawn of the Internet. Of course, many developed countries have their own idiosyncratic defining moments. Japan, for example, has recently faced difficult economic times, while the rest of the world has prospered. And there are likely many more events that are not defining moments for Americans but that, while felt in the United States, are defining moments in other nations. As a result, each country really deserves special investigation. This is particularly true when targeting people over 23 years of age. For them, the cohort structure in different countries is much more likely to be different than it is to be similar. However, for the youngest adults — those 17 or 18 to about 22 — a truly worldwide cohort may be emerging from the impact of the Internet, and the MTV/CNN/satellite globalization of communications. If this is the case (and we believe it is) it could usher in a new era of "world marketing" programs, at least for the developed countries.

In less-developed countries, illiteracy and poor communications prohibit the spread of information and dampen the effects of what could be defining moments. However, AIDS, with its devastating effects, must be a defining moment in many African countries, while the drug trade could similarly impact some South American countries. Once again, each country deserves its own cohort investigation.

That said, we can attest to the value of understanding cohort-specific values in other cultures. Because they do not change over one's lifetime, they provide anchors that can open doors to marketing success. If you are doing business abroad, this is your challenge. We hope you will take us up on it. In fact, we can help you take us up on it with a well-developed, multi-stage process for ferreting out different cohort structures in different cultures. Just remember that by developing products and marketing executions that tap into deep-seated cohort values and by matching them up with other aspects of Multi-Dimensional Marketing, the world can quickly become your "cohort oyster."

ENDNOTES

1. Jacqueline Scott and Lillian Zak, "Collective Memories in Britain and the United States." *Public Opinion Quarterly,* No. 57, Issue 3 (Fall 1993): 315–331.

2. Howard W. French, "Japanese Teens Pick Night Life Over Class." *The Wall Street Journal* (3 March, 2000): sec. A, pp. 1 and 25.

EPILOGUE

An ancient Arab proverb states that men resemble the times more than they do their fathers, and we couldn't agree more. Defining moments that happen when we are becoming adults shape values that remain with us, essentially unchanged for life.

We began this journey by pointing out that age — particularly coming of age — plays an important role in binding us together into distinct generational cohorts. And this provides marketers with a tremendous opportunity for meeting the very real and very different needs of various cohorts as they enter new lifestages.

For a social theory, such as generational cohorts, to be most valuable, though, it should aid not just in understanding different societal segments *now,* but in predicting the *future* as well. We have seen in certain cases how Multi-Dimensional Marketing™ and the Lifestage Analytic Matrix™ can do precisely this — for example, by projecting that Leading-Edge Baby Boomers will react to retirement in a completely new way than their parents did.

This is a very useful tool for marketers planning for the near-term future. Longer-term projections, however, require that a recurring historical pattern be established.

THE FOURTH TURNING'S CYCLES OF HISTORY

In their widely acclaimed book *The Fourth Turning: An American Prophecy*,[1] authors William Strauss and Neil Howe offer an intriguing theory based on predictable cycles of societal change. They trace Anglo-American history back to the War of the Roses (1459–87) and make a remarkably compelling case for their argument that in a lifetime of 80–100 years, each of us witnesses four stages, or turnings. Those stages are:

- ✦ Crisis
- ✦ High
- ✦ Awakening
- ✦ Unraveling

These are recurring periods; thus every 80 years or so the cycle repeats itself: A Crisis period is followed by a High, followed by an Awakening, followed by an Unraveling, leading to another Crisis.

Although Strauss and Howe derived their cyclical patterns from historical research, and we discerned our cohorts from market research and empirical marketplace data, the two match up quite closely (see the table on p. 346). The key difference is that over the period from the 1920s to the present, we postulate that seven distinct cohorts exist, with their formative coming-of-age periods from 5–18 years in length based on the critical defining moments. Strauss and Howe, on the other hand, see five generational cycles during that period, each of which is (or will be) 20 years in length (because that is the time it takes for one "generation" to be born, marry, and have children of its own.) Over that 80-year time period there have been four "generational cycles" (a new one is just beginning), and four "turnings," one of which (a Crisis) is about to repeat. However, there is no fundamental conflict between our "cohorts" and their "generations." Rather, they are complementary, and we accept the recurrent cycles that Strauss and Howe put forth. *The cohorts are*

smaller, shorter **waves** *with peaks and troughs overlaying the longer,*
recurring 20-year-long generational **swells.**

For Strauss and Howe, the last Crisis occurred with the Great
Depression and World War II. Their G.I. Generation (for General Issue,
a reference to World War II foot soldiers) experienced these key events.
The hue and cry of those times was about abandoning the social structures
and values held prior to 1929 and honing in on, first, the rebuilding of
America and, second, thwarting the common world enemy during the
war. These shared experiences reshaped social institutions to assist in
reaching these overriding societal goals. This Crisis period was followed
by a placid, stable postwar era — a "High." During this time, social
institutions were solid. Marriage was strong. Government was applauded.
Schools and families were the primary social units. This, of course,
reflects the coming-of-age experience of our Postwar Generational
Cohort. Strauss and Howe call this group the "Silent Generation."

Then came the Baby Boomers, who gave us an "Awakening."
Strauss and Howe call them the "Boom Generation." They challenged
almost every social institution with their "Don't Trust Anyone Over 30"
mantra and "Hell No, We Won't Go" chant in reference to the Vietnam
War. They rejected the values of older cohorts, and it clearly showed in
their dress, their ideals, and their actions.

Strauss and Howe tell us that we are now in a period of
"Unraveling." And there is good evidence that the social institutions of
the High are indeed crumbling. We have children shooting each other
in schools. We have half of all marriages ending in divorce. We find
professional athletes openly "dissing" their coaches, umpires, and other
authority figures. We have provocative movies, such as *Pulp Fiction* and
American Beauty, given Oscar-level applause. And as noted earlier, the
general public looked the other way at President Clinton's indiscretions.
Those in the Generation X and N Generation Cohorts — what Strauss
and Howe respectively refer to as the "Thirteenth Generation" and the
"Millennial Generation" — either have come of age, or are coming of
age, during this time, and our theory suggests that this unraveling social
environment will shape their values throughout their lives. The following
chart compares the Strauss and Howe generational cycles to our cohorts.

THE FOURTH TURNING: DEFINING MOMENTS

Strauss and Howe's Generational Cycles		Our Generational Cohorts		
Generation Birth Years	Key Events	Cohort Birth Years	Coming of Age Years	Defining Moments
G.I. Generation (Crisis part of cycle) 1901–24	World War I Prohibition Depression	Depression Cohort 1912–21	1930–39	✦ Great Depression
	World War II	World War II Cohort 1922–27	1940–45	✦ World War II
Silent Generation (High part of cycle) 1925–42	Affluence Civil Rights	Postwar Cohort 1928–45	1946–62	✦ End of World War II ✦ Good economic times ✦ Moving to the suburbs ✦ Cold War ✦ Korean War ✦ McCarthyism ✦ Emergence of rock and roll ✦ Civil rights movement
Boom Generation (Awakening part of cycle) 1943–60	Kent State Watergate	Leading-Edge Baby Boomer Cohort 1946–54	1963–72	✦ Assassination of JFK, RFK and Martin Luther King, Jr. ✦ Vietnam War ✦ First man on the moon
		Trailing-Edge Baby Boomer Cohort 1955–65	1973–83	✦ Fall of Vietnam ✦ Watergate ✦ Nixon resigns ✦ Energy crisis
Thirteenth Generation (Unraveling part of cycle) 1961–81	Not yet known	Generation X 1966–76	1984–94	✦ Reaganomics ✦ Stock market crash of 1987 ✦ *Challenger* explosion ✦ Fall of Berlin Wall ✦ Gulf War ✦ AIDS crisis
Millennial Generation (Crisis part of cycle) 1982–?	Not yet known	N Generation 1977–?	1995–?	✦ The Internet ✦ Good economic times ✦ Columbine school shootings ✦ Clinton's impeachment ✦ Terrorist attack on World Trade Center and Pentagon

While we agree with Strauss and Howe's basic theory, we believe that for marketers, our cohort segmentation enables more precise targeting of smaller, distinctly different segments. For example, we see a clear distinction between the Depression and the World War II Cohorts. Anyone — male or female — turning 18 between 1940–45 in America was indelibly marked by the war. They were, and remain to this day, more romantic, more group-oriented, more optimistic, and less preoccupied with financial security than those just a little older, who came of age during the Depression years. Interestingly, these two cohorts even have a self-awareness that they belong to different groups. To lump them together, as do Strauss and Howe, is to miss major distinctions critical for marketing. Another example pertains to the Boomers, which we believe are two very different "cohorts," not one 20-year "generation."

PREDICTING THE FUTURE

We don't have the data to go back in time past the twentieth century to determine the cohort structure back to the War of the Roses. But then, there's no compelling reason to do so, since those cohorts are all long gone and thus not very attractive market targets. *However,* the Fourth Turning allows us to project forward into the future in a way that goes beyond what our empirically-based generational cohort theory permits.

Based on their 20-year generational cycles, Strauss and Howe suggest (and we concur) that another Crisis is coming, one that will restructure society away from its present self-focused value and behavior system to more of a cause orientation. They believe that this will happen sometime between 2006 and 2012 — roughly 80 years after the onset of the last Crisis, the crash of 1929 when society moved from the self-focus of "The Roaring '20s" to the cause of defeating fascism. The precise nature of this future crisis, and its triggering event can only be speculated. But based on the cyclical pattern Strauss and Howe have found extending back to the fifteenth century, it will come. And it will be a major defining moment with significant social consequences.

On September 11, 2001, a major terrorist attack on the World Trade Center and the Pentagon took place. Was this the "trigger" defining event that brings on the Crisis? On balance we believe the tragedy of September 11 was not the trigger. For one thing, according to the cyclical theory, a Crisis in 2001 would come from five years to a decade too early — not totally unprecedented, especially given the faster pace of modern life, but still well ahead of Strauss and Howe's schedule.

If we're right, when the Crisis does come, the nation's leaders will for the most part be aging members of the Leading-Edge Baby Boomer Cohort. The followers, who will embrace solidarity and teamwork and respect the institutions they defend, will be N-Gens. And because the crisis itself can confidently be predicted to be a cohort-defining event, those who come of age during those years (and who will be those heading the charge to cope and rebuild in the aftermath) will be of a new cohort as yet unnamed and undefined.

Strauss and Howe do not stand alone in predicting a coming crisis. In his widely acclaimed book *The Roaring 2000s,*[2] Harry S. Dent, Jr., found economic conditions highly correlated with the demographic structure of our society. He investigated the changes in the stock market (as measured by the Standard & Poor's 500, adjusted for inflation) and overlaid changes in population size lagged by 49 years — the year of peak earning power for most people. He found a remarkable correlation. This led him to predict that when the Leading-Edge Baby Boomers start retiring and the Boomer's peak earning period crests, the market will decline. This is because the Leading-Edge Boomers will need significant income streams to replace their salaries — and because one of their cohort characteristics is to spend, not save, their inadequate savings alone will not suffice. Thus they will draw down their 401(k)s and stocks will plunge, leading to a Depression, most likely coupled with severe deflation. This is demographically predictable, and Dent predicts it will happen about the year 2010. Sound familiar? To us, it sounds like a) a defining moment, and b) a crisis. While Strauss and Howe are unsure of the nature of the crisis — possibly economic, possibly political — Dent is positive it will be financial.

That writers coming from as diverse viewpoints as Strauss and Howe, and Dent both persuasively forecast an upcoming crisis at about the same time is highly provocative. It is also suggestive that the so-called Kondratieff Long Wave cycle predicts a trough or global depression around 2010.[3] Again, these prognostications all take place almost a decade from September, 2001. Only time will tell about September 11's final overall significance. But what *is* known is that the future will hold a series of significant events — some will be like small hills, while others will be larger, more consequential mountains, and still others huge, Everest-like defining moments, which will change the system of social values, create a new generational cohort, and restructure society's mind-set.

This book has been about generational cohort theory and how it can help you better understand, reach, and motivate your customers. Existing cohorts can be mined with new and repositioned products and services that tap into their value structures. And for emerging cohorts, marketing strategies and tactics must be refashioned to reflect their different value systems. In devising future marketing plans, the key thing to remember is this: In a world of ever more rapid change, values are the one constant.

We believe this generational cohort approach will result in marketing executions that will take you to new heights of understanding and effectiveness, and we wish you great success.

ENDNOTES

1. William Strauss and Neil Howe, *The Fourth Turning: An American Prophecy.* New York: Broadway Books, 1997.

2. Harry S. Dent, Jr., *The Roaring 2000s: Building the Wealth and Lifestyle You Desire in the Greatest Boom in History.* New York: Simon & Schuster, 1998.

3. Nikolai Kondratieff was a Soviet economist who studied pricing and related economic cycles in some cases (for example, salt prices) going back to the fourteenth century. He was made into a semi-cult figure in Russia in the late 1920s for predicting a coming economic collapse in the capitalist economies, since that prediction obviously aligned with the Communist ideology. In 1930, he made the mistake of saying that the Great Depression that he had predicted was just part of an 80-year cycle, and would at some point be replaced by good times. This was *not* what Stalin wanted to hear, and lacking tenure, Kondratieff was sent to the Gulag, where he perished shortly thereafter. His so-called "Long-Wave" cycle theory still has adherents, and seems to have some validity if you move the dates and events around a bit. A more thorough description and analysis is found in *The Long Wave in Economic Life* (1983) by J. J. Van Dunn.

INDEX

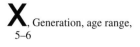